How to Make
the Rest *of* Your Life
the Best *of* Your Life

How to Make
the Rest *of* Your Life
the Best *of* Your Life

Mark Victor Hansen
and Art Linkletter

THOMAS NELSON
Since 1798

NASHVILLE   DALLAS   MEXICO CITY   RIO DE JANEIRO   BEIJING

Published in Nashville, Tennessee, by Thomas Nelson. Thomas Nelson is a trademark of Thomas Nelson, Inc.

Thomas Nelson, Inc., titles may be purchased in bulk for educational, business, fund-raising, or sales promotional use. For information, please e-mail SpecialMarkets@ThomasNelson.com.

Scripture quotations noted KJV are from The Holy Bible, KING JAMES VERSION.

Library of Congress Cataloging-in-Publication Data

Hansen, Mark Victor.
  How to make the rest of your life the best of your life / Mark Victor
Hansen and Art Linkletter.
     p. cm.
  Includes bibliographical references.
  ISBN 0-7852-1890-4 (hardcover)
  ISBN 978-0-7852-8926-5 (tradepaper)
  1. Older people—Life skills guides. 2. Aging—Psychological aspects.
  3. Old age—Social aspects. I. Linkletter, Art, 1912– II. Title.
  HQ1061.H3368 2006
  646.7'9—dc22

                              2006013614

Printed in the United States of America
07 08 09 10 RRD 5 4 3 2 1

*This book is dedicated to the 76.9 million Baby Boomers,
the Echo Boomers who will come after them,
and the millions of people over sixty-five today.
May the next fifty years of your lives be the most amazing ever.*

Acknowledgments

E very great book is a dream before it becomes a reality. Art Linkletter and I are longtime friends. I asked him to do a book with me, and bless his heart, he said it would be fun.

When I was invited to dinner with Sam Moore, chairman of the board of Thomas Nelson Publishers, we liked each other from the get-go. I told him that I wanted to write a book with Art Linkletter. Sam pointed his finger in my face and said, "I want it." It is a beautiful thing in the publishing business to be wanted, loved, cherished, respected, encouraged, and paid to write something that will serve a vast amount of hungry readers. Thank you, Sam.

Jillian Manus, the best agent in the world, said, "Let's do it." With the brilliant legal, accounting, and permissions help of my wife, Patty Hansen, and our extraordinary attorney, Ken Browning, we were ready to write.

Our superb helper of helpers was Tim Vandehey. What he did touched our souls. Tim captured the essence of who we are and where we wanted to go. We loved him, had him on every interview, and gave him assignment after assignment, and he handled each one flawlessly. Together, we roared with laughter, had fun, learned a tremendous amount, and believe we have created an important book that will serve our readers well.

My executive assistant, Debbie Lefever, was indispensable as always, arranging conference calls with celebrities and making scheduling nightmares look like child's play. Art's executive assistant, Jennifer Kramer, smiled and navigated the world's busiest nonagenarian's calendar masterfully.

Jonathan Merkh, Publisher of Nelson Books, has confidently listened to and agreed to our endless requests. We deeply thank him for his unwavering belief in this project. Ted Squires, an executive vice president with Thomas Nelson, has been a friend, confidant, and marketer's dream since the conception of this project. Many thanks to Belinda Bass for her wonderful design work, and to our editor, Paula Major, for her boundless patience with our endless revisions and rerevisions and her help making this a timeless read.

We thank our many old and new friends who generously gave their time in interviews: Dr. Ken Dychtwald, Dan Burrus, Norman Lear, Dr. Walter Bortz, Sallie Foley, Dr. Steven Austad, Dr. Michael Elstein, Jack LaLanne, Dr. Gary Small, Paul Zane Pilzer, Donald Ray Haas, Cheryl Bartholomew, Barbara Morris, our incredible Senior Acheivers and Senior Athletes, and any others we may have overlooked inadvertently. We dreamed this book; you were all part of the Dream Team that made it a reality.

Finally, nothing would have been possible without the loving support we receive each day from our wives, Patty Hansen and Lois Linkletter. They are the solid bedrock from which we can soar in our flights of breakthrough thinking. They also contributed generously with specific insights to each iteration of this book.

We treasure you, our fans and readers, for reading, absorbing, and using the principles in the book and sharing them with those whom you love and care about. Again, thank you for reading our work.

In the many areas of life, it's customary to save the best for last. Thus, we acknowledge and honor the presence of the Higher Power from whom we receive so many gifts and enlightened insights. As you'll see in this book, the Higher Power comes first in our lives.

—ART LINKLETTER AND MARK VICTOR HANSEN

Contents

Foreword *by Art Linkletter*

This book is a love letter to the Baby Boomers of America, all 76 million of you men and women born between 1946 and 1964. You have precipitated many economic changes in our country in the last half-century, and as you age, you're going to bring about many more—drastic ones—especially in the cost of Medicare.

In the last one hundred years, think about how much health-care costs have risen. Instead of living until forty-seven (the average life expectancy at the turn of the twentieth century), we now live to seventy-seven, with many of us, myself included, living far beyond that. The spending per capita for health care has gone from $143 in 1960 to over $5,670 in 2003. Even adjusted for inflation, that's an enormous increase. In 1985, as a nation we spent $427 billion for health care. But that's nothing; one projection has future costs by 2008 at $2.055 *trillion*, with one-third of the lower income group uninsured! Medicare now costs as much as Social Security, and by 2015 it will cost more than the budget for Social Security and the Defense Department combined.[1]

In short, we are living at a time when change is happening everywhere . . . turbulently and rapidly. The Industrial Revolution is over, and we are living in the era of Information and Communication. By 2050, one of every four Americans will be over 65. But while older Americans have been growing as a class, since 1965 there has been a dearth of birth. The younger generation is marrying later and having fewer children than the Boomers, so there are fewer "under-20s" looking for beginning or part-time jobs. This opens the door for retiring Boomers who have spent all their money on careless living and must work at least part-time to pad their so-called "entitlement" pensions. And even those entitlements must change. They *will* change. It's inevitable.

This book, then, aims to answer the Big Question: "Fine, I can live longer, but can I live *better*?" Mark and I have assembled a cast of outstanding authorities on health, business, sex, money, and more to share their wisdom on the ways that older Americans can take advantage of every opportunity in the coming years.

When I go to a doctor or a business consultant, I believe in what's called "due diligence." In other words, I find out his qualifications and his past record and then decide if I find him pleasant and accommodating to work with. So fair is fair. I should expect to provide you with the same kind of information about me. Following are some of my experiences in the field of gerontology.

To begin, I'm ninety-four years old. I have lived through the most amazing century in the history of mankind. I have written three auto-biographies. The first, when I was forty, covered the preceding twenty years, which took me from being a hobo riding freight trains to a college education, then to a radio career as a national celebrity and the beginnings of a family that now numbers five children, eight grandchildren, and fifteen great-grandchildren. I wrote my second autobiography twenty years later at the age of sixty. It covered tumultuous years when tragedies took the lives of two of my younger children, when the invention of television changed my career, and when I arrived in the top moneymaking ranks in business. The final book came when I was eighty and reported the big final change in my life, when I became a top professional lecturer on drug abuse, positive thinking, and gerontology as one of the founders of the UCLA Center on Aging, of which I'm currently chairman of the board.

I've been worldwide spokesman for World Vision (one of the largest missionary fund-raisers in Africa), traveled through Africa, India, South America, and Haiti filming TV specials, and became chairman of the board of the John Douglas French Alzheimer Research Foundation, which has raised millions of dollars to fight this dreaded disease. I'm also the national chairman of USA Next (a national project of United Seniors Association, Inc.) that has several million Americans enrolled to help in Washington with Social Security, Medicare, and death tax reform. I lecture some fifty times a year across the nation, raising money for Christian schools and many humanitarian organizations such as the Red Cross, YMCA, Leprosy Missionaries, Salvation Army, and a number of colleges. I have seventeen honorary doctorates. And I received the Humanities Annual Award from President Bush in 2004.

I could go on, but it would sound like I was bragging. The only other thing I'll mention is that being married for seventy years to the same lady has given me a good share of experience in the area of matrimonial harmony. It's funny, but when at events they announce that I've been married to the same girl for seventy years, that gets the biggest applause. I'm also proud that I've remained the tent pole of my family—the support right at the center. I'm in every business my kids are in, involved in all of it. I'm making up for the things I didn't have, growing up as a foundling in poverty.

I was the son of an evangelical preacher and shoemaker. My parents were living a sweet life as they saw themselves approaching heaven. When I was seventeen, I told them I was going out to see the world with five dollars and the shirt on my back. They told me, "God will take care of you." We always felt God would take care of us. During the holidays, baskets of fruit and food appeared at our doorstep, and we never knew who brought them. My father had absolute faith that I would go out into this world and go absolutely everywhere, and I would be okay. God would take care of me. And He always has.

Don't ask me if I'm going to retire. Retire to what? I love what I'm doing because I think it *matters*. And I think this book can matter to anyone who is getting into the later years. Don't stop living and learning.

I never want to be
What I want to be,
Because there's always something out there yet for me.

There's always one hill higher—with a better view,
Something waiting to be learned I never knew.
So until my days are over
Never fully fill my cup.
Let me go on growing—up.

John Wooden, the UCLA basketball wizard and philosopher, says, "Things turn out best for the people who make the best of the way things turn out."[2] I can't think of a better message to send you into this book. May you enjoy the journey.

—ART

Foreword *by Mark Victor Hansen*

You are reading this because you are going to live the rest of your life in the future. You deserve a new future view—a future view that is worthy of you, helps make you ageless and youthful, happy and proud. We offer you a future of all that you ever imagined and more, much more.

Obviously, you want to know how to make the rest of your life the best of your life. Hope gives each of us options. You have greatness in you, and we want to be the catalyst to help you realize it. The world is depending on you to fulfill your potential, and we want to help you do it. We want to help you make a difference that leaves a lasting legacy. This is the operating manual that will help you create a future that is worthy of you and your contribution to the world.

It's time to be inspired to serve your enlightened self-interest. Enlightened self-interest makes everyone better off and no one worse off. It means that you take care of yourself, your loved ones, your company, your community, and then as many others as possible to make the world better. On the journey, we'll show you models of individuals who are doing great work; living fully, vitally, and dynamically; and contributing mightily. They are self-actualizing, fully-functioning self masters.

I call this "discovering God's destiny for you." My walk with God began early in life. My parents were devoted church attendees and believers. My mother grew up in a Baptist home where my grandmother attended church multiple times per week and taught Bible stories on a flannel board every Sunday night to my brothers, cousins, nephews, nieces, and me. On Sunday we would attend the Baptist church or the Lutheran church my father, a Danish immigrant, grew up in.

During my time at university, I decided that I wanted to know about the Spirit, God, and Jesus, so I decided I would take a minor in theology just because I was so interested. Frequently, I am asked the question, "If you hadn't become a professional speaker, what would you have become?" My answer: a minister.

When I lived in New York, I attended two different churches. I attended Dr. Norman Vincent Peale's church and then a black church in Harlem called United Palace. I have continued that practice even to this day. Now on Sundays, I go to an interdenominational church in Los Angeles and then come back to attend one of several churches in Orange County with my family, including Dr. Robert Schuller's church. I am blessed to say that I am on a first-name basis with most of the major ministers in America.

I have always hung out with and learned from individuals older than me. In graduate school at Southern Illinois University, I was invited by my physiology teacher, Dr. Alfred Richardson, to hear Dr. R. Buckminster Fuller, the chairman emeritus of the SIU Design School, talk live to 5,000 students. Fuller's message wowed my soul. Before the afternoon was over, I went to his office and asked him for a job as a research assistant, and got it. At the time, Dr. Fuller was seventy-one years young. He said, "Most greats don't even come into their own until they are in their 80s. The system cannot retire you unless you retire yourself." This is what we say: Let's trade "retirement" for "refirement!" Fire up your passions and your knowledge and get back in the game. You are needed, wanted, and can do things no one else can do.

As I write this, I am fifty-seven years young, and I feel twenty-eight. Last year I climbed the highest mountain in the continental United States, Mount Whitney. I am elated to be working with a living icon, Art Linkletter, who is the model for the future. I have gigantic goals, over 6,000 of them. It is true that you live longer with many big and little goals. Goals give you a sense of adventure and excitement. Goals stimulate your *will to live* and make a difference.

I share all this for the simple reason that Art and I are dedicated to ending negative aging. People who keep the idea in their mind that age has only negative consequences—decay, disease, degeneration, death—help to create those outcomes. We want to create a new kind of ageless aging. We want to create a new image of maturing, a way to see that *chronology* is irrelevant. It is just a number, one that Art says he never even gave heed to until after he was eighty. We want you to know your *biological age*; then we want you to reverse it with nutriceuticals and exercise that will take twenty years off of you.

Most importantly, we want to teach you about *experiential age*. Satchel Paige asked, "How old would you be if you didn't know how old you are?"[1] I told you that I feel twenty-eight years old, and Art, at ninety-four, says he feels like forty-five. However, experientially, Art feels he is 358 years old. I feel 158 years old from the perspective of what I've experienced. We have compressed a great deal of life into our lives . . . and we're not done.

We believe that age sixty is the new forty, the new middle age, because people have a new image of themselves and are living longer than at any time in human history. More of you are choosing to write a new self-prescription for the good, happy, healthy, and long life that is worthwhile, important, significant, and helpful to others.

What if you could live longer, earn more than you ever imagined, serve greatly in surprising ways, and see your great-great-grandkids like Art has? It's possible, and more so everyday, especially if you heed the many recommendations in this book. Art and I want to inspire you to entrepreneurship and volunteerism at levels previously unimaginable. You probably have already worked full-time on a job and/or career. It is time that you work on your fortune and future, and it is never too late. The world has big needs, and that means you have big opportunities to use potential you never knew you had. Art and I offer you the magic ingredient: *permission*. You don't have to believe you can do small things in a great way or great things in a great way; all you need to believe is that we believe you can.

You need to work on you. You need to work on you harder than you ever worked on a job. Because when you get better, the world gets better.

You are worth it, or you wouldn't be holding this book in your hands right now. We have done everything we can as great friends, colleagues, and writing partners to translate over 150 years of life experience for your benefit.

With this book, we are making individuals who embrace agelessness, youthfulness, energetic vitality, lifelong learning, goal setting, and significant contributions that last forever. My hope is that I can help you discover God's destiny for you, that you will feel empowered not only to thrive but also to serve. Because the greatest amongst us is servant of all.

—MARK

Forget Entitlements—Introducing
the Ten Empowerments

I f you're lucky, you're going to grow old.

If you're very lucky, you'll grow so old that morticians will follow you around with a measuring tape to save time. You'll need a fire marshal on hand for your birthday cakes. When someone mentions they've spoken to you, people will gasp and exclaim, "Is he/she still *alive?*" That's old.

Wait a minute? *Lucky* to grow old? That's what we said. But you protest: "Doesn't everybody want to stay younger longer?" Of course they do, but it's not possible. No matter what you do on the outside, you're going to become older on the inside. The only alternative to growing old is getting dead. And while we've never been dead, we can safely say being old and alive is a heck of a lot more fun.

Grow Old, Don't Get Old

Aging is not optional. That means if you want to enjoy your life, there's only one thing you can do: don't *get* old. *Grow* old. Growing old means that as you age, you grow. You learn. You discover new passions, new wisdom, new things that excite you. You learn from your mistakes and make new ones instead. You create new relationships even as you keep cherished old ones. You take care of your body, exercise, eat right, take risks, learn to play an instrument—you *live*. You grow and change and improve with the decades.

Getting old means you fossilize, watching the years pass you by, complaining but never acting, regretting but never reaching out. Getting old means you're dead years before your body gives out. Who wants that?

The philosophy of *How to Make the Rest of Your Life the Best of Your Life* is not to apologize for old age or try to avoid it, but to show you that it can be an incredible time of freedom and discovery and learning and purpose—if you approach it in the right frame of mind. Old age is a privilege. How are you using it? Are you attacking life head-on, going after new challenges, using your time and money for some cause close to your heart? Are you defying expectations and horrifying your grandchildren by learning to surf, hiking the Appalachian Trail, or starting a business? Are you growing old or just getting old?

The 60s Are the New 40s; the 80s Are the New 60s

Many of the technologies, medications, nutritional and fitness discoveries, entrepreneurial opportunities, and social networks people need to make their later years incredible already exist. What's lagging behind are people's mind-sets. Many of us have not embraced the idea that we can be more vital and alive at seventy than we were at forty. We're stuck in obsolete ideas about old age, ideas that whisper in our ears that our only options are to sit in a rocker, complain about new music, forget about sex, learn shuffleboard, and pray we don't outlive our retirement savings.

Nonsense. Today, we're living so much longer and more productively that age sixty has truly become the new age forty—the prime of life when our careers are in full swing, our minds are at their most creative, and our passions burn their hottest. If you had what you thought was your prime of life when you were in your 30s or 40s, count yourself lucky. You get to have a Second Prime, a time in your 60s, 70s, or even 80s when you can use your wisdom, experience, and financial resources to start fresh, create something marvelous, discover a new purpose for your life, and revitalize and replenish your body.

We're going to open your eyes to the latest findings in genetics, finance, psychology, fitness, and more. We'll share stories from "Senior Achievers" and, in doing so, reveal the secrets for keeping your body, mind, and soul vibrant and full of purpose and energy . . . for experiencing a true Second Prime that makes your first prime look like a dress rehearsal.

We've even created an online community, www.SecondPrime.com, for Baby Boomers with a life-affirming attitude and anybody else who wants to live long and live brilliantly. Once you've finished this book, visit and meet other people just like you.

You know you're getting older . . .

- When your friends compliment you on your new alligator shoes and you're barefoot.
- When your doctor doesn't give you x-rays anymore but just holds you up to the light.
- When a sexy babe catches your fancy and your pacemaker opens the garage door nearest you.
- When you remember when the Dead Sea was only sick.
- When your wife says, "Let's go upstairs and make love," and you answer, "Pick one!"
- When going braless pulls all the wrinkles out of your face.
- When you don't care where your spouse goes, just as long as you don't have to go along.
- When you and your teeth don't sleep together.

THE SOCIAL SECURITY/MEDICARE TIME BOMB

We're going to start by shaking up the conventional wisdom and ruffling a few feathers. We're not advocating that Social Security and its fellow programs be eliminated; they have helped many older Americans lead better lives. But there are two aspects of government entitlements that we cannot support: debt and dependency.

Consider the financial projections for the Social Security trust fund. According to the Social Security and Medicare Boards of Trustees, negative cash flow into the trust fund is expected to increase rapidly after 2010, when many of the 76.9 million Baby Boomers will start retiring. After that, the shortfall will accelerate as the number of retirees collecting benefits gradually overwhelms the number of workers paying into the system. The government projects that by 2017, tax income will fall short of payouts, and by 2041 the fund will only be able to finance 74 percent of benefits. By that time, the trust fund will be gone.[1]

Medicare is in even worse shape, especially as Boomers get older and sicker and their healthcare costs rise. By 2079, the cost of Medicare benefits is projected to reach a staggering 14 percent of gross domestic product. That means 14 percent of every dollar produced in the United States would be going toward paying Medicare hospital and drug benefits! Medicare assets would drop below payouts by 2014 while the Medicare Hospital Insurance Trust Fund, which pays hospital benefits, will be exhausted by 2020.[2]

THE TEN EMPOWERMENTS

Social Security and Medicare could put America into even more debt while fostering dependency among seniors. Fixing them is a political issue, so what we're suggesting instead is this: exchange these entitlements for the Ten Empowerments, gifts you give yourself by making smart, courageous choices. You're entitled to all ten, but only if you develop the right mind-set and make smart, brave choices about your future.

If you embrace the Ten Empowerments, you will find that you can make more money after "retirement," be healthier and more active, and be independent. You'll get what you earn, find greater purpose and passion in what you do, make new social contacts and meet amazing human beings, do real good in the world, and keep your mind sharper and more powerful. You won't need the monthly checks from Social Security, you'll be healthier, so your medical bills won't be as high, and you can use your financial resources to buy health coverage that's exactly what you want. There are many options out there if you know where to look.

Empowerment #1: You can defy the stereotypes of old age.

Society is filled with outdated ideas about people over sixty-five: they're frail, they're losing their marbles, they're cranky, they're out of touch, they have no interest in sex. Those ideas are part of the "conventional wisdom" about growing old, and if you listen to them, they will rob you of your power to create the life you want.

Instead, why not adopt some "unconventional wisdom" of your own? This is the first step to making the rest of your life the best of your life: convincing yourself that you can create the life you want rather than being bound by archaic ideas. You can and you will, once you empower yourself with statements like these:

- I will never retire but, instead, work at something that gets me excited to get out of bed in the morning.
- I will make myself fit and healthy and athletic.
- I will prevent disease and improve my health by improving what I put in my body.
- I will embrace adventure, travel, and new experiences.
- I will live independently.
- I will create new relationships with all kinds of human beings.
- I will live each day with passion and purpose.
- I will discover or rediscover my spiritual life.

Say these things, then write them down. If you write down your intentions, you are ten times more likely to achieve them than if you just talk about them.

Empowerment #2: You can determine your longevity.

Research has shown that longevity has more to do with the lifestyle choices you make than with your genes. Your DNA gives you a basic framework to work with, a predisposition for or against conditions such as high cholesterol, cancer, heart disease, or diabetes, but what you build on that frame is a matter of choice—the lifestyle you choose to lead. You are not the slave of your DNA; you have the power to decide whether you are healthy enough to hike ten miles at age seventy-five or obese, hypertensive, and dependent on prescription medication.

The diseases that kill millions of Americans every year are diseases of lifestyle—coronary artery disease, cancer, high blood pressure. Sure, there are inherited factors involved, but what you eat every day and how much you exercise have a lot more to do with your developing these killer diseases than who your grandfather was. If you're eating five servings of fresh fruits and vegetables every day and working out at the gym five times a week, you could still develop diabetes or heart disease, but your genetic programming will have to work a lot harder to make that happen. It's more likely that you'll defy your genes and keep your blood pressure low, build a healthy heart, have strong, flexible joints and muscles, and as a result, live longer.

You know you're getting older . . .

- When your back goes out, but you stay home.
- When you wake up looking like your driver's license picture.
- When it takes two tries to get up from the couch.
- When your idea of a night out is sitting on the patio.
- When happy hour is a nap.
- When you step off a curb and look down one more time to make sure that the street is still there.
- When your idea of weight lifting is standing up.
- When it takes longer to rest than it did to get tired.
- When your memory is shorter and your complaining is longer.
- When the pharmacist has become your new best friend.

Gerontologists expect members of the Baby Boom generation to live routinely into their mid- to late 80s and beyond. But that's not a birthright; it simply means that due to medicine, science, and knowledge about nutrition, you have that potential. Whether or not you tap it is up to you. How? By eating fresh, antioxidant-rich foods. Exercising and moving your body. Finding ways to let go of stress. Challenging your mind. Meeting new people. Finding a spiritual community. Maintaining a great sex life with your spouse. And by taking pure joy in the true pleasures of life, from a piece of gourmet chocolate to your first time holding your new grandchild.

Studies have shown that once you get past your mid-80s without succumbing to the diseases of age, you've got a good shot at living a century. Are you living a lifestyle that gives your body and mind the best chance of aging well? You can take charge of your mental, physical, and emotional health and maximize your odds of celebrating your one hundredth birthday, or you can let it all ride on the genetic roulette wheel. It's up to you.

Empowerment #3: You can make new friends and create rich new relationships.

All too often, seniors seclude themselves in retirement communities where the only people they come into contact with are in the same age group and share the same race, social status, economic background, and political beliefs. That's a recipe for stagnation. If variety is the spice of life and you've spent the first sixty years of yours around all kinds of people of all ages, why on earth would you want to spend the rest of your life around people who are just like you?

If you want to empower yourself, use your knowledge, memory, and passion for life to reach out to people of all ages and from all backgrounds and forge new relationships. You can do it at a church, through volunteer work, or simply in your neighborhood. You can even do it if you live in a retirement enclave where everybody's over the fifty-five-year-old hill and picking up speed. Just get yourself out there, stick out your hand, and introduce yourself.

Why is this important? When we have social networks and a wider circle of friends, we live longer and more richly. People who don't share your political beliefs, who come from a different culture, or who are half your age are inherently interesting; they view the world differently. You learn from them as they learn from you. Seek out people who are nothing like your friends, put yourself into situations where you'll come into contact with artists, activists, entrepreneurs, missionaries, and college students. Develop the art of conversation. Become a great listener. It's a wonderful skill.

Empowerment #4: You can be financially secure as long as you live.

Do not retire. We're going to say that a lot. Retirement is like taking a classic car, one that's been running for forty years, and garaging it. Eventually, that finely-tuned engine is going to gum up with old oil, the battery will give out, and the car is as good as dead.

The key is to make the transition from working because you *have* to into working because you *want* to. Decades of gold watch retirement ceremonies have brainwashed us into believing that reaching sixty-five means sitting in a rocking chair. And that's more than wrong—it's tragic. Human beings are builders, creators, and entrepreneurs. We need challenge, a reason to get up in the morning. Simply shutting up shop at retirement and spending the rest of your days playing golf is a recipe for dying early. There is no reason why in your 60s, 70s, or even 80s, you cannot take the knowledge you've gained through decades of working and find something new to do, whether it's getting a job, starting your own business, or volunteering.

There's a good reason for doing this too: it will give you the freedom not to need Social Security. One of the saddest things we hear people say in our travels is, "I hope I don't outlive my money." That is terrible. If you're healthy and have all your marbles, you should be hoping for every minute of life you can savor because it's all you're getting. But many seniors assume that after they leave their corporate job, they won't be working for the rest of their lives. With today's longevity, the woman who retires at sixty-five has a great chance of living to ninety. But does she have enough money to make it to ninety? The prospect of running out of money is terrifying.

It doesn't have to be that way. Instead of dreading the idea of "going back to work after I retire," why not say to yourself, "After I quit working for someone else, I'm going to take a year off to travel and then go to work doing something I really love." As the saying goes, if you do what you love, you'll never work a day in your life. Increasing numbers of Americans over age fifty are going back to work, some because they must, but more because they want to work. They want a reason to hop out of bed and be excited about the day and a way to earn supplemental income. If they have some retirement savings and very little debt, they can find the perfect occupation. They are becoming teachers' aides and retail clerks, volunteers at nonprofit organizations and precinct walkers for political candidates. Many are starting their own businesses.

We are going to talk a great deal about senior entrepreneurship. We think it's a fantastic idea. When you have forty years of experience in a field and a network of contacts, why not start a business? That's exactly what millions of seniors are doing. Thanks to the Internet, many are doing it at home, which means no commute, the ability to care for a spouse with health problems, and the freedom to control your time. If you think entrepreneurially as you near "retirement" age, and if you make enjoyment your top criterion for a new occupation, you will keep your spirits high, your mind vigorous, your skills sharp, and your body younger . . . and you'll probably make enough money that you won't need to worry about what Social Security is able to pay out.

Empowerment #5: You can be more fit than you were at thirty.

It's never too late to start exercising, adopt healthy habits, and reap the benefits. Studies have shown that people in their 60s, 70s, and 80s who start a regular exercise program for the first time in their lives gain just as great a benefit as younger people: increased muscle mass, greater strength and flexibility, improved endurance, weight loss, enhanced energy and appetite, and even a more agile mind.

By developing a physician-approved exercise regimen and eating healthy foods every day, you can get back a great deal of the vitality and physical freedom that many seniors assume are gone forever. Later in this book, you'll meet athletes in their 60s, 70s, and 80s—men and women who have been competing for years at an elite level. They're fit, lean, and agile—all the qualities that seniors are supposed to have left behind. How does such fitness happen? By you making a commitment. Turning back the clock to have strength, flexibility, energy, and speed in your old age is a matter of doing three things as part of your everyday lifestyle:

1. Exercising aerobically (running, walking, cycling) and anaerobically (weight lifting), and stretching. Aerobic exercise develops your endurance and improves your cardiovascular health, while anaerobic exercise builds muscle, improves your strength, and helps you keep off the weight you lose.

2. Eating generous amounts of fresh fruits and vegetables, lean meats, fish, whole grains, and raw nuts. All these foods contain the vitamins, minerals, essential oils, and phytonutrients you need to prevent disease and keep body and mind vital.

3. Getting enough rest. Americans are notoriously poor at getting enough sleep; our culture discourages it. But then we quit working a regular job and don't have to get up every morning to commute, and we still don't get enough sleep! It doesn't make sense. Your body really does need eight hours of sleep a night. Rest helps you recover from exercise, improves your energy and concentration, and boosts your immune system.

Remember, smart exercise and eating are the only things you can do for your body that have no negative side effects! All you'll do is improve the health of your heart and cardiovascular system, stave off cancer, lose weight, reduce or eliminate joint pain, become more mobile and flexible, feel more energetic, look better, and live happier.

Empowerment #6: You can keep your mind agile and sharp.

Art Linkletter here. This section is written from my perspective because as a ninety-four-year-old man who's also Chairman of the John

Douglas French Foundation for Alzheimer's Disease, I can say that there is nothing more important than keeping your brain active and challenged. The brain is just like a muscle; if you don't work it, it will atrophy, and you'll lose function.

But what's more important is that you have the power to slow or even prevent loss of mental abilities simply by working your brain like you would work your bicep. If you work your mind every day and live a life where you're constantly learning new things, science and human experience show that you'll keep your mind sharper longer.

You know you're getting older . . .

- When it takes twice as long to look half as good.
- When the twinkle in your eye is only the reflection of the sun on your bifocals.
- When you look for your glasses for half an hour, and then find that they were on your head all the time.
- When you get two invitations to go out on the same night, and you pick the one that gets you home the earliest.
- When you give up all your bad habits and you still don't feel good.
- When you sit in a rocking chair and can't get it going.
- When you confuse having a clear conscience with having a bad memory.
- When your hip sets off an airport metal detector.

You must always be thinking, solving problems, engaging other people, challenging your brain to work and struggle. Do games and crossword puzzles. Take on volunteer work in an area you know nothing about. Dedicate a summer to reading a dozen new books, or learn a new language. You cannot spend too much time giving your brain a good, hard workout. Our brains are our minds, and our minds are who we are.

Attitude is just as important. Avoid "catastrophizers," people who feel victimized by life, who always see the cup as half empty: those grouchy, grumpy old people you see rocking on their porch and complaining about the world. They're letting their minds rot because of a negative attitude. If you have a positive, life-affirming attitude, you're going to do all the things that keep you alert, sharp, and "in the game" of life: communicating, pursuing an area of curiosity, staying connected with your family, community, church, or political party. The more you do, the more you'll find that your mind is a tool you can use to shape any future you have in mind.

Empowerment #7: You can make a positive difference in the world.

Another of the unfortunate stereotypes of old age is that elders are powerless. Right. Who runs nations and companies? Men and women over fifty. Who possesses most of the money? Older Americans. Who has all the contacts, the business savvy, and the experience to make change happen? Seniors. You have tremendous power to change the world; you've just been brainwashed into thinking it belongs to someone else.

If you see something that you feel needs to be changed, whether it's a new law or a boarded-up building that would be a perfect community center, you have the power to make it happen. There are many community, state, and national activist groups dedicated to mobilizing people to effect change. Organizations like Volunteer Match (www.volunteermatch.org) exist to connect people who are passionate about making a difference with opportunities to do so. There are as many ways to create positive change as there are problems that need fixing.

If you don't have the time or inclination to get involved, give your money to a cause you care about. You do not have to sit idly by while younger people make decisions that affect your future. You have power to change policies, support or oppose political candidates, and even advance legislation. Never doubt your own ability to shake the halls of power. All you need to do it is the willingness to act.

Empowerment #8: You can discover and nurture your creativity.

When we talk to seniors, three-quarters of them have a secret desire to play piano, write poetry, paint, or something else wonderfully creative, but when we mention it they usually say, "Oh, but that's stupid. I would not be any good at it."

That's missing the point. The point at trying something creative is not to be good at it; creativity is its own reward. We think 90 percent of human beings have creative energy inside them. People are creators by nature, but most become sidetracked by the demands of making a living and raising a family. A lucky few get to make a living writing, singing, sculpting, or acting, but most of the rest of us carry that secret longing to be creative around inside us for the rest of our days.

If you have that longing, don't keep it a secret. If you're no longer working on someone else's schedule, why not try the creative field you've been watching with envy for forty years? It doesn't matter if you haven't picked up a guitar since high school or only painted the siding on your house. The aim is not to produce great art but to let loose your creative spirit and the power of your ideas.

You can create nightly in front of an audience or alone in an art studio. It doesn't matter, as long as you're serving that longing. There are many ways to express the creative side you've suppressed all these years. Be original in finding a creative outlet. What's to stop you from starting your own jazz combo or writing group? There are many sources of energy that you can tap to energize your old age and make your post-work years thrilling. Nurturing your creative side is one of the best.

Empowerment #9: You can look forward, not back.

Raise your right hand and repeat after us: "I will not be an old crank." You know the people we're talking about, the crotchety seniors who live in the past and complain about the present. Nothing is good enough, everybody is dishonest or stupid, and the hurts of decades before are more important than the people in their lives today.

We feel pity for seniors who live this way because they are missing out on life. They are wallowing in the pain and misfortune of yesterday because it's easier than facing the challenges of life now. Such souls are on the expressway to the grave; there's nothing like resentment and regret to make you neglect your body and mind.

You're not that kind of person. You have the ability to make peace with what's gone before, savor each moment you live in now, and look forward to a bright future. That's not to say that it's not important to look back; you never want to lose wonderful memories or stories, which is why we're big believers in writing journals. But as you look back, apply the lessons of your past to what you're doing today and tomorrow. Approach today with relish and joy. Stop and live in the moment.

Americans are not very good at *the moment*. But when you're older and you have more control of your time, enjoy the freedom you have to stop, really stop, and enjoy the moment you're in. You don't have to wait until you're walking across the Golden Gate Bridge; you can do it at any time. Chances are, no matter where you are or what you're doing, there's something extraordinary happening: a baby chattering, flowers waving in the wind, music playing, a classic car passing on the street.

Most of all, look ahead. If you're fifty-five today, you have a good chance of living into your 90s. What are you going to do with all that time? What will be your purpose? If you have the freedom that comes with controlling your time, your future is a blank slate where you can create anything. Dream big. Sail around the world. Start a company. Write the novel that's inside you. Run for congress.

Empowerment #10: You can create a life filled with new experiences, inspiration, and great achievements.

There's another bit of conventional wisdom that says as you grow older, you become more conservative. Hogwash. When you're seventy, have the money you'll need to live until you're a hundred, and have no boss to answer to, what have you got to lose by taking a risk or two? Risk makes great things possible. What's to stop you from trying skydiving for the first time, investing in a start-up company that you believe in, or getting on stage to do stand-up comedy?

Old age is not the time to sit back in your comfort zone. It's when you should rip big, dripping chunks out of life and let the juice run down your chin. It's the time when, as long as you're in solid financial shape, you should embrace the uncertain. Uncertainty makes you grow, keeps your mind young, and electrifies your spirit. Mastering a new skill or getting through a new experience—even if it makes you uncomfortable—is one of the most exhilarating feelings in the world. It becomes addictive. That's the ultimate independence. You become unstoppable.

The Ten Empowerments are your alternative safety net. But unlike entitlements, which are out of your control, the Ten Empowerments are completely in your control. You can choose to be fit and healthy, creative and passionate, vital and active. If you do, you will have the choice to depend on those entitlements or to reject them. The key is *choice*. Get old or grow old? The choice is yours. It's always been yours. By building your future on the Ten Empowerments, you'll be helping us create the new alternatives to Social Security and Medicare:

Self Security and Insteadicare

The names alone imply self-reliance and independence, and that's what they're about. We're about to start a revolution. Come along for the ride.

Part I

It's Not "How Old Are You?" But "How Are You Old?"

As you'll see in this section, age is many things: how old the calendar says you are, how old your body says you are, and how old you feel. The last is the most important. We are coming to see that longevity is as much an act of will as a dedication to exercise and healthy diet. That's why the right question is not "How old are you?" That assumes that the entire truth of your age—of your life—lies in the birth date on your driver's license.

The question "How are you old?" means far more. It asks you how you feel, how you view life, how much passion and purpose and vitality you're bringing to each day. It says, in essence, "You're in control of this whole scene. How have you decided to age?" There are a million ways to do it. In this section of the book, we're going to start out with some fundamental ideas about aging that will suggest the many ways you can have a spectacular *seniorhood*.

chapter one

The Eight Great Myths About Growing Old

Years ago we discovered the exact point, the dead center of
middle age. It occurs when you are too young to take up golf
and too old to rush up to the net.[1]

—FRANKLIN P. ADAMS

We live in deeds, not years; in thoughts, not breaths;
In feelings, not in figures on a dial.
We should count time by heart-throbs. He most lives
Who thinks most, feels the noblest, acts the best . . .
Life's but a means unto an end; that end,
Beginning, mean, and end to all things—God.[2]

—PHILIP JAMES BAILEY

In 2003, Art Linkletter, who has known every American president since
FDR, administered his famous Old Geezer Test to one George W. Bush.

"We were standing in the Oval Office. I was in Washington to get the
Humanities Award, and I asked to meet with President Bush privately. We
were sitting around and talking about all the things I'm doing, and he said,
'I can't believe at ninety-one you do all these things. I hope when I'm
ninety-one I'll be living that way, with the same vitality, curiosity, and
enthusiasm.' And I said, 'Would you like me to give you a test? Based on a
UCLA study proving that lifestyle is more important than genes, we
believe you can live longer no matter what your genes say.' He said, 'Go
ahead. Let's see how I make out.' So I stood there with the president of the

United States, and I started firing questions at him: Do you smoke? No. Are you abusing alcohol? No. Do you get eight hours of sleep? Not quite. That's understandable for a man with a high-stress job.

"I went down the list. Low-fat diet. Exercise. Good breakfast. Humor. Curiosity. A passion for what you do. A happy marriage. All these things add to your life because they cut down on stress. He gave good answers, and at the end I said, 'Mr. President, you passed the test. I now proclaim you an honorary Old Geezer.' He laughed. It was probably the first time in the history of the presidency of the United States that the president had an examination on how to get older better, and I gave it to him."

> Three elderly men are at the doctor's office for a memory test. The doctor asks the first man, "What is three times three?" "274" is his reply.
>
> The doctor rolls his eyes and looks up at the ceiling and says to the second man, "It's your turn. What is three times three?" "Tuesday," replies the second man.
>
> The doctor shakes his head sadly then asks the third man, "Okay, your turn. What's three times three?" "Nine," says the third man.
>
> "That's great!" says the doctor. "How did you get that?" "Simple," he says, "just subtract 274 from Tuesday."

It's Not Dying, But Living Old That Scares Us

You don't find many folks aspiring to become Old Geezers. They are either spending fortunes in a fruitless search for potions that will keep them eternally young, or they are hustling themselves toward the grave in the hope that their bodies will call it quits before they end up broke and in a home somewhere waiting in vain for a grandchild to visit.

In other words, they buy into the eight great myths about growing old. According to a *USA Today/ABC News* poll of 1,000 adults taken in 2005, the average age people want to live to is eighty-seven. Just 25 percent of those surveyed said they wanted to make it to one hundred. And what did the same group cite as their main reason for not wanting to live to 100, 120, or beyond? Being disabled by health problems and becoming a burden to their loved ones.[3]

Baby Boomers say they fear death less than they fear the idea of falling apart when they hit old age. The specter of spending ten, twenty, or thirty years immobile, bereft of memory and identity, and utterly dependent taps the deepest fears of today's active, vibrant Boomers, and who can blame them? Compared to that kind of life, death looks like a viable alternative.

Those grim images of old age are outdated. Today, seniors compete in world-class Olympic events, run ultramarathons, start and manage billion-dollar companies, publish bestsellers, climb Himalayas, act, sing, dance, travel to the farthest corners of the world, and make breakthrough discoveries in medicine, science, history, geriatrics, and human sexuality. People over fifty have broken the tape into the twenty-first century with vigor, but our concepts about what it means to be old are languishing in the nineteenth century. It's time they caught up.

Where We Were Then, Where We Are Now

In case you think this is all a lot of hype, witness some of the more remarkable examples of older people who are not just getting by but are at the top of their games:

- Clint Eastwood, 76, won his second Academy Award for Best Picture at age 75.
- Paul Newman, 80, remains a race car driver and a leading producer of natural foods, much of the profits from which he donates to charities.
- Sophia Loren, 71, continues to make films regularly in her native Italy and is widely regarded as one of the world's great timeless beauties.
- John Wooden, 95, former UCLA basketball coaching legend, continues to travel the country speaking to audiences about his Pyramid of Success.

- Sandra Day O'Connor, 75, was widely regarded as the most influential justice on the Supreme Court of which she was recently a member.
- Warren Buffett, 75, known as the "Oracle of Omaha," is one of the world's wealthiest men, the champion of value investors, and the leading mind in smart, risk-managed investing.
- Paul Harvey, 87, continues to tell listeners the "rest of the story" and wish us all "good day" on radio stations throughout the United States and around the world.
- Etta James, 68, is one of the most vibrant, virtuoso female blues singers in the world and performs at dozens of blues festivals annually.
- Chita Rivera, 73, still regarded as "The Goddess of Broadway," continues to tour and perform, singing and dancing all over the nation.
- Betty Ford, 88, has become synonymous with drug rehabilitation and persists in her crusade to find new ways to prevent and treat drug abuse.

Those are just a few examples of well-known people who are leading the way in their professions at ages that, a few decades ago, would have gotten them laughed into the rest home. Society's acceptance of what seniors can accomplish has undergone a marvelous transformation. We don't even blink today when a seventy-year-old launches a new Internet company, sets a record in the discus throw, or releases a hit music CD. The younger generation takes it for granted now that older Americans will live longer, be healthier, get more active, and achieve more in their later years than ever before. The only problem is the older Americans themselves still don't get it.

In 1903, the average US life expectancy was forty-seven years. Today, according to the Centers for Disease Control and Prevention, the average US citizen can expect to live just over seventy-seven years as of 2004.[4] And people in some other cultures, such as Okinawa and Sardinia, are living even longer. What's even more surprising is the increase in the number of centenarians—those over one hundred. According to the US Census

Bureau, there are more than 71,000 Americans over age one hundred today, with that number expected to boom to 241,000 by 2020.[5] We owe that in part to improved health care, medicines, public sanitation, and better nutrition. But millions have access to those things, and only a small percentage of us live to triple digits. What do they know that we don't?

The Art Linkletter "Old Geezer Test"

Are you a future Old Geezer? Answer the questions to find out, then check your score at the bottom.

1. Do you refrain from smoking?	YES / NO
2. Do you abstain from alcohol consumption?	YES / NO
3. Do you get eight hours of sleep a night?	YES / NO
4. Do you eat a low-fat diet?	YES / NO
5. Do you exercise every day?	YES / NO
6. Do you eat a good breakfast every day?	YES / NO
7. Do you have a sense of humor?	YES / NO
8. Do you have a sense of curiosity about the world?	YES / NO
9. Do you have a passion for what you do?	YES / NO
10. Do you have a happy marriage?	YES / NO

Scoring—Count your "Yes" answers and determine your odds of becoming an Old Geezer.

9–10 "Yes" answers: You are well on your way to Old Geezerhood, if you're not there already.

6–8 "Yes" answers: You're a good candidate to become a Geezer, but you've got some work to do in a few areas.

3–5 "Yes" answers: You're not maintaining the best habits to keep you vital as you age. Old Geezerhood is going to take some work and commitment.

0–2 "Yes" answers: You have a will, right?

AGING FEARLESSLY

Today's super-old refuse to accept the idea that age-related losses of health, mental clarity, mobility, passion, and purpose are *inevitable*. Aging and decline, for now, are inevitable (though medical and scientific research are now challenging even that long-held belief), but they can come at the end of eight or nine or ten decades of healthy, vigorous, fulfilling living. We're not talking about denying aging or chasing some nonexistent fountain of youth but about *extending healthy life by years or even decades*.

The people who will make the rest of their lives the best of their lives are those who stubbornly refuse to believe that life is a one-way slide into dissolution once you pass age sixty. These people—you're one of them—look at aging fearlessly, as a time when adult life is just entering its second half. You've made your money, had your kids, made your sacrifices, earned your wisdom. Now it's time to travel, build, eat, drink, dream, create, speak truth, cherish friends, learn from past mistakes, make all new mistakes, take risks, make peace with the things you cannot change, and raise Cain over the things that need changing. As Norman Lear, creator of such television icons as *All in the Family*, said in an interview for this book, "'Next' is more important than 'Over.'"

As aging expert Dr. Ken Dychtwald stated in an extensive interview for this book, "We are witnessing the emergence of a *gerontocracy*, a powerful new old age. And we have the largest generation in American history barreling toward it." More than any other time in history, you have the power to take your place in that gerontocracy. It all begins with understanding the Eight Myths and how to defy them.

A husband and wife, both sixty years old, were celebrating their thirty-fifth anniversary. During their party, a fairy appeared to congratulate them and grant them each one wish. The wife wanted to travel around the world.

The fairy waved her wand and poof!—the wife had tickets

in her hand for a world cruise. Next, the fairy asked the husband what he wanted. He said, "I wish I had a wife thirty years younger than me."

So the fairy picked up her wand and poof!—the husband was ninety.

Myth #1: Sickness

According to the conventional wisdom, old age means a breakdown of the body's systems. But advances in science and new discoveries about the power of lifestyle changes mean that age does not have to be a time of constant sickness and diminishing health. Only about 5 percent of seniors today live in nursing homes.

As with so much related to health, avoiding sickness in old age comes down to *prevention*. Most of the diseases that disable or kill older Americans—heart disease, stroke, cancer, diabetes—are in large part the result of lifestyles that include too much bad food, too little exercise, excessive stress, lack of rest, and killer habits such as smoking and drinking. By the same token, the factors that extend healthy life are also matters of lifestyle: eating lots of fresh fruits, vegetables, whole grains and nuts, getting plenty of regular exercise (including playing sports), drinking enough water, and so on. The problem is, it seems that many Americans lack the foresight to understand that doing these things when they're fifty can keep them living well at eighty.

"Sadly, too much of modern medicine appears to still be driven by the pharmaceutical industry and the sickness model and does not concern itself with health, energy, and vitality," wrote Australian antiaging physician Dr. Michael Elstein, author of *Eternal Health*, in response to questions for this book. "Many doctors are ignorant when it comes to matters of wellness, largely because they are unhealthy themselves." Worse, what some call the "harmaceutical" industry is now focused on selling "continuity" drugs that you take forever. We remember when you took a drug for a week, got better, and stopped taking it.

In other words, sickness is as much a matter of the culture in our society as of the culture of bacteria. If you're waiting to become ill before taking action, you're going to be sick.

An Ounce of Prevention . . . Your vital organs, especially your kidneys, become less efficient with age (healing massage may help). Your metabolism slows down. Your vision and hearing become less acute (though some claim the Bates method may help prevent some sight impairment; learn more at http://en.wikipedia.org/wiki/Bates_Method). These aren't surprises to anyone, but it's amazing that some people never make the changes necessary to compensate.

The keys to avoiding chronic sickness as you age are anticipation and prevention. This is why it becomes so vital not to deny old age but to accept and embrace it as a time when your greater freedom and possibility come with a price: investing time, planning, and money in measures designed to prevent the early breakdown of your body. There are so many things you can do that might seem insignificant but have an enormous cumulative effect on your risk of disease:

- Wash your hands regularly. Just using regular soap and water (expensive antibacterial cleansers are no better, according to the FDA) reduces your risk of infection by bacterial and viral diseases. Wash your hands as long as it takes to sing "Happy Birthday."
- Regularly dust and clean bedrooms and other rooms where you spend lots of time to reduce the risk of allergic reactions, eradicate dust mites, and eliminate mold and bacteria.
- Get your annual flu vaccination, and make sure your grandchildren are vaccinated for pneumonia. Recent studies show that when children and infants are vaccinated against pneumonia, deaths among seniors from the disease drop dramatically.
- Talk to your physician about an "aspirin a day" regimen. It purportedly thins blood clots and thereby helps prevent strokes, aneurisms, and heart attacks.
- Get an annual checkup, even if you feel perfect. Men over fifty

should always have a prostate exam, and everyone over fifty should have a colonoscopy at least every five years, more often if you are at higher risk.

As Elstein points out, today there is a remarkable battery of tests that measure risk factors for heart disease and other killer diseases: CT scans, glucose metabolism tests, "biological terrain assessments" that measure free radical levels, cellular acid/alkali balance, inflammatory levels, and more. Today's advanced diagnostic tools can detect the root causes and inform the treatment of illnesses years before they cause symptoms.

Wellness Insurance? You may be familiar with "wellness medicine," a collection of alternative therapies ranging from chiropractic to therapeutic massage. These types of health care focus less on treating illness than on reducing stress and getting the body in an optimal state to fight off illness and maximize overall health. Many Baby Boomers who came of age in the 1960s, and are big proponents of alternative care, still rely on wellness providers to help them stave off the ailments of old age. In fact, we invest three times as much on alternative therapies as we do traditional medicine.

> *You are as young as your faith, as old as your doubt; as young as your self-confidence, as old as your fear; as young as your hope, as old as your despair.*[6]
>
> —SAMUEL ULLMAN

Good news. The insurance industry has finally caught up with you. Through companies such as Health Action Network Society, you can purchase "wellness insurance," which combines life insurance, accidental death and dismemberment insurance, and coverage that pays part of the cost of such wellness caregivers as massage therapists, osteopaths, naturopathic physicians, and psychologists. This makes it easier and more affordable to get the preventive care that can help keep muscles supple, reduce stress and detoxify your body, ease pain from injuries or arthritis, and recommend beneficial regimens of food, supplements, and nutrients that will truly enhance your well-being.

Myth #2: Frailty

This is one of the classics: old people are brittle and fragile, and if they fall down, they'll break a hip and be dead in a year. Is that true for some seniors? Yes. All stereotypes have some basis in fact. But it doesn't have to be true for you. You can be active and robust and sturdy deep into the second half of life.

The most common villain when it comes to the myth of frailty is osteoporosis, the loss of bone mass that often occurs with age and affects millions of Americans. Women are four times more likely to develop the condition because of the effects of menopause, but it also affects men. Osteoporosis makes bones more brittle and easier to break, especially bones in the hip and spine. That's why many seniors are so afraid of falls; a broken hip can result in severe disability, long hospitalization, and a heartbreaking loss of mobility and independence.

Relentlessly Active. It turns out that a lifetime of strenuous physical activity is not just good for controlling your weight and keeping your heart healthy, it also keeps you mobile and tough, keeping bones strong and muscles supple and flexible. Look at some of the isolated cultures that are known for their longevity:

- Natives on the Caribbean island of Dominica, which has the highest longevity in the western hemisphere and boasted the incredible Elizabeth "Ma Pampo" Israel, who died on October 14, 2003, at the unconfirmed age of 128.[7]
- Farm and sheep herding families in remote areas of Sardinia, like those profiled in "The Secrets of Long Life" by Dan Buettner, *National Geographic*, November 2005.
- Okinawans, also profiled by Buettner and the subjects of the Okinawa Centenarian Study.[8]

These people lead different types of lives, consume different diets, and have little in common but their advanced age. However, they do have one thing in common: agrarian societies where hard work goes on daily with no reprieve because one is seventy-five and feeling sore. It's not uncommon at all to see men and women in their 70s and 80s in these regions putting in full days of work in fishing boats, on farms, or tending cattle work that would leave people in their 30s and 40s gasping for air and sore to the core. Ask these individuals about their daily regimens of walking, weeding, building walls, and hauling wood, and they inevitably shrug; such exertions are an ordinary part of their lives, and have been for years. It really does come down to, "Move it or lose it."

Agelessness Secret #1

Universal Pluripotent Cell Research

The Stowe Foundation, under the direction of Dr. Lawrence Stowe, has discovered a type of pluripotent (meaning it can become any kind of cell in the body) adult stem cell existing in any individual's own bone marrow. These cells can become any other tissue in the body. The foundation is developing a technique to harvest these Universal Pluripotent Stem Cells (UPS) and then rapidly reproduce them so that they can be transplanted in large number into a damaged organ. This technique of harvesting the bone marrow yields a significantly greater number of these pluripotent cells than any other source.

These cells may possibly be used in treating conditions such as heart disease, stroke, diabetes, and liver cirrhosis as well as knee and joint repair, spinal cord injuries, wound and ulcer repair, and tendon and ligament surgery. In addition, all varieties of cosmetic surgery will benefit from the healing powers of the UPS.

The FDA considers the expansion of the UPS to be the same as creating a new blood product, so current restrictions apply to actual use in the United States. Please watch the news or look online for the latest updates on restrictions and on possible new therapies involving these extraordinary cells.[9]

The 105-Year-Old Javelin Thrower. Case in point: John Whittemore, who set a record for his age group in the javelin throw in October 2004 before passing away in April 2005. Now, given that he was 105 when he made his record throw, his age group wasn't all that big (685 men as of 2000, according to the Census Bureau), and his record toss of 11 feet wouldn't have made the evening highlights on ESPN. But Whittemore had been competing in track and field—and setting records—since his boyhood. As recently as the autumn of 2004, Whittemore was working out with weights daily and still thinking about new records. Since his death, USA track and field is thinking about creating a competition group for athletes aged 105 to 109.[10]

You read that right: 105 to 109. It's never too late. So says fitness legend Jack LaLanne, ninety-two, who has been preaching the benefits of diet and exercise for more than sixty years. LaLanne, who still works out for two hours every morning and has a forty-six-inch chest and a thirty-inch waist, tells people they can benefit from exercise no matter how long they waited to get started. "I hate to get up at 5:00 AM and leave a [warm] bed to work out in a cold gym," he said in an interview for this book. "But I love the results."

The Corrosive Power of "I Can't." A summer 2005 study at Yale University revealed that the more television seniors watched—the more they were bombarded by negative, derisive stereotypes of bumbling, decrepit old fogies—the more negative their ideas about aging became. Participants between sixty and ninety-two were divided into two groups and filled out viewing diaries for a week, with one group adding its views about how the elderly were portrayed on television. The characterizations ranged from "nonexistent" to claims that the aged were constantly the brunt of jokes.[11]

This is precisely the kind of input from the wider world that makes seniors say the words that guarantee an old age of tragic decline: "I can't." I can't play softball at my age. I can't do a three-mile hike. I can't lift weights. Those two words corrode the spirit and turn the idea of the frail, incapable senior into a self-fulfilling prophecy. In response we say, no, you can't hike three miles today. But you can hike one mile. And if you do it three times a week, soon you'll be hiking five miles and wondering what was the big deal.

Research from a wide range of sources agrees that it's never too late to start a program of strength, endurance, and flexibility training. But just as important to a well-developed exercise regimen is the will to practice it. One thing we've noticed in common among senior athletes and adventurers is a defiant attitude. These are folks who relish the fact that other people are stunned when they reach the top of a mountain trail, do fifty reps on the bench press machine, or a perfect warrior pose in a yoga class. It's up to you to cultivate that defiant attitude about exercise, movement, and activity.

Just Get Moving. Naturopathic physician Dr. Andrew Myers believes being fit and strong is less about exercise and more about *movement.* Movement doesn't require the gym or expensive equipment. Movement means gardening, walking, dancing, or playing with the grandkids. For more information about Dr. Myers's "Simple Health Value," visit http://www.simplehealthvalue.com/simplehealth.asp.

Just get your body moving:

- Lift weights.
- Do stretching exercises to elongate your muscles and improve flexibility and mobility.
- Swim. It's the best low-impact exercise around.
- Garden.
- Cycle.
- Go dancing.
- Climb hills, then mountains.

Frailty comes with disuse. When you use what you've got, consistently and with variety, it won't be a concern.

Myth #3: Senility

This is probably the most dreaded myth about growing old: the slide into dementia and the eventual loss of identity. That's understandable.

After all, we live between our ears; our bodies are tools evolved to follow the directives of our brains. If that marvelous, trillion-celled computer breaks down, the fittest body on the planet isn't much good.

The best way to refute this myth is to look around at the millions of seniors engaged in demanding, thought-intensive activities all over the world. Seniors are running businesses, governing nations, making new discoveries, writing best-selling novels, and that's just for starters. Their minds are as sharp and quick as when they were in their 30s.

As with most aspects of aging, some decline in your cognitive powers is inescapable; it's biology. Cellular death happens in the brain as early as your 20s, and your brain shrinks for your entire life after that. But we're discovering that old age doesn't mean losing your marbles. For example, a 2003 Duke University study revealed that high blood pressure does not accelerate age-related cognitive decline as was thought. Your brain is tough. You can protect your mind and work your brain so that you're gaining more cognitive ability than you lose. We're discovering now that it is possible to train your brain and retain more of your memory and mental ability as you grow older.[12]

A Boot Camp for the Brain. Dr. Gary Small is Director of the UCLA Center on Aging, author of *The Memory Bible* and *The Memory Prescription*, and one of the medical minds on the vanguard of improving brain function and memory through specific activities and lifestyle changes. Later on, we'll go more into Dr. Small's work and other ground-breaking discoveries regarding keeping the brain and mind vital, but look at what the simple existence of his book, UCLA "memory boot camp" program, and books and programs like them tell us: just like you work a muscle to improve its function, you can work your brain to do the same. You're not stuck with a fading memory any more than you're stuck with small biceps. Dr. Small says in *The Memory Prescription*:

> The search to uncover our risk for dementia and what deter-
> mines the rate at which our brains age has revealed a startling fact:
> for the average person, only about one-third of this determination

comes from genetics. So if two thirds of what determines our future risk has to do with our environment and the lifestyle choices we make today, we clearly have more control over our future than many might imagine—two-thirds control.[13]

That's an extraordinary idea. But research backs it up. If you're worried about dementia and memory loss as you get older, you can take action. And there's no such thing as starting too late.

Age and Deceit Beat Youth and Speed. There's a credo that goes, "Age and deceit will defeat youth and speed every time." That's a bit cynical, but there's an aspect we agree with. As you grow older, particularly as you move into your 80s and 90s,

> *I like old people when they have aged well. And old houses with an accumulation of sweet honest living in them are good. And the timelessness that only the passing of Time itself can give to objects both inside and outside the spirit is a continuing reassurance.*[14]
>
> —M.F.K. Fisher

you are going to lose some of your cognitive ability even if you never develop Alzheimer's disease. You'll find it harder to remember the events of a few days ago even though the distant past is crystal clear. Problem solving will be a bit tougher. Age happens. Changes will too.

Senior Achiever

Dr. Solomon Margolin, 86, founder and president of MARNAC, Inc.

With doctorates in physiology, biochemistry, and genetics from Rutgers University, Dr. Margolin spent decades in the pharmaceutical industry, holding research and director positions for several major pharmaceutical laboratories. He also has developed more than twenty FDA-approved drugs, including drugs carrying the brand names Dimetapp and Coricidin that are sold worldwide. So why start MARNAC in 1990 at age seventy, when most of his peers were retiring?

To develop treatments that truly change lives for sufferers of multiple sclerosis.

"In my recent work with multiple sclerosis, I work with secondary progressive, the worst kind," says Margolin. "These people are paralyzed: they either have to be in wheelchairs or can't use their hands. We give them the drug and after three months or six months half of them start to walk again and use their hands."

With his MS drug in the FDA approval pipeline, Margolin, a three-time winner over cancer, still works with his wife, a physician board-certified in internal medicine, on research and treatments for conditions such as restoring lung function to patients whose lungs have been scarred due to asbestos or smoking.

What keeps him going? "I'm ornery," he says. "I've never had [retirement] in my blood. Because of my age, I occasionally encounter younger people who just find it hard to believe that an old codger should know so much. I don't get upset about it. I just keep on pushing on, pushing on.

"Also, my sense of curiosity goes back to when I was three years of age. My mother told me that I once was out in the back yard on a little tricycle, and I was screaming and hollering, so she ran out to find out what had happened. I said, 'Look. I've discovered where the clouds came from!' There was a steam locomotive making steam, and that's where the clouds came from. And that's the story of my life."

Dr. Margolin can be reached at www.marnac.com.

However, there are factors that can compensate for the loss in pure mental horsepower. When you've lived seven or eight decades, you have more experience, sounder judgment, and greater wisdom than someone who's thirty or forty years younger than you (or you should). You possess the ability to judge people, assess a situation from all sides, and make a sound, rational decision. There's no teacher like experience.

Why Reread the Same Books? Brain health professionals offer many recommendations for preventing dementia, and we're going to touch on them in our chapter on the mind. But we feel like the easiest to do is also the most important and enjoyable: challenge your mind constantly. Research has shown that challenging activities such as travel, crossword puzzles, and learning to play a musical instrument can build up your brain and decrease your risk of developing Alzheimer's as well as other, milder forms of dementia.

It turns out that testing your intellect can preserve your intellect just as exercise can preserve your muscle mass and bone density. But since many seniors become complacent as they age, not seeking out new challenges and learning new things, they don't demand greater activity from their brains. Like any other part of the body, when the brain goes unused, it atrophies. There's no excuse for it, especially with the array of educational programs available for seniors at universities and community colleges. For example, the Bernard Osher Foundation has enabled universities across the nation to create Osher Lifelong Learning Institutes, which offer courses for people over fifty in a huge range of subjects. Seniors can participate in university courses, attend lectures, go on field trips, conduct research—all marvelous ways to keep the mind vibrant and alive.

There are many other simpler ways to challenge yourself:

- Read new books; don't reread old ones.
- Learn a foreign language.
- Learn to read music.
- Do crossword puzzles or word games daily.
- Read maps and study geography.
- Get into debate or public discussion groups.
- Discover and challenge yourself to do something that can't currently be done.
- Solve one of the world's problems.
- Invent something.
- Write your book.

Anything that stretches your mind beyond the routines of your day and forces you to learn things you didn't know yesterday is pure brain food.

Dig In Up to Your Elbows. Nothing we've seen appears to have a greater impact on mental sharpness into old age like a sense of passion, purpose, and involvement in something that you care about deeply. We encounter it all the time in discussions for this book: people in their 80s and 90s who are running businesses, running for office, and competing in sports are doing so with minds that are wonderfully keen and senses of humor that are remarkably nimble. The common denominator: they're up to their elbows in life, doing something that they love doing, something they would pay to do if they had to.

One more thing: laugh. Tell jokes. One of the great things about being old is that the humor a forty-year-old couldn't get away with is fine for a ninety-year-old. Never lose your sense of humor, particularly about yourself. It will keep you young.

Myth #4: Sexlessness

Art Linkletter jokes, "At my age, the greatest form of contraception is nudity." Funny, but why do we laugh? Is it because once you get past a certain age, you lose your sexual drive? There's a common public perception that after age sixty-five, seniors don't want sex, don't have sex, don't enjoy sex, and shouldn't talk about sex. The younger generations don't even want to think about the idea of senior sexuality. Yuck.

Let us set the record straight: married couples over fifty-five love sex. They want it, enjoy it, and talk about it. There is zero evidence to show that being over fifty-five means you stop wanting sexual activity. That's the propaganda of a youth-obsessed culture that sees anyone over fifty as obsolete and anyone over seventy as dead. Too bad: just as Baby Boomers are driving changes in medicine, science, and finance, they're bringing on some new perceptions about being sexy in your 60s, 70s, or 80s.

No Kids, No Pregnancy, No Problem! Sophia Loren once quipped, "Sex appeal is 50 percent what you've got and 50 percent what people think you've got." Sex appeal is more than a matter of physical appearance—a fact that adults, as we age, come to know more clearly. The knockout without a brain in his or her head becomes less attractive as we get older and travel around the block a few times. Confidence, a sense of humor, wit, a romantic flair—these all become much greater aspects of sexual attraction as we hit middle age.

If sixty is the new forty, mustn't sixty-year-olds be enjoying rumpling the sheets as much as today's forty-year-olds? The answer is a resounding yes. A study on "Sexual Interest and Behavior in Healthy 80- to 102-year-olds" published in the Archives of Sexual Behavior back in April 1988 showed that 63 percent of men and 30 percent of women were still having sexual intercourse.[15] More recently, a 2004 AARP study revealed that nearly half (49 percent) of Americans between ages 45 and 70 who had a regular sexual partner were engaging in sexual intercourse at least once per week. More important, 63 percent of them reported being extremely or somewhat satisfied with their sex lives.[16]

Perhaps more important is the enjoyment level of sex for seniors these days. Plenty of anecdotal evidence found in survey after survey suggests that senior men and women enjoy sex as much in their Second Prime years as they did in their younger years. And why not? If you're physically healthy, there are plenty of reasons to enjoy sex more. You're not worried about pregnancy. You're not worried about the kids bursting in on you. You're more familiar with what your spouse wants. You're more communicative and a lot more experienced at romance and foreplay. You're better at sex.

Rewriting the Rules. Exercise is changing the paradigm already. Seniors who haven't worked out in years are discovering that no matter what your age, it's never too late to get in shape. As a result, older Americans look better. They're shattering the stereotype that old age means saggy pecs and scrawny knees and no energy. As they're hitting the weights and doing lung-burning sessions on the stationary bike and elliptical, they're also redefining what it means to be attractive in our society. Women like Sophia Loren, Lauren Bacall, Raquel Welch, and Julie Christie, and men like Paul Newman, Sean Connery, Clint Eastwood, and Harrison Ford prove that older people can not only be sexy, but out-and-out hot.

If You're Not, Why Not? There are valid reasons not to be sexual later in life:

- You're not married, or you're widowed.
- You're not in shape and are ashamed of your body.
- Your relationship with your spouse is not good.
- It's too much work.
- You're having problems with your physical health.

Every one of these problems has a solution: exercise and diet, counseling, joining a social organization or dating service, and so on. Then again, maybe you're just an old sourpuss who has decided that sex is for young people. If that's your attitude, no wonder you're not having sex! Sexuality is a very real, vital part of growing old and comes with a host of wonderful physical and psychological benefits.

Myth #5: Loneliness

One of the saddest myths about growing old is the picture of the wizened old man or woman, abandoned in a nursing home or left living alone in a dingy apartment, forgotten by family, never visited, depressed and alone, slowly decaying. And while that sort of thing, sadly, does occur, there is absolutely no reason for anyone, no matter how bereaved by a death or reduced by infirmity, to be alone in old age. More than ever before, there are countless opportunities for older Americans to get out, meet people, network, and rediscover the energy that comes with relationships.

Social Networks Are Good for You. The facts are in: having a close circle of friends helps you live longer. The Australian Longitudinal Study of Aging, which in 1992 began studying nearly 1,500 people to determine the impact of social, economic, behavioral, and environmental factors on health, has revealed that over ten years, having a strong network of friends increased longevity, even more than having close family ties. The researchers who conducted the study theorize that a tight circle of friends and confidants influences peoples' habits more, boosts mood, and helps members of the group cope with life's difficulties.[17]

Combine this with the common practice in Okinawan society of the *moai*, a mutually supportive circle of long-term (often lifelong) friends, and the pattern becomes clear: having a network of friends is good for your health. Being with other human beings lifts us out of depressing reveries and dwelling on the past, improves mood, motivates change, triggers the sense of humor, offers a path to new challenges, and reminds us that for all its vagaries, life is good.[18]

It gets better for social butterflies. According to a report published by Dr. Robert H. Coombs, professor of Biobehavioral Sciences at UCLA, married couples enjoy greater longevity than the unmarried, need healthcare services less often, have an 8 to 17 percent higher rate of cancer cure than single people, and even suffer from schizophrenia less frequently.[19] That's for better, not worse.

A young man saw an elderly couple sitting down to lunch at McDonald's. He noticed that they had ordered one meal and an extra drink cup.

As he watched, the gentleman carefully divided the hamburger in half, then counted out the fries, one for him, one for her, until each had half of them. Then he poured half of the soft drink into the extra cup and set that in front of his wife. The old man then began to eat, and his wife sat watching, with her hands folded in her lap.

The young man decided to ask if they would allow him to purchase another meal for them so that they didn't have to split theirs.

The old gentleman said, "Oh no. We've been married fifty years, and everything has always been and will always be shared, fifty/fifty."

The young man then asked the wife if she was going to eat, and she replied, "It's his turn with the teeth."

So Many Opportunities. There's a staggering array of organizations that offer seniors the chance to meet others, do good works, and make discoveries:

- Groups like United Planet, Earthwatch, Meals on Wheels, the American Red Cross, Habitat for Humanity, Operation Smile, Northwest Medical Teams, and Global Volunteers give seniors the chance to volunteer overseas for weeks or months, doing everything from teaching reading to participating in scientific research.
- Dating services like Silver Singles give seniors an easy, safe way to meet new people.
- Internet-based tools like Meetup.com make it simple for older folks to connect with like-minded individuals of all ages in their area.
- Organizations like the Red Hat Society simply offer women fun, companionship, some healthy silliness, and some wonderful events and perks.
- Venerable groups like the Elks, Lions, and Rotary perform important duties in many communities and give seniors a great way to connect with people in their area.

There are even organizations who recruit volunteers to visit lonely seniors who crave company! There is no reason anyone has to be lonely or isolated in later life, not when there are so many opportunities to make contact, achieve, and do good things. These days, if you're alone, it's probably because you choose to be.

Myth #6: Purposelessness

People need purpose. It's that simple. We all need something that gives us a reason to get up in the morning and lets us feel at the end of the day like we used our time wisely. That's especially true for seniors. When the daily rigors of going to a job are over, the kids are gone, and there's nothing more strenuous to strive for than making a hair appointment, it's critical to your well-being to find something meaningful that challenges you, makes you feel needed.

With Baby Boomers likely to remain healthy and active into their 80s and beyond, their need to find purpose and make a difference will only increase. While there is no research to support the idea that having a demanding purpose extends life, look at the highest-achieving older people you've heard of, from celebrities to folks in the community. Almost all of them have a calling or goal that gets them moving each day and keeps them from giving in to age. There's no reason you can't do the same thing.

What Is Purpose? In his 1999 book, *The Adult Years: Mastering the Art of Self-Renewal*, Frederic M. Hudson provides an excellent list of the types of pursuits that can make up a purposeful later life. They include:

- Continuous lifelong learning and earning
- Maintaining multiple tasks in parallel that add commitment and reward to your life
- Keeping up with new fields of expertise and areas of interest
- Living on the edge of your possibilities and knowing how to lose, adapt, and recover[20]

What is purpose? It's that pursuit, goal, or activity that you feel like you were "meant" to do, something you could do all day, everyday, for no pay and not feel tired at day's end. It's your passion. It could be starting a company, relearning a hobby that you set aside fifty years earlier, volunteering, becoming a political activist or advocate for the homeless, setting the goal of running a marathon, restoring a sailboat so you can sail around the world, or any of a million other things. Purpose is something that gives back to you more than you put into it—that feeds your soul and dreams and desire to exceed your limitations.

When you're younger, following your purpose isn't always easy. The world is full of people who had passionate dreams in their youth but let them slip away on the currents of practicality and least resistance. You start a job, buy a house, get married, have kids, have bills to pay. Purpose and passion are forgotten. But then comes your Second Prime. No kids. No regular job. No mortgage. You've got time to fill, and you need ways to fill it. Now is the time when you should be questing for meaning, searching for your sense of purpose. What do you care about most? What group of people do you want to help? What do you want to change? What lofty goals would you set for yourself if you didn't care what anyone else thought?

Volunteer. One of the most common and satisfying ways seniors discover their sense of purpose is through volunteering. By the time you've reached the later part of your life, you have a host of skills and talents that would be useful to others: business knowledge, trade skills, and teaching experience to name a few. With organizations like VolunteerMatch and Literacy Volunteers of America always on the lookout for people to fill needs throughout the country, there's no reason why, if you're healthy and mobile, you can't find a way to give back through volunteering.

Purpose gives back more than you invest: according to the Council on Aging for Southeastern Vermont, people who volunteer—who gain the social networks that such activity brings—are in better health than non-volunteers. Volunteering builds self-esteem, teaches new skills, and has been shown to enhance health because of an increase in endorphin levels. Apparently, the satisfaction of volunteering can even reduce stress. Mark Victor Hansen wrote a book called *The Miracle of Tithing*, which states that you can contribute with four T's: your *thinking*, your *time*, your *talent*, and your *treasures*. The greatest is your thinking. The best thinking for charities has not been done yet, and you can do it, helping them to solve problems and raising more money, awareness, and exposure.

Activism. Seniors who are of a political or environmental mind can also embrace activism as a way to discover a sense of purpose. When you've seen so much and have strong views, it makes sense to promote those views. Seniors have been a huge part of everything from the National Organization for Women and antiwar movements to the environmental movement. Why? They have the time, the money, and the expertise that younger folks lack. From AARP to the Gray Panthers, seniors are becoming a more powerful voice in politics and social change by virtue of their sheer numbers and economic power. Your opportunity to be heard and to make a difference is not only here, but growing.

Personal Goals. Purpose can be all about a cherished goal. What have you always wanted to do? Travel to Spain? Learn the piano? Lose fifty pounds? Write a bestseller? Paint a masterpiece? Once you have the time to devote to it, a goal like one of these can become your purpose. With dedication and discipline, you can turn a purpose into a way of life as well. For example, the exercise regimen required to get in shape to run a marathon will likely become a regular part of your life, leading to a healthier, longer life.

Many seniors discover a buried creative side after they shed the layers of work, debt, and children. The cities and towns of America are filled with gray-haired painters, sculptors, composers, poets, novelists, dancers, and radio personalities. Do you have a creative soul dying to be let loose?

Myth #7: Passivity

Depression is commonly undiagnosed among seniors. It's a debilitating clinical illness. Among people sixty-five and older, about 3 percent experience clinical depression. Fortunately, these people can be treated with a combination of powerful drugs and psychotherapy. But even for seniors who do not suffer from depression, old age can be a time of passivity and resentment.

It's understandable when you look at all the negative aspects of old age: loss of loved ones, health problems, lack of mobility, difficulty making the transition from working life to retirement, and similar causes. Some people *learn* how to think about age from a negative, angry place, developing neural pathways in the brain that serve that purpose. For these seniors, the later stages of life are all about refusal, disapproval, and a sense of what psychologist Martin E. P. Seligman called "learned helplessness."[21]

Defiant, Stubborn, and Willful. The opposite of being passive is not being active, but *taking initiative.* Seniors who get past the passivity myth are the ones who refuse to allow outside forces to wield control over their lives. Rather than sit around and complain, they find reasons why things aren't working and develop solutions. The aging Boomer generation, with its strong-willed attitude and refusal to go gently into that good night, is likely to take initiative to a new level. You can do it. All you have to do is make a habit of saying:

> "I am in control of my old age. No one can do anything to me without my consent, and if I see something that demands to be changed, I will take steps to change it."

Defiance and stubbornness are not vices when they're deployed in the defense of one's own independence. You have a right to speak out, to act, to refuse to stand by and let things happen to you. Exercise it.

Myth #8: Poverty

Remember "I hope I don't outlive my money"? Living in poverty or dependence on family is a major fear of seniors. But you won't be able to count on Social Security to bail you out if you fail to do the proper financial planning. Even defined benefit pensions, such as those offered by the government to public sector workers, are far in the red.

The hard truth is some seniors who have allowed themselves to become dependent on what they see as "guaranteed" entitlements may fall into poverty, which is certainly likely to spur government action. The fact that Americans are saving less than ever—about one percent of our incomes per year compared with 11 percent in the 1970s—is another factor that will put some seniors on the brink of financial ruin.[22]

Choice One: Plan Wisely. The main problem is a good one: Baby Boomers are expected to live longer than any American generation that came before them. If you walk away from your regular job at fifty-five, you can reasonably expect thirty to thirty-five years of life ahead of you. That was a whole lifetime at the turn of the century. It's a long time to keep paying out when you have nothing coming in. So unless you plan on winning the lottery, the first step to avoiding financial struggle in old age is planning and making some sacrifices while you're working.

You would be wise to save 10 percent or more of your income, tithe 10 percent, and invest 10 percent. This is great lifelong advice. If you are starting late, you have to accelerate the amount of money earned, saved, given, and invested. John Wesley, founder of the Methodist church and the richest preacher of his time, said, "Do all the good you can, by all the means you can, in all the ways you can, in all the places you can, at all the times you can, to all the people you can, as long as ever you can."[23]

You can't have it all while you're earning and live without financial worries when you're eighty. It's vital to retain the services of a good, smart financial advisor, preferably one who's been certified by the American Institute of Financial Gerontology, an organization that specializes in the financial and investment issues related to aging. Work with this advisor on figuring out what kind of assets you'll need to maintain the lifestyle you want when you retire, then figure out what you'll need to save to accrue those assets. It's really not more complex than that, though there is a dizzying array of investment vehicles. Sprinkle it all with some clarity and lack of self-deception about the return you'll earn on your money, and you're on your way.

Oh, and the earlier you start, the better.

Keep Working. Hold on. We're not suggesting you never quit working for The Man. We're also not suggesting that you take a desperation job at minimum wage. What we are suggesting is that you never stop creating, contributing, or working. Instead of retiring, you need to "refire" your passion and create a second career that allows you to make a living doing what you want. It doesn't have to be much; a few hundred dollars a month might be enough to pay your expenses and let you enjoy your lifestyle. Whatever you decide to do, it's time to become the CEO of You, Inc.

You have assets you may not have realized:

- A lifetime of marketable experience
- A network of business contacts
- Time to pursue opportunities
- The Internet, the most powerful information-sharing tool ever created

Now is the time to tap into your fondest interests or area of greatest expertise and start your own business! Whether it's an online antique mall or a business crafting handmade furniture, there's nothing stopping you. Okay, you may not be entrepreneurial and dislike the idea of working for yourself. No problem. Why not consult for your former employer or other companies in the same industry? Most corporations would kill to have access to a mind with decades of experience. Your expertise is an in-demand asset. Take advantage.

Maybe It's Time to Cut Back. If you can't increase your income enough, try the other end: lowering costs. Before you throw the book across the room because you think we're asking you to give up the lifestyle you've worked so hard for, wait a moment. We're not. What we are suggesting is that you look at *simplifying*.

"Simple living" is a growing movement that says, "We have too much stuff that we're living to service, and we spend too much time running around. Let's clean out, slow down, and really live." It's a great sentiment, and living simply works and saves money. Seniors who live more simply can lower costs while actually improving their quality of life by doing things like:

- Driving less and walking more
- Growing food in the garden
- Cooking at home more and eating out less
- Camping instead of staying in expensive hotels
- Getting rid of one car or getting a high-mileage hybrid
- Keeping clothes longer and shopping at garage sales
- Spending less on costly toys like flat panel TVs and more on books
- Reviving your library card
- Entertaining more at home with friends instead of having expensive nights out

You don't have to give up all your expensive, guilty pleasures to live simply and save money. Just cut back. As you see from this list, simple living means living closer to nature and people and at a slower, more peaceful pace. And those are things that make life feel richer.

You Don't Have to Be Rich . . . not to be poor when you're old. You just have to plan: get a financial strategy, look at businesses you could start, look at ways to cut back and save more today.

That's it for the Eight Myths. They have only as much power as you grant them. There's not a single part of defying the myths that doesn't lie in your control. It's your choice how you want to grow old. It always has been. Now, here are the Eight Truths about your Second Prime:

Eight Truths About Your Second Prime
- As you live longer, you will have generations of relationships.
- For the first time, products are being designed exclusively for you.
- Technologies such as genetics and nanotechnology could allow you to slow the aging process.
- Digital technology will allow you to leave an oral and visual history to your descendants.
- The business world will welcome you back to employment on your terms, seeking to capitalize on your experience.
- The Internet will help you connect with others, make money, and learn in ways you've never imagined.
- Travel services designed for older people will open the entire world to your adventurous spirit.
- The culture is rediscovering your wisdom and creating new ways to share it with the young.

Don't forget, you can find out even more about living your Second Prime at our Web site, www.SecondPrime.com. Meet other Boomers who share your interests, read about more Senior Achievers, and much more.

Let's move on and take a look at the endless argument between genes versus lifestyle. Guess what? Somebody won.

chapter two

Final Score:
Lifestyle 70, Genes 30

The older I get, the greater power I seem to have to help the world; I am like a snowball—the further I am rolled the more I gain.[1]

—SUSAN B. ANTHONY

A man's age is something impressive, it sums up his life: maturity reached slowly and against many obstacles, illnesses cured, griefs and despairs overcome, and unconscious risks taken; maturity formed through so many desires, hopes, regrets, forgotten things, loves. A man's age represents a fine cargo of experiences and memories.[2]

—ANTOINE DE SAINT-EXUPÉRY

Blueberries versus bioengineering. In essence, that's what the current landscape of antiaging science breaks down to: lifestyle versus genetics. On one hand are those whose primary focus is on extending human life span though the diligent, preemptive application of the science we know works today: testing and screening for disease, healthy diet (the antioxidant-filled blueberries), exercise, mental challenge, social contact, and the like. These advocates, led by such figures as best-selling author Dr. Andrew Weil, tend to hold the position that while cutting-edge, antiaging research has exciting potential, it has not yet yielded any proven advances that can slow down or reverse aging, so let's work with what we know gets results. There's logic to this: why sit around and let your body decay waiting for some genetic miracle when you can act now, make lifestyle changes, and add decades?

On the other side are the antiaging scientists, led by such individuals as Steven Austad, PhD, professor of Cellular and Structural Biology at the University of Texas Health Science Center at San Antonio and a leading advocate for the aggressive pursuit of new antiaging research, usually occurring in the human genome. This work suggests the possibility of fulfilling the greatest of human desires—the substantial extension of human life span—in the coming decades while laboring under the burden of enormous expectations. How can it not, when some members of this movement utter the highly charged word *immortality* at the drop of a hat?

Lifestyle or Genes?

We've said that aging is inevitable and that the wise person accepts that fact and does the most he or she can to make the best of the rest of life. And that's true—*today*. Many researchers in the field of experimental gerontology believe that medical science will make inroads against age-related degeneration and may even eventually halt the cellular death that leads to the aging of our bodies. Right now, that's not possible. Ten years ago, we couldn't look into the human genetic sequence to find the causes of disease. Today, we can. It would be foolish to assume that because we don't yet know how to manipulate genes to give humans 300-year life spans that we won't in the future.

The only bullets we can fire at the Grim Reaper today, though, are the ones we've known about for years: eating fruits and veggies, working out, and so on. Wisdom dictates that we focus on what we can do now while supporting legitimate research that might yield breakthroughs in treating the underlying causes of aging.

But that raises a question: Which factor has more to do with how we age, lifestyle or genetics? Let's take a look at that, though as you may have guessed by the title of this chapter, you're not as much of a slave to what mom, dad, and your grandparents bequeathed you as you might think.

An Unequal Ratio

A woman at a retirement home where 80 percent of the residents are women sees a new arrival lying poolside—a man in his early 60s, quite good-looking. Hoping to snare him before any of the other women, she goes down to introduce herself. After some pleasant small talk, she asks him, "So, how did you end up here?"

The man says, "I killed my wife, dismembered her body, and dumped it into the ocean," he says. "I was tried for murder, but they didn't have enough evidence and had to let me go. So I moved here, because I heard there were a lot of rich widows."

The woman takes this all in for a moment then says, "So, you're single then?"

You Are Not Doomed

In 1984, the John D. and Katherine T. MacArthur Foundation convened a group of sixteen elite researchers from a variety of disciplines to embark on a decade-long series of studies of aging. The goal was to create a "new gerontology" that would counter the hoary, debilitating cliché that old age doomed one to a later life of senility, immobility, and obsolescence.

The findings of what has become known as the MacArthur Foundation Study of Aging in America were galvanic. According to its results, seniors in America do not view their lives as hopeless and view their health as generally good. Furthermore, it appears that illness, declining mental performance, and detachment from life are not inevitable for the elderly. But the most important outcome of the study was that genes are only responsible for *25 to 30 percent* of our longevity. The other 75 to 70 percent is a little bit of luck but mostly lifestyle choices. This finding is accepted as fact by gerontologists and antiaging scientists around the world.[3]

You really do have control over your life span and your "healthspan," the period of time in your life that you are well, active, vital, and mentally sharp. Where some researchers are primarily concerned with the length of life, others believe that science should zero in with equal intensity on the quality of life—helping people stay healthy and active years or decades longer, even if their life spans don't increase appreciably.

We think it should be a balance between the two. No one wants to live 150 years but spend the last fifty of those years blind, crippled, and bedridden. At the same time, if you told us we'd live to eighty-five but be dancing the tango until age eighty-three, we'd take it.

"The focus is so much on the length of life, not the quality of life," says Dr. Austad in an interview for this book. "I think that's why the public is dubious about this whole enterprise to lengthen life. I think if you said, 'How about making people healthier for 50 percent longer,' people would say, 'Yeah.' But the easiest way to measure research is to talk about longevity." Let's face it, for most of us quantity of life isn't enough. We want all the best parts of our lives to be longer:

- *Workspan*—The period of productivity and achievement
- *Lovespan*—The period of sexuality and rewarding relationships
- *Soulspan*—The period of volunteering, giving back, making a difference, and being spiritually alive and awake
- *Mindspan*—The period of clear thought and brilliant ideas

You should accept nothing less. And it's becoming clear that more than ever, that means making smart, healthy lifestyle choices.

THE LIFESTYLE FACTOR

Every so often we'll see the sentiment on a bumper sticker: "Eat right. Exercise. Die anyway." Funny, but telling. There's no question that certain lifestyle choices have been shown to extend healthspan and life span, but then every so often a George Burns will come along and live to a hundred despite years of smoking and throw all the theories to the wind. Mark Twain said it perfectly at his seventieth birthday celebration in 1905:

I have made it a rule to go to bed when there wasn't anybody left to sit up with; and I have made it a rule to get up when I had to. In the matter of diet, I have been persistently strict in sticking to the things which didn't agree with me, until one or the other of us got the best of it. I have made it a rule never to smoke more than one cigar at a time. As for drinking, when the others drink I like to help. I have never taken any exercise, except sleeping and resting, and I never intend to take any. Exercise is loathsome.[4]

Twain would live to seventy-five, some twenty-seven years beyond the average life expectancy of his contemporaries. As the author of *Roughing It*, his denunciation of exercise was probably a bit of curmudgeonly role-playing. But the fact remains that some individuals who defy the accepted "no smoking, no drinking, hard exercise, and smart diet" wisdom do outlive those who adhere to it. Why? Is there some other aspect of lifestyle that affects longevity as much as what we put into our bodies and how we move them? As it turns out, yes. All aspects of lifestyle merit some examination.

You can see the effects of lifestyle on life span simply by looking at the root causes of the major diseases that kill us: cancer, heart disease, hypertension, stroke, and diabetes. Time and again, we see the incidence of these diseases rise in countries that become wealthier and adopt more Western lifestyles: heavy meat consumption, less exercise, higher levels of obesity. A 2003 report released by the World Health Organization showed that due to tobacco use, unhealthy diets, and aging populations, global cancer rates were on the rise, with fifteen million new cases expected by 2020. Cancer was once thought of as a Western disease; it now kills more people in the developing world than in industrialized nations. Diabetes may be the biggest scourge; statistics suggest it will be our number-one killer in a decade.[6]

> *The great secret that all old people share is that you really haven't changed in seventy or eighty years. Your body changes, but you don't change at all. And that, of course, causes great confusion.*[5]
>
> —Doris Lessing

Doris "Granny D." Haddock, 96, ran for US Senate in New Hampshire at 95

When Doris Haddock was "only" eighty-nine, she decided she was fed up with the corrupt US campaign finance system, which led to corporations having all the influence over which legislation was passed in Congress. Did she write a letter? No. She walked across the United States.

"I could see that the House was not going to do anything about the McCain/Feingold bill," she says. "The Senate began sending us notes basically saying, 'Dear little old ladies, we're going to pass that bill,' and the same thing happened: nothing. I knew the only way to get it passed was to wake up the public. The only thing I could see was to do the walk."

Her son was dubious that she could walk 3,200 miles at her age, so he made her do a training regimen to prove she could handle it. "I went out and laid on the ground in a sleeping bag in November," she says. "I begged for food and shelter, like a pilgrim. I had to learn to thumb a ride..I lived on trail mix for a week and walked ten miles a day with twenty-nine pounds on my back. At the end of the year, I came to him and said, 'I'm ready.'"

In 2004, having already become a celebrity in New Hampshire, she decided to run for the Senate as a Democrat against a well-funded Republican opponent. Despite entering the race only three months before the election and being out-fund-raised, $2.8 million to $166,000, she garnered 34 percent of the vote and is widely credited for giving New Hampshire to John Kerry in the presidential election.

Today, despite throat surgery, she remains active as a speaker. "I'm just an ordinary old woman," she says. "People write to me all the time and tell me I'm an inspiration, but anyone could have done what I did. Having a purpose gives you a reason to keep on living after sixty-five."

To reach Doris and find out about her upcoming book, visit www.grannyd.com.

A Growing Body of Research

Logically, if we can bring on many of the diseases of aging by engaging in foolish habits, we can stave them off by engaging in healthy ones. That's borne out by an increasing body of research:

- Clinical studies are underway throughout the world to confirm what many scientists already know anecdotally: turmeric, the Asian spice that gives curry its yellow color, wards off such diseases as Alzheimer's, cystic fibrosis, and colorectal and other cancers.[7]
- A ten-year study in Japan, in which researchers from Gifu University in Japan looked at the consumption of soy and oil-rich fish by nearly 30,000 residents of a single town, showed that the men and women who consumed the highest levels of soy were the least likely to die during the study. Fish oil also appears to play some role in women's longevity.[8]
- A study by Gary Fraser of the diet and lifestyle of Seventh-day Adventists found that their lifestyle—largely vegetarian diet, regular exercise, no tobacco or alcohol use, strong spiritual beliefs—substantially reduced their risks of coronary artery disease and cancer.[9]
- A 2001 study published in the Official Journal of the American College of Sports Medicine looked at 347 elderly Dutch men and assessed the effects of their exercise habits on their cognitive abilities. The authors concluded that engaging in more than one hour per day of physical activity at an older age may reduce the risk of cognitive decline.[10]
- A Norwegian study of 15,000 men and women linked higher dietary calcium intake to lower blood pressure. Other research also points to calcium as a preventive factor for colon cancer.[11]

- A long-term study by Dr. William Strawbridge and other researchers published in the *American Journal of Public Health* in 1997 showed that individuals with a strong religious faith who regularly attend religious services have lower blood pressure, are less likely to suffer from depression, cope better with illness and injury, have a greater sense of well-being, have stronger immune systems, and live 23 percent longer than those with no religious faith.[12]
- A 2005 study by American and Japanese gerontologists revealed that while obesity had little effect on the longevity of adults over age seventy, being obese after seventy gave them a far greater probability of spending their remaining years disabled.[13]
- A six-year study of Chicago residents has shown that eating fish once a week provides omega-3 fatty acids that boost brain function, reduce the risk of stroke, and delay age-related dementia. The research of Joe Mercola, M.D., suggests that omega-3 also prevents skin cancer when taken daily.[14]
- A study led by a Yale University researcher of 660 men and women in Ohio showed that adults with positive attitudes about aging lived an average of seven years longer than those with negative attitudes.[15]
- Researchers at the University of California–San Francisco found that women under chronic stress may suffer damage to the DNA of their immune system cells, causing cells to reach the end of their reproductive lives faster, die sooner, and accelerate the aging process.[16]
- And of course, there's the so-called French Paradox, in which the French and Italians, who eat rich foods and fats and cheeses in abundance, have much lower rates of heart disease. Scientists now think the paradox has to do in part with the Mediterranean diet, rich in olive oil and other beneficial fats, and also with the drinking of red wine, which contains resveratrol, a powerful antioxidant thought to lower the risk of cancer, atherosclerosis, heart disease, and brain diseases such as Alzheimer's.

In an article in *Time* magazine, Dr. Bradley Willcox of the Pacific Health Research Institute in Honolulu said it best: "You could have Mercedes-Benz genes, but if you never change the oil, you are not going to last as long as a Ford Escort that you take good care of."[17] Surprisingly, gerontologists and other scientists who study the progress of aging say that many who reach one hundred and beyond are in surprisingly good condition, presumably because they have passed the age, thought to be around ninety, where if they were going to develop the destructive maladies of age, they would have done so already. The thinking now is that if you can make it to your 90s, you stand an excellent chance of making it to triple digits in good shape.

The wise man does not grow old, but ripens.[18]

—VICTOR HUGO

There are false starts and contradictory findings, but with studies and hundreds of clinical trials planned or underway around the world to study lifestyle factors from diet and smoking to stress and remaining employed in old age, a clear picture is emerging: genetics may be the foundation on which you build your health, but the lifestyle choices you make determine the quality of the house that rises and how long that house will endure.

MISCONCEPTIONS AND MYTHS

One of the most common assumptions about lifestyle is that taking loads of antioxidant supplements helps fend off a strike force of diseases from cancer to macular degeneration. When our bodies metabolize food, our cells throw off extra electrons called *free radicals*, which can also form from immune system activity and as a result of environmental factors such as pollution and pesticides. These solo electrons need to pair with other electrons, so they steal them from healthy cells. The result, over time, is cellular damage, cell death, and even genetic damage. So life really is a fatal disease with no cure.

Antioxidants such as vitamin E and vitamin C "donate" electrons to the free radicals, preventing them from damaging cells. Millions of people down billions of dollars in antioxidant tablets and vitamins every year to achieve this effect. Unfortunately, research suggests that supplements may not be the answer. Multiple studies have shown that while eating plenty of antioxidant-rich foods does reduce the risk of some cancers, heart disease, and other afflictions, taking supplements may not. For example, a Danish study of more than 170,000 people considered at high risk of gastrointestinal cancer determined that antioxidant pills—with the exception of selenium—were "useless" in preventing GI cancers. Some speculate that there may be other compounds such as phytonutrients in fruits and vegetables that make the antioxidants more effective.[19]

So if you want to get the full benefits of antioxidants, you can't be lazy, eat garbage, and pop a handful of pills each morning. You've got to hit the farmer's market and chow down on your daily dose of green leafy vegetables, red peppers, carrots, and the like.

Another lifestyle choice open to question appears to be Caloric Restriction (CR), which has become a *cause celebre* in many antiaging circles. The idea is that if you restrict your calorie intake to 1,200–1,500 calories per day (the average adult man needs 2,500–3,000 calories daily), you reduce the metabolic activity that produces free radicals and in so doing reduce cell damage. However, cutting calories by one-third appears to increase life span in worms, insects, and mice, but there is no evidence yet that it does the same for humans. The few people who have put themselves on a restricted-calorie diet have shown, however, some health improvements such as dramatically lowered cholesterol and healthy weight levels thanks to less food intake. Chances are, we'll know more in a few decades.

Our big gripe with CR is about quality of life. Is it worth an extra ten or twenty years of life if you can never eat the foods you love or sit down to a meal with friends because you're watching every single calorie? No doubt some people will say, "You bet it is." That's fine, but we think there are just as many who would refuse to give up the pure pleasures of food. So the jury remains out.

But the biggest myth is that people who live to one hundred while retaining their ability to work, play, and engage in life are the beneficiaries of some genetic secret. They're not. According to a 1988–1998 study conducted by researchers at the University of Georgia, healthy centenarians show a wide variety of traits that seem to affect their ability to remain vital and active. There does not seem to be a magic bullet, but factors of function, ability, and personality appear to have a great deal to do with a person's ability to stay vibrant past one hundred. In other words, a long life span and a long healthspan appear to be equal-opportunity events. "We interpret these results from the optimistic perspective that any person may have a chance of living a long and productive life," said Leonard Poon, director of the UGA Gerontology Center. The university is currently engaged in Phase 3 of its centenarian study, set to conclude in 2006.[20]

LIVING TO 200 MEANS GENES

What about our genes? Are they just the foundation for the edifice of our longevity or something more? Could the secret to slowing or even reversing aging lie within the human genome? It's a controversial topic among scientists, but most agree that if humans have the capacity to live well beyond the current accepted ceiling of 120 years with any sort of health and function, our genes hold the key.

Lifestyle, you see, can only do so much. Leonard Hayflick, professor of anatomy at the University of California–San Francisco, the father of modern gerontology, and the discoverer of the point where cells reach the end of their ability to divide and replenish themselves (now called the Hayflick Limit), makes that point in candid terms. He says that if you cured all the diseases that ravage us in our dotage—cancer, heart disease, stroke, diabetes—you would only add thirteen years to life expectancy.[21] Still desirable, of course, and we would doubtless live healthier and happier, but because our cells still wear out and break down, our bodies will still inevitably deteriorate.

Clearly, if we're going to extend healthy, useful life by many decades or even centuries, as some antiaging evangelists claim is possible, we need to focus on our genes. And that is a field that is complex, controversial, and not without promise.

GENES DON'T DETERMINE EVERYTHING

But what role do genes play in life span? Turns out they're not the allpowerful force we thought they were. Ever since James Watson and Francis

Crick published their findings about the structure of DNA in 1953, most people have assumed that you were the slave of your genetic code; with it set, the balance in your life's bank account was deposited, and when it was used up, so were you. The belief in the power of the gene led to a dangerous fatalism, in which some individuals who became morbidly obese or developed cancer simply blamed their genes instead of making lifestyle changes to prevent disease. Why bother when longevity is determined by the genetic blueprint, which can't be influenced?

Today we know better. We understand that genes determine inherited characteristics from our eye color to our propensity to develop plaque buildup in the arteries. In effect, your genes decide the *likelihood* of your developing a disease, being overweight, losing your hearing, and a million other aspects of living. But except in the case of incurable genetic diseases like Huntington's, your DNA does not hand down an ironclad sentence that states, "You will live sixty-three years and five months and not a day longer." Genes determine what could *potentially* occur in your body; lifestyle decides whether that potential becomes reality or not.

We also know that genes *do* change. The damage caused by free radicals can damage the DNA in your cells, and it's this damage that some researchers believe may be behind many types of cancer. Conversely, if you eat a diet rich in antioxidants, you will protect your cells and your DNA from damage from rogue molecules. So your genes are neither all-powerful nor beyond your influence. Far from it: every lifestyle decision you make influences how much of your genetic inheritance you manifest.

THE ENGINE OF AGING

Where genes take center stage in antiaging research is when the talk turns to the root causes of aging. Why do our bodies break down? Why do cells live a certain amount of time and then inevitably decay? Researchers are just beginning a deep investigation of the genetic and molecular causes behind aging. It's a field regarded with some skepticism by the rest of the scientific community, but antiaging researchers are united in their passion for what they say is not only real, hard science, but of potentially world-changing benefit to the human race. Research is looking into a staggering variety of areas of human cellular biology seeking the mechanisms that cause our cells to age, lose their ability to function and reproduce, and ultimately die. The goal is not just to find the causes of and prevent the diseases of aging, but in the end to slow or even reverse aging itself.

In his book *Merchants of Immortality*, Stephen S. Hall presents one such example of the thousands going on worldwide: a company called Sierra Sciences in Reno, Nevada, which claims to have discovered molecules that might allow cells to replenish the control devices at the ends of our chromosomes, called *telomeres*, that determine how often a cell can divide before it starts to die. If such a molecule could be turned into a drug, then in theory people could take a pill that would lengthen their telomeres, allowing cells to go on dividing and resetting the aging clock. It's an extraordinarily complex, speculative possibility, but it suggests the incredible potential for life extension that cellular biologists and geneticists are only beginning to tap.[22]

Agelessness Secret #2

Consume Antioxidants

Antioxidants are organic compounds, including vitamins C and E, vitamin A (which is converted from beta-carotene), selenium (a mineral), and a group known as the carotenoids, which are the pigments that make carrots orange. Found mostly in brightly colored vegetables and fruits and leafy greens, they are thought by most health professionals and aging experts to be crucial to maintaining your health as you age.

Antioxidant-rich foods you should eat regularly include:

- Citrus fruits
- Tomatoes
- Broccoli
- Apricots
- Red peppers

- Spinach
- Blueberries
- Strawberries
- Garlic

Antioxidants are powerful because of the basic chemistry our bodies use to turn food into fuel. When our cells use oxygen as a catalyst to metabolize food molecules into energy, an extra oxygen electron called a *free radical* is often left over. Oxygen molecules hate to be alone, so they try to steal an electron from a healthy cell, damaging that cell in the process. That damage, occurring billions of times in our lives, can cause serious damage to cell walls and cell structure and can even damage DNA, which can lead to uncontrolled cell growth, also called cancer. Your body can also produce free radicals when exposed to cigarette smoke or pollution.

Antioxidants "lend" an oxygen molecule to pair off with the rogue free radical molecule, preventing it from damaging cells. That's why conventional wisdom now suggests that consuming plentiful amounts of antioxidant-rich foods (supplements don't appear to have the same beneficial effects, though they may have some) can keep you healthy longer.[23]

In response to questions for this book, Dr. Michael Elstein, the Australian antiaging physician and author, writes about some of the most promising aging research going on now:

- The development of so-called *genome remedies*, drugs which could be engineered to target and repair damage in DNA and would be individualized based on each patient's genome.
- Extensive research taking place at the University of Colorado, the University of Texas Southwestern Medical Center in Dallas, and

other locations to discover the genes of aging. These studies include isolating longevity-causing mutations in worm genes, finding genetic pathways that imitate the effects of insulin in a manner similar to restricting calories, and the discovery of an amino acid that declines in aging muscle, heart, and brain tissue but has been found to extend the life spans of mice.

- Work with telomeres in controlling and killing the growth of cancerous cells, the only cells in the body that can reproduce indefinitely. Elstein writes that using telomeres to slow down aging is difficult. However, he adds that "Geron Laboratories in the United States has already employed telomerase (the enzyme that regulates telomere growth) to increase the life span of human cells from the skin, blood vessels, eyes, muscles, and immune system."

- Animal models of aging. "A big aspect of the research today is about gene variants associated with longer life," says Dr. Steven Austad in his interview. "There have been dozens of genes discovered in worms, mice, and flies that if you disable them, they live longer. Some of these are the same genes in all cells. This is hot news because I don't think anybody's ever thought you'd find the same genes in animals as different as a fly and mouse that would have the same effect. Nobody is proposing that we genetically alter people to make them live longer, but these genes suggest there are molecules in our genes that can be targeted to make us live longer."

> *When I was forty, my doctor advised me that a man in his 40s shouldn't play tennis. I heeded his advice carefully and could hardly wait until I reached fifty to start again.*[24]
> —Hugo L. Black

So, Can I Buy an Immortality Pill Next Year?

Where antiaging science gets contentious and dicey is where people start talking about what can be achieved and when. Mainstream scientists like Austad insist that "hard" science is making progress but in slow, measured stages. Then there are the immortality prophets like the epically bearded Aubrey de Grey, a researcher at Cambridge University in England, who has become the poster boy for the aggressive science side of aging exploration. This movement takes a much more gung-ho view of longevity research, promoting claims of sometimes dubious scientific standing through organizations with names like the Immortality Institute.

Writing in response to our questions, de Grey insists that with proper funding, "we have a fifty/fifty chance of seeing advances in twenty-five years" that will extend human life spans to potentially millennia. "Should our culture see aging as inevitable? Absolutely not! It is obviously something we can defeat, just as rust on a car is."

Austad takes a different view: "There's a huge divide appearing in the literature between real science and pop science," he says. "There's a difference between being an amusing eccentric and being a salesman. I think longevity evangelists are actually doing a great deal of harm making these outrageous statements about making people live longer."

Whether you believe antiaging science must proceed slowly and cautiously or that dramatic breakthroughs are on the horizon with the right attention and funding, one fact remains: right now what we can do is make lifestyle changes to make the most of our 120-year potential. Says Hayflick, "I do not expect that intervention in the fundamental aging process will occur in our lifetime—or in the lifetimes of our children."[25]

So what can you do today?

- Eat a varied diet rich in a wide range of fruits and vegetables and with a balance of protein, carbohydrates, and healthy fats (mono- and poly-unsaturated fats). See the World's Healthiest Foods Web site (www.whfoods.com) for great lists of healthy foods.
- Get enough fiber, 40 grams or more a day. The average American is lucky if he or she takes in 15 grams per day.
- Shop the perimeter of the supermarket, where the least processed foods are. Stay away from the middle aisles unless you need toilet paper.
- Include soy in your diet. The Chinese have extremely low rates of breast cancer, and they claim that soy is the reason.

- Drink decaf and white or green tea instead of coffee.
- Take supplements including vitamin C, vitamin E, selenium, folic acid, calcium, ginger, turmeric, and fish oil. Or try taking nutriceuticals, formulations of vitamins, minerals, and other compounds designed for specific effects on the body.
- Drink at least eight glasses of water a day.
- Lift weights. Studies show that even people in their 90s who have never lifted weights before can see huge benefits.
- Take the supplement alpha-lipoic acid for memory.
- Work puzzles, take classes, keep working—anything to keep your mind stimulated and challenged.

THINK VITAL

But perhaps the most important thing you can do is to think like a vital, energetic person who is determined to defy the idea of getting old. Life is full of people like George Burns or Bob Hope, who lived very long, productive lives while ignoring the conventional wisdom about staving off age and disease. Are such people just winners of the genetic lottery? We don't think so. There is something most centenarians appear to have in common: a love of life and a stubborn refusal to think of themselves as old.

"I believe the key to avoiding the debilitation of old age is staying productive, doing something that's going to help not only yourself, but somebody else," says Barbara Morris, R.Ph., who at a fabulous-looking seventy-six is a practicing pharmacist and author of *Put Old on Hold*. Interviewed by us for this book, she maintains there are five keys to keeping old age at bay:

1. *Have a clear vision of you and your life twenty-five years from now.* "When I was ten years old, I knew I didn't ever want to get old, she says. "I saw a picture of a pretty young woman in *Ladies Home Journal*, and I told myself, 'That is how I always want to look.' That picture is just as sharp and clear in my mind today as it was then. That vision has motivated me to achieve what I have."

2. List the youthful attributes you want to have in twenty-five years. "I think we need to stay aware of what it means to be old. We need to observe old people to see what it is about their oldness that we want to avoid and appreciate the youthful attributes we have right now. You're going to have to work to maintain those attributes. Youth is a gift; it's free. Old age takes effort." Make a physical list.

3. Develop daily antiaging habits. Morris, who works a ten-hour day as a pharmacist, says she doesn't sit down during that long day. After work, she first jumps onto the treadmill and walks for thirty minutes, lifts weights, and does other exercises. "Staying young is going to take a cultural shift," she says.

4. Engage in positive mental management. Morris suggests practicing positive self-talk and affirmation—you are energetic and full of life, and you are *never* too old to do something.

5. Believe it's possible to put old on hold. Morris writes, "You can control the aging process—believe it. Here's a great goal: as each day goes by, experience freedom, good health, and independence, fully able to enjoy the best years of your life."

In other words, people who live to ripe, active, old ages all seem to refuse to let anyone else define their idea of old age. "Students in California can define their own gender, meaning they can define their own identity, appearance, or behavior," Morris said during her interview. "And I say if that's legal, it certainly ought to be legal for people to determine their perceived age on an employment application or something like that. Everybody knows what's in them. We shouldn't allow chronological age to limit our potential."

What *How to Make the Rest of Your Life the Best of Your Life* is really about is changing your definition of age. We have three different categories of age:

1. *Chronological,* which measures how old you are by the clock and the calendar. Unless you're after senior citizen discounts at the movie theater, this is irrelevant.

2. *Biological*, which measures how old your body is according to cellular damage, toxins, and many other metrics.

3. *Experiential*, which is how old you feel based on your experience and your attitude toward life. Mark has tested over 10,000 audience members at his live seminars, and no one feels their chronological age. Most seniors feel twenty to forty years younger. Experientially, those who have *really lived* feel older.

We're proponents of living by your experiential age because judging from the purposeful, self-possessed folks in their 80s, 90s, and 100s who are still out there working, creating, and enjoying life, your mind-set may be the most important longevity technology of all.

In his interview for this book, Dr. Dychtwald, psychologist, gerontologist, and author of eleven books on aging, including the recent *The Power Years*, says, "There are plenty of people who are just not acting their age. They're not doing the 'roll over and play dead' thing. When John Glenn went up into space at seventy-seven, everybody said, 'What's an old guy doing that for?' I think people who have lived this longer life and are still reinventing themselves, still growing, and still contributing, in many ways, are the real social pioneers of the twenty-first century."

It's Who You Know

Growing old is no more than a bad habit which a busy man has no time to form.[1]

—ANDRÉ MAUROIS

Age: that period of life in which we compound for the vices that we still cherish by reviling those that we no longer have the enterprise to commit.[2]

—AMBROSE BIERCE

We asked many of the seniors we interviewed for this book a simple question: "What's the worst thing about growing old?" The common, rueful response was, "Watching my friends die." This was often followed by, "I'm the only one left." People who live long tend to perceive themselves as young until life reminds them that they're old. No matter how we may strut through the decades feeling untouched by time, there's one clock we cannot ignore: the deaths of others.

Another stereotype of old age is the elder sitting around on his porch or in her room at the nursing home, utterly alone and forgotten. Like all stereotypes, this one has some basis in truth; there are many seniors who, once their friends begin dying, lose their connection to the world. They have not made an effort over the passing years to form new relationships with younger people, so when their lifelong companions are gone, they turn inward—brooding, unwilling to extend a hand to new people, depressed. In fact, according to Dr. Eric Kaplan, a specialist in geriatric psychiatry with Columbia St. Mary's in Milwaukee, Wisconsin, about 30 percent of elderly patients report depressive symptoms to their primary care physicians, with about half of those suffering from nonclinical depression.[3]

The antidote to this kind of debilitating isolation is obvious: people. With the passage of time, it's becoming clearer that there's more to a long life span, healthspan, workspan, soulspan, lovespan, and mindspan than what you eat and who your grandparents were. Factors that cannot be easily measured in a laboratory—purpose, will, passion, desire, faith, humor, the support of others—all appear to have a profound effect on how long and how well we live. The truth appears clear: who you know and the quality of the relationships you keep as you age, both with lifelong circles of pals and with new friends you make along the way, help you live a richer, more rewarding life and may indeed help you live more of it.

A 1999 study published in the *British Medical Journal* by Harvard's Thomas Glass seems to confirm this belief. Glass observed how various forms of social involvement impacted the health of more than 2,700 men over sixty-five in New Haven, Connecticut. The findings were conclusive: "Social engagement was as strong as anything we found in determining longevity," wrote Glass. "It was stronger than things like blood pressure, cholesterol, or other measures of health."[4] A 2001 study by A. Faber and S. Wasserman also confirmed the opposite end of the equation: severing social ties "leads to disability, depression, and even death for the elderly."[5] A similar report from the University of Dayton concluded that people without close interpersonal ties are twice as likely to die as their counterparts with close interpersonal relationships.[6] In other words, the song is right: people who need people are the luckiest people in the world.[7] We would like to personally invite you to attend our seminars around the country where you can meet new people. Visit www.SecondPrime.com for information.

WITHDRAWING FROM LIFE

"Sigmund Freud said the two things that matter most in life are love and work," says Dychtwald. "One of the reasons that people worked was that it was a great socializing force. It brought people together of different backgrounds and different ages, so if I was fifty-five and working in the field, and you were twenty-seven, we might talk about our families and our lives, and I might show you a picture of my grandchild, and you might talk to me about your wife who was about to give birth, and we might have each other over for dinner. Work was a part of our lives that caused people to come together." Dychtwald claims that all started to change with the New Deal, which institutionalized old age, made retirement the dream of every working adult, and perhaps, inadvertently separated the generations from each other.

Today, work is no longer at the center of the lives of people over sixty. They're trying to leave work behind so they can . . . what? Play golf? Travel? Those are fine, but you can't do them every day. In the work environment, we're always around other people. We're thrown into situations where we have to communicate, even with people we don't like. Clients become friends. Colleagues become business partners. The social dynamic is a hugely important part of the working life. But when seniors turn their backs on work, what's there to fill the void? If they haven't cultivated other social circles during their working life—club memberships, creative groups, churches, volunteer organizations—there's nothing. Couple this with the fact that many seniors move away from their longtime homes when they retire, and you have a generation of people with no social connections, floating free, unengaged in life.

"Successful, ideal aging is not just biology. It is actually the intersection of the three basic domains of biology, psychology, and sociology—the three fundamental components of humanness," says Walter M. Bortz II, M.D., in his book *Dare to Be 100*. Bortz says that as they age, many seniors systematically disengage from life, doing everything from driving less to ending memberships in organizations to making fewer and fewer phone calls. They interpret this as freeing, as a shedding of responsibility, when in reality it represents a withdrawal from the idea that there's anything left to accomplish in life. In effect, these seniors are ceding control over their lives to someone or something else. That makes them vulnerable to disease, depression, and poverty, especially during times of stress. As Bortz writes, "It seems that while stress itself may not be so bad, it is lonely stress that causes real trouble."[8]

"Lemming Syndrome" and "Light Partners"

We all know the story: a couple is married for fifty years, totally dependent on one another, then one gets sick and dies. The survivor grieves for a few months, then his or her health hits the skids and in no time there's another funeral. We call it the "lemming syndrome," where one partner follows the other over the cliff. Why does it happen? In large part because survivors have no one else to turn to. They fix all their emotional needs on one person and don't build much of a social network outside the marriage. Sure, they have friends, but that's not the same as having confidants, people who aren't your spouse to whom you can say anything, who are always there for you, and who can pull you back into the light after grief covers you in shadow. That's the power of social networks. We know about "life partners." Friends who stick with you for years are "light partners."

Father Time is not always a hard parent, and, though he tarries for none of his children, often lays his hand lightly upon those who have used him well; making them old men and women inexorably enough, but leaving their hearts and spirits young and in full vigour. With such people the grey head is but the impression of the old fellow's hand in giving them his blessing, and every wrinkle but a notch in the quiet calendar of a well-spent life.[9]

—Charles Dickens

A 2003 study of 7,524 women sixty-five and over published in *Psychosomatic Medicine* showed that women with large social networks were at less risk of dying than women with small or nonexistent social networks. The combination of marriage and active outside social lives seemed to offer the greatest benefit, helping women live one to two years longer, no matter what their health. "Both marriage and larger social networks may provide a protective effect on their own, whereas the combination of the two seems to be most beneficial," said researcher Thomas Rutledge of the University of Pittsburgh in the article.[10]

Another rather creative study confirms the power of mood to improve the quality of life. A 2001 inquiry by Rutgers University reviewed the reports of one hundred seniors in the test group, some of whom received flowers regularly, while others did not. The researchers found that seniors who received flowers had lower rates of depression, better recall of recent events, and a greater desire for companionship than those who didn't.[11] In short, flowers make people happy, and happy people live longer, healthier lives.

> An elderly husband and wife are sitting side by side, rocking on the porch. Suddenly, the wife reaches over and slaps the husband.
>
> "What was that for?" he asks.
>
> "That was for forty years of bad sex," she replies. He thinks this over for a minute, then reaches over and slaps her back.
>
> "What was that for?" she asks, shocked.
>
> "Knowing the difference," he says.

A LITTLE WILD SPECULATION

In his book *AgeLess*, Edward Schneider gives readers a "longevity quotient" test that, in part, looks at their engagement with life. The test looks at factors such as habitual outlook on life, ability to cope with stress, family and social connections, availability of people in an emergency, sex life, volunteerism, and interest in education.[12] (You'll find similar tests later in this book; go to Chapter 9 for an exercise called "Live Regretless!")

That's about as close to empiricism as the subject of "why maintaining social contacts extends life" gets these days. So why not engage in a little idle speculation about the reasons why?

Support during hard times. Circles of close friends offer shoulders to cry on and words of support and courage during times of illness or bereavement, a factor that some researchers believe has a great deal to do with increased longevity. When you become sick or someone dies, instead of allowing you to retreat into grief or seclude yourself into a sickbed, your circle draws you out, brings you food, reminds you that life is still good. This type of activity can prevent depression and even suicidal thoughts and encourage people who are suffering to remain engaged in life.

Motivation to reach goals or try new things. Have you ever had a regular group of pals or colleagues who challenged you, who were always asking you to step outside your comfort zone? That's what a strong social network does for the elderly. Since it's becoming clear that will, determination, and desire for life can extend and improve life, looking ahead to new challenges and achievements—hang gliding, travel, publishing your first book of poems—can help keep life rich, exciting, and rewarding.

Improved mood. Friends are good for your mood. That's obvious. Social interaction stimulates the pleasure centers of the brain, boosting mood, warding off depression, and giving you a boost of adrenaline in the bargain. Interacting and having fun with people you've known for years and with whom you have similar interests are proven ways to create a more positive outlook on life, which has been shown to have a beneficial effect on life span and health.

More likely to access health care. Married couples are known to access health-care services more often than singles, and the same "nagging" effect holds true for people with strong, tight social circles. When you're older, you are likely to have health problems that require some kind of regular attention, and being part of a vibrant, active, communicative gang of bosom companions not only lets you find out about new health-care resources from them, it gives you people to harass and cajole you into going to the doctor when you know you should—even when you don't want to.

Exposure to new ideas. Constantly being around new people—people you might not ever meet if you stuck to your small circle of close pals—exposes you to new ideas, new ways of life, new trends, and new thinking that can be exciting and give your mind a strenuous workout.

Competitiveness. Having a social network of people who are all trying to get in shape, earn more money, travel to the most exotic location, or just outdo each other in all areas of life can compel even the most complacent individual to get off the couch and test his limits. Give yourself and others challenges. When Mark became interested in mountain climbing and took on Mt. Whitney, individuals begged to be on the trek. Ultimately, thirty-three people went up Whitney together.

Sense of humor. It's not known whether or not a sense of humor actually extends life, but we do know that laughter has a horde of beneficial physiological effects: reduced blood pressure, the release of endorphins that reduces the short-term effects of stress, even reduced heart rate and stomach acidity. Beyond those benefits, associating with a group of people where humor, wit, and cleverness are prized and encouraged is a wonderful way to improve mood and develop creativity.

Agelessness Secret #3

Thermal Body Scans

You may have heard about the body scans that many clinics make available as a way to catch health problems such as arterial plaque buildup or tumors before they become incurable. The advertising has been pretty aggressive, but there's a problem: your risk of developing disease due to the radiation that these body scan machines employ can actually be higher than the risk of having heart disease or cancer. "The radiation dose from a full-body CT scan is comparable to the doses received by some of the atomic bomb survivors from Hiroshima and Nagasaki, where there is clear evidence of increased cancer risk," says David J. Brenner, PhD, DSc, professor of radiation oncology and public health at Columbia University in New York.

Not much room for doubt in that kind of statement. However, since many health-care professionals believe there is a preventive benefit to be gained from getting a preemptive view of the body, a new type of scanning technology has been developed: thermal scanning, also known as clinical thermography. This system uses infrared scanners and computer systems to scan your body for varying heat sources. The creators of the technology claim that by detecting the temperature changes created by various neurochemical transmitters, thermal scanning can actually detect the early beginnings of diseases ranging from stroke to cardiovascular disease to hormone imbalances—conditions a CT scan or MRI can rarely detect if at all—years before they affect your health.

The best part? No radiation. The cost for a thermal scan is about the same as for a body scan that uses radiation, a few hundred dollars. But for well people who want early warning of possible serious health issues, it's money well spent on a procedure that, so far, has proven safe and effective.[13]

We've All Got Friends, So What?

So what's the difference between the senior with a few close friends and the senior with a large clique of people she's known for years? It appears to be the sense of *community*, the ability that a large group has to buoy the spirits and, at the same time, provide a needed kick in the seat of the pants. Apparently, it's not just how well you know people, how long you know them, or even how many of them you get together with, but the dynamic of the community that really makes a difference in your quality of life. When people who know each other well, respect each other, and have a strong sense of self-worth get together in an environment where candor is the rule and anyone can say anything without fear of sanction, good things happen. Everyone becomes everyone else's safety net.

> I refuse to admit I'm more than fifty-two, even if that does make my sons illegitimate.[14]
>
> —Nancy Astor

The same does not appear to be true of family members, which is strange. Several studies, including the Australian one we cited earlier, make a point of stating that the "light partner" effect doesn't seem to occur when the people the senior is associating with are family members. We can think of several reasons why this might be the case:

- Family members do not hold the senior to high standards for health, mental activity, etc.
- Family members sometimes enable passive, self-defeating behavior.
- Some family members may be more interested in an inheritance than the well-being of their relation.
- Family members who are not of the same age as the senior may be completely uninterested in interacting.

However, we can think of many circumstances where proximity to family enhances quantity and quality of life. For example, in Asia and parts of Europe, it is quite normal to have multigenerational households where grandparents live with the rest of the family, care for the children, pass on wisdom and stories, and so on. So long as these seniors are given what they need to live independently, we can't think of too many arrangements that are more revitalizing for body and mind.

When You Are an Old Woman, You Shall Wear . . .

You may have seen them on the streets of your town from time to time: middle-aged and elderly women, tittering and high-stepping, garbed in gowns of royal purple and topped with hats of flame red that dominate the peripheral vision. Are they circus folk? Escapees from a psychiatric ward? Fashion victims on their way to a reality show taping? No. They are members of one of the fastest growing, most successful social networks in the country, the Red Hat Society.

The Red Hat Society (called a *disorganization* by its members, tongue firmly in cheek) started unofficially in April 1998, when five women went out to tea, wearing purple clothing with red hats. A few months previous, Sue Ellen Cooper, now known as the Exalted Queen Mother, had given her good friend the fifty-fifth birthday gift of a red hat and a copy of the poem "Warning," by Jenny Joseph, which begins with the line, "When I am an old woman, I shall wear purple . . ." Inspired by the poem's spirit of mischief and defiance of the popular image of middle-aged women as fuddy-duddies, Sue Ellen encouraged a few friends to don purple clothes accessorized with red hats and matching gloves, then to go out to tea in their full outfits. The women had so much fun the first day that they continued to go out together in this regalia. Eventually, they attracted the attention of the media. After being featured in a national magazine and a newspaper article that hit the wire services, the Red Hat Society formally established itself in the spring of 2000.

As the delighted women spread the word, more and more women asked how they could be a part of the group, and the Red Hat Society spread like wildfire. Today, it's a huge organization just for sassy, spirited women over age fifty (and some younger women, who wear pink hats and lavender clothes) that boasts books, its own credit card, licensed products, and roughly one million members in over forty thousand chapters in the United States and at least thirty countries. It's a phenomenon.

"People needed permission to play. It was Recess 101," says Cooper in an interview conducted for this book. "Nobody's engineering this. It just happens. I was just a typical woman who felt that she wasn't anywhere near done and wasn't ready to be invisible or ignored. At first it was totally silly, but then it took on more important undertones. Women began doing wonderful bonding and connecting, and now my favorite thing about this is connecting women all over the world, putting them in touch with each other. It's networking that we couldn't have done without the Internet, which is ironic, because I had to learn to use the computer when this all started. Good thing I can use the left side of my brain a little bit."

The Red Hat Society parts company, however, with groups like Rotary or the Lions when it comes to public service work, according to Cooper. Its service is to its members. "We have a lot of chapters who do wonderful things, like walk against breast cancer or raise money occasionally, but I tell them we're not trying to raise funds, we're trying to raise fun," she says. "If we start letting them turn these things into philanthropy, the next thing you know they've lost their recess. I'm trying to get it through their heads that it's okay to take a little time to play with your friends. We have no rules: you get together when you want, where you want, do what you want, wear what you want. They're like little kids when you tell them there are no rules. We just tell them that no rules does not mean no manners. Most people just relish the silliness of getting those clothes on and going out with their girlfriends. It invariably becomes like what it was like to be ten years old, having fun with your friends. They're happy, positive, silly women.

"It's not about rocket science," says Cooper about her mission for the Society, which has grown from her and an e-mail account to more than sixty employees. "I ask members, 'Do you wish you had gone to that wonderful art museum? Do you wish you could go to the movies at midnight? Do you wish you could go out for ice cream?' That's what this is about. Finally, you have somebody to do this with. There's no reason you can't take an afternoon off and go to the movies with your girlfriend, even if the ironing doesn't get done. It's really a very small rebellion. You come back to your families and your duty revitalized if you give yourself a break once in a while."

Cooper sees her loosely organized, fast-growing group—which has clearly struck a deep chord in women all over the world—as a way for women to stay vital. "It's about staying alive and involved and engaged," she says. "I don't care how old people are. I just care about what kind of person they are and what they're interested in doing. I like the idea of having friends of all ages. I've got friends of all ages, and it's very enriching. Women love it because they go out and young guys say, 'You ladies go, you're cool.' There is an age at which you become invisible to our culture. You're just this older woman; you're boring. But these people have lived the most amazing lives and had the most amazing careers. They are not just little old ladies."

JOIN OR CREATE

Sue Ellen Cooper, founder of the Red Hat Society (www.redhat society.com), has a vision, but you don't have to start your own international organization to have a vitality-enhancing social network. There are endless options available to you for connecting with others:

- You can go back to school. Seventy-three universities around the country have Osher Lifelong Learning Institutes funded by the Bernard Osher Foundation, dedicated to helping seniors develop new skills and quench their hunger for knowledge. There are also community colleges and programs like the Learning Annex. Education is an incredible way not only to meet others and grow your social circle, but to keep your mind active and challenged.
- Travel. Organizations like Elderhostel are designed to bring older adults together to travel to destinations all over the world.
- Be active in church. Studies have shown that church groups offer regular participants some of the best benefits to longevity and quality of life. If you belong to a congregation, consider getting more involved. If you're still not part of a church, find one that suits you and join.
- Volunteer. Groups like VolunteerMatch, ProLiteracy, and Idealist.org are always on the lookout for caring people willing to share their

time, knowledge, and compassion to do everything from teaching children to read to building new homes for disaster survivors.

- Join a hobby-based group. Whatever your interest, from Harley-Davidson motorcycles to classic jazz recordings, there's probably a group in your area that meets to talk, play, or obsess about it.
- Become part of a political, social, community, or activist movement. You can turn your passion into action, whether you're interested in helping the homeless, are pro-business, or want to do beach cleanup. Joining a movement with a political or social mission is a wonderful way to come into contact with impassioned people who care about the same things you care about.
- Get a job. Work isn't just about earning money or having something to do with your day; it's about meeting people who are younger than you, older than you, and have different life experiences. If you don't need the money to live on, take a part-time job at a business that interests you, such as a children's bookstore or an ecological co-op. Mark is a partner in the Enlightened Wealth Institute and invites you to one of their quarterly meetings as his guest. Visit www.enlightenedwealthinstitute.com or call (888) ONE-MILL.
- Join a civic club. These organizations offer wonderful settings where people can meet, swap stories, and connect based on similar backgrounds.
- Get creative. Getting a part in a play or singing in a chorale are both excellent ways of growing your personal community while expressing your artistic side. Creative individuals tend to be passionate and communicative, and as a bonus, activities like learning to read music are even good for brain health!
- Get online. We're going to talk a great deal about the Internet in this book; it's simply the most powerful tool for finding information, communicating, and connecting with others that's ever been created. If you're not on the Internet, get on it. You taught your kids how to read; have your grandkids teach you how to use the Internet. Mark's mother-in-law, Shirley Shaw, eighty-seven, just learned how to use the Internet and loves it.

If you don't like any of the things we've suggested above, try something even simpler: organize the friends you already have. If you're only getting together in small groups or one-on-one, it's likely that some of your friends are lonely. Take charge and create an occasion: a dinner, an outing, a regular get-together. Remember, the Red Hat Society started organically, with a few women going out and wearing funny clothes. Start your own audacious social club with six or ten or seventeen friends, old and new, and hold regular events, everything from hikes to trips to the theater. Don't just do "old" things; try daring activities that are supposedly only for the young—going to a rock concert or a poetry slam, for example. Remember, your only limits are self-imposed.

Senior Achiever

Arthur Winston, 99, employee of the Los Angeles Metropolitan Transit Authority since 1934

By the time you read this, Arthur Winston will be retired. His plans are to retire on his hundredth birthday, March 22, 2006. Winston has worked for the Los Angeles MTA, the agency that manages the city's mass transit system, for more than seventy-five years. He directed a crew that cleans and maintains the agency's buses. He has missed only one day in that time: the day his wife died in 1988.

Getting up at 4:00 AM every morning to go to work hasn't dulled Winston's health or his sense of humor. "I don't know what I'll do when I retire," he says. "I'm afraid if I sit around, I'll freeze up." He doesn't have any of his teeth and misses a few words here and there but is remarkably fit and healthy, able to walk around the busy MTA yard, dodging buses and waving to coworkers often one-third his own age.

The age difference doesn't concern him. "I think my bosses would like me to retire, but none of the younger people I work with resent me. I like everybody I work with," he says. Born in Oklahoma in 1906 (a year before it became a state), Winston comes from a long-lived family—his father lived to ninety-nine, his mother to eighty-eight. He hasn't seen a doctor since an appendectomy decades ago—when he was young.

Winston is a hero in his South Los Angeles neighborhood and in city government. He received a Congressional Citation from President Clinton in 1996 as "Employee of the Century," but he remains the same humble, good-humored man who seems to wonder what all the fuss is about. He laid out his simple, eloquent philosophy in a February 22, 2004, interview with Kurt Streeter of the *Los Angeles Times*:

"Working men are simple and humble people. They use the money they earn wisely. They do not rush. They arrive fifteen minutes before every shift. They keep their uniforms crisp. They see to it, even if the boss doesn't ask and the job doesn't call for it, that no bus leaves with grimy rims. And they absolutely do not fuss or mope or complain."

Note: Arthur Winston passed away peacefully in his sleep on April 13, 2006, at age one hundred, less than a month after retiring.

It's About the People, Not the Group

All too often older people stick with a circle of friends they've known for years not because they have anything in common anymore but because it's familiar and easy. It's normal for a few individuals or couples in a group of older friends to be more adventurous and younger at heart than their peers, but it's not normal to ignore the voices inside you shouting, "Travel, dream, be bold!" because you don't want to offend old pals. It's vital to be part of social circles that empower and magnify your desires. When you're seeking social networks, focus on associating with people with certain characteristics:

- Optimism
- Positive outlook on life
- Positive body image

- Many wide interests
- A hunger for knowledge and new experiences
- Sense of humor
- Creativity
- Passion
- Storytellers
- People with healthy habits like exercise and good diet
- People who "refuse to get old"
- Travelers
- Risk takers

Being around other seniors who have a lust for life and see their Second Prime as a time of great adventure and opportunity will bring out those same qualities in you. By getting a taste of other lives that are as vivid and varied as your own, you grow your vision and discover what life can be, if you're willing to look beyond today.

The "How Are You Old?" Self Test

You know how old you are. But how are you old? Other tests can tell you how long you'll live. This one will tell you how well you'll live.

For each question, circle a number from 1–5. 1 means you disagree with the statement completely; 2 means you disagree somewhat; 3 means you're neutral; 4 means you agree somewhat; 5 means you agree completely. Figure out your scoring at the bottom.

	Disagree				Agree
1. Purpose I have one or more things in my life that I feel compelled to do, that give me a sense of accomplishment at day's end.	1	2	3	4	5
2. Passion I'm spending part of my time doing something that makes me excited just to get out of bed in the morning.	1	2	3	4	5

3. Work I don't ever see myself quitting work. If I stop working for someone else, I'll start my own business or become a full-time volunteer.	Disagree 1 2 3 4 5	Agree
4. Self-Image I'm becoming more powerful, more capable, and more full of life with each passing year.	Disagree 1 2 3 4 5	Agree
5. Friends I have a circle of friends I've known for years. We kid each other, keep each other honest, and never let each other quit.	Disagree 1 2 3 4 5	Agree
6. Beliefs I believe that the most important factor in my aging well is my belief that I can age with vigor, wonder, and a sense of adventure.	Disagree 1 2 3 4 5	Agree
7. Attitude What society believes about getting older has nothing to do with me. I defy the stereotypes about my age, no matter what age I am.	Disagree 1 2 3 4 5	Agree
8. Independence I will remain independent until I simply cannot take care of myself.	Disagree 1 2 3 4 5	Agree
9. Risk I embrace risks and new experiences. If I'm uncomfortable, it means I'm alive.	Disagree 1 2 3 4 5	Agree
10. Goals I'm always setting goals for ten, twenty, and thirty years into the future.	Disagree 1 2 3 4 5	Agree

SCORING: Add up your total points for a possible score between 10 and 50.

41–50: You are *Unstoppably Old.* You are a force of nature. Your mind and spirit are going to carry you to a long life filled with achievement and joy.

31–40: You are *Enticingly Old.* You still place some limits on yourself, but overall you're living a life most people will never know.

21–30: You are *Uncertainly Old.* You're not quite sure how you want to grow old. You're still searching, which means that in this book, you'll hopefully find some answers.

11–20: You are *Fearfully Old.* You're buying into the stereotypes of old age, not your own vision of what your old age could be. Time to start changing things.

0–10: You are *Powerlessly Old.* You're well on your way to an old age of dependence, frailty, and loneliness. Get help fast.

Resources—It's Who You Know

Education
- Bernard Osher Foundation (www.osherfoundation.org)
- Elderhostel (www.elderhostel.org)
- Learning Annex (www.learningannex.com)
- American Association of Community Colleges (www.aacc.nche.edu)

Volunteering
- VolunteerMatch (www.volunteermatch.org)
- Help Your Community (www.helpyourcommunity.org)
- ProLiteracy (www.proliteracy.org)
- Idealist.org (www.idealist.org)
- World Volunteer Web (www.worldvolunteerweb.org)

Internet Tools
- AARP (www.aarp.org)
- Sojourners (http://sojo.net)
- Women of Faith (http://womenoffaith.com)

See the Second Prime Resources section at the end of the book for a complete catalog of print, Web, commercial, and organizational resources.

Part II

You Can't Turn Back the Clock, But You Can Rewind It

We've laid the foundation for our philosophy about rejecting the dependency of Social Security and Medicare and choosing the empowerment and independence of Self Security and Insteadicare. Now it's time to move on to specifics: eight chapters, each focusing on a different part of the whole person as you age. Each has the power to help you age well or age poorly. As always, the choice is yours.

In Part II, you'll find new information on health, money, sex, and more from leading experts, more incredible Senior Achiever stories, exercises, and ideas to help you shatter your own preconceptions about your own aging and transform your thought process. You'll also acquire the knowledge and insight to begin embracing the Ten Empowerments, creating your own Self Security and Insteadicare programs, and living your Second Prime.

Let's get going!

Work and Money *or* The Only Thing You Should Re-Tire Is Your Car

Our society must make it right and possible for old people not to fear the young or be deserted by them, for the test of a civilization is the way that it cares for its helpless members.[1]

—PEARL S. BUCK

We do not grow absolutely, chronologically. We grow sometimes in one dimension, and not in another; unevenly. We grow partially. We are relative. We are mature in one realm, childish in another. The past, present, and future mingle and pull us backward, forward, or fix us in the present. We are made up of layers, cells, constellations.[2]

—ANAÏS NIN

We have a serious problem with that Pearl S. Buck quote, eloquent though it is: the old are anything but helpless. We adore the Anais Nin quote because it represents all that we believe and know about aging: as one facet of the self ages, another grows younger, and all of it is contained as much in the mind as in the body. We're going to tell you how to choose empowerment every single time.

RETIREMENT IS A FAILED EXPERIMENT

Retirement is an idea whose time has come and gone, a relic of an age when few people lived past fifty-five, most worked for big corporations that offered pensions and retirement packages, and if you made it to sixty-five, you probably only had about five years of rocking on the porch before you were in the ground. Heck, we could spend five years just catching up on the books we've been meaning to read!

Then something happened. Retirement failed to keep up with the changes in our culture, our healthspan, and our expectations for old age. But what really happened was that the minds of Baby Boomers bifurcated and somehow managed to hold two contradictory ideas at the same time: on one hand, an insistence on a vivacious, adventuresome old age, and on the other, a comfortable retirement where money would never again be a concern and work would be a thing of the past. The two aren't compatible, but since the 1970s, we've been deluding ourselves that they are.

Ken Dychtwald has strong views on the subject, and he's been working to change the minds of those at the crest of the "age wave," as he has famously called it. As part of his extensive interview for this book, he said, "If you examine the history of retirement, you see something quite interesting that happened in the 1920s and 1930s. In the 1920s, the industrial era was in full bloom. For the first time, we began to glorify the look and style and capacity of youth, and all the experience and wisdom and perspective of maturity was seen as less valuable. But what really turned the wheels was the Depression. During the Depression, the unemployment levels reached 25 percent. Roosevelt had all of these young men and women who were not able to earn a living, and therefore, were holding off on getting married and holding off on starting their families, and there was a real question as to whether they would ever get a chance for the American dream. What struck him was that if he could somehow remove some people from the workforce, he could make room for the young. So he made a thoughtful and probably sensible decision: he institutionalized old age and retirement and formalized the notion that older people were no longer able to make a contribution.

> *Old age is far more than white hair, wrinkles, the feeling that it is too late and the game finished, that the stage belongs to the rising generations. The true evil is not the weakening of the body, but the indifference of the soul.[3]*
>
> —ANDRÉ MAUROIS

"Life expectancy the day that Social Security was passed was only sixty-three," Dychtwald continued. "There were forty workers for each recipient, and so there wasn't a sensitivity that there'd be a strain on the economy from the small number of anticipated retirees. A little-known fact is that for the fifteen years after Social Security was passed, the average age at which people retired was seventy. Even though people were told that they should step out the door, the elders back then resisted. Why? Because they wanted to earn a living. They felt good about the contributions they made, and they thought, 'Well what am I going to do if I sit at home all the time?' Retirement started getting a head of steam during the 1940s, '50s, and '60s. Life expectancy continued to grow, and the financial wherewithal of older adults picked up substantially. All of a sudden, you had more and more sixty- and seventy-year-olds who were living longer and longer with some money in their pockets. Industries began to realize that retirees were not just a group of older people sitting at home in rocking chairs but America's first true leisure class.

"What was born during that period, I think, was part fantasy, part myth, part wishful thinking: this notion that retirement was a fantastic stage of life, that work was degrading, that everybody should retire, and that if you retired and never worked again, you would just be grinning from ear to ear. It was almost like a biblical metaphor—retirement was like heaven on earth. It was better than work. You'd be happier than when you worked. In fact, if you were seeking any stature at all in your community, retirement was the way to achieve it. We have grown up in a recent era where we have this idea of how happy everybody is when they're not working for decades. Not only that, but we've also created the notion that people are entitled to decades of retirement and other people should help pay for that. The truth of it is, nobody really knows if that's right or not. It's like a pharmaceutical company selling a pill to cure a disease, but never really testing it.

"Today's retirees are the guinea pigs of this experiment. As we look around, what we're seeing is that about half of today's retirees are bored out of their wits. Today's retirees have the lowest volunteer rate of any age group in the country. And many older people are very nervous about their financial state, obviously because they're dependent on what they might have earned previously or on their employer or their union or the government."

Financial Freedom Calculator

How financially free will you be in your Second Prime? The goal is to work because you want to, not because you have to, and not to be a slave to your lifestyle. Use this calculator to get an idea of where you stand now.

---

1. Based on your retirement savings, Social Security, and any other source of income, estimate what your annual post-work income will be:
$

---

2. Describe the lifestyle that income allows you to have—your house, travel, cars, and other toys, entertaining, etc.

---

3. Describe your ideal post-work lifestyle. What's different about it? More travel or a bigger house?

	Points
4. How much more money will you need each year to live that ideal Second Prime lifestyle? If you don't need more money, give yourself 1 point. For each $10,000 more you will need, add another point. $	
5. If you don't have enough money to live your ideal lifestyle, you'll either have to work in your later years or scale back your standard of living. Which is it? Pick one: • Time—How many hours will you need to work each week after you leave your job? Hours: _____	Points

- Lifestyle—What are you willing to cut back to lower your cost of living? List up to 3 things:

1.

2.

3.

If you chose Time, add 1 point to your score for every 10 hours you'll need to work per week. If you chose Lifestyle, take 1 point away from your score for each thing you're willing to cut back.

TOTAL POINTS

SCORING: Calculate your Financial Freedom Quotient, or FFQ. The lower your score, the more freedom you're likely to have when you're in your Second Prime. Just take your point total and multiply it by the number of years you have until you retire from full-time employment. Example: if you scored 2 points and you plan to leave work in 10 years, your FFQ is 20. FFQ scoring:

0-10: You should be free to do anything you want and enjoy decades of security.

11-30: You're in pretty good shape. With a few lifestyle changes, you should have no financial worries.

31-50: You have some work to do in planning and saving better, or you're going to be working when you'd rather be traveling.

51+: You should be nervous. You haven't planned well, and unless you start saving big or make drastic lifestyle cutbacks, you may not be able to afford to stop working.

RETIREMENT EQUALS EXTINCTION

When you look up *retirement* in the dictionary, you see a variety of definitions. We looked, and we found definitions like:

- To go to bed
- To fall back or retreat
- To withdraw from use or active service

These definitions speak volumes. Retirement, for most people, does not mark a new start, but a stopping point where growth and momentum cease and the purpose of life becomes to do less, be less, and turn the course of the world over to others. How can that kind of disappearing act be healthy? Yet that's what millions have been brainwashed into accepting as gospel.

If we could get away from using the word "retirement" in the rest of this book, we would, but it would complicate things too much. The bottom line is that retirement is a death sentence. It is extinction. We are what we do—for our careers, for others, for our families, and for our communities. We are the sum total of our works. When you meet someone new, what does he ask you? "What do you do?" We define ourselves by the works of our lives. We're bankers, doctors, teachers, engineers, senators, farmers, printers, boat builders, mothers, students, artists, ministers. So what is a person who has hung up the many-colored coat woven by fifty years of working life? A person without a definition. Here's our twist on the old Satchel Paige saying about age:

If you don't know what you do, how do you know who you are?

Your Safety Net Is Torn

Even with Social Security in trouble, Baby Boomers are stubbornly holding on to the idea of retirement as worry-free, work-free, and money-rich. That's simply not going to happen. The era of the New Deal is long past, and most financial experts agree that the traditional picture of retirement is not going to be an option for many Boomers.

"Huge hard trends are taking place when we think of an aging population, and we look at health care," said futurist Dan Burrus in an interview for this book. "Medicare will cost more than Social Security and the Department of Defense combined. And beyond Social Security and

Medicare and Medicaid, there are so many government employees at the state and federal level, and they have all been promised pensions that the states have no money to pay. So we have a huge, predictable problem coming our way and the politicians don't even want to think about it."

Top financial and investment minds concur with Burrus' view. Says Harold Evensky, a principal of the financial planning firm Evensky & Katz in Coral Gables, Florida, in a *Fortune* magazine round table: "We're beginning to see a rethinking of the whole concept of what we've called retirement. Many people simply are not going to be able to have the traditional stop-working-at-sixty-five, enjoy-life-with-what-you've-saved retirement."[4]

Boomer couples of typical means put together a retirement income plan using a process that looks something like this:

- Determine how much they need each month to live the lifestyle they want, say, 80 percent of their current working income.
- Work with their financial planner to determine how much they'll need to save and invest to have those assets by retirement.
- Factor in Social Security payments.
- Figure out if they'll have to make lifestyle changes to reduce expenses, such as taking one trip a year instead of two.
- Adjust their savings accordingly so they'll have the nest egg they need to live on.

All this figuring and planning reminds us of a mountain climber descending a sheer, dangerous rock face on a rope, but he doesn't know exactly how long the rope is. When you're creating your retirement financial plan, you're making one enormous leap of faith: that your retirement nest egg won't run out before your time runs out. That's like being on that rope and having it run out 200 feet above the ground.

Okay, so maybe you've planned well and wisely, and you're confident that you will have enough assets accumulated to keep you and yours going until age ninety-five. Does your plan also depend on Social Security and pensions remaining stable and dependable? What if they don't? With forty-four million Americans dependent on some kind of defined benefit pension, the mass retirement of millions of Boomers is a perfect storm poised to drive the pension system onto the rocks.

A premonition of that crisis came on July 23, 2004, when United Airlines announced it would attempt to terminate the pensions of some or all of its 134,000 active and retired employees. As the Labor Research Association states:

> The pension disaster at United underscores the larger crisis that workers face as more companies attempt to shed their defined benefit pension plans. It also raises serious questions about the ability of the Pension Benefit Guarantee Corporation to protect workers when their pension plans fail.[5]

In other words, the safety net you may be counting on to rock you into a bucolic retirement is frayed and torn. Depend on it, and you're likely to fall through—if not to the poorhouse, then at least to a demeaning minimum wage job that you need just to pay for your prescriptions. Now is not the time to stick your head in the sand and pretend everything is all right. Instead, it's time to swallow hard, face the facts—and your fears—and see that there is hope . . . if you can reclaim control of your financial future.

Don't Retire. Refire!

Seniors are working longer, and their longer working years are transforming the American landscape. We're not the only ones who see it. In an article called "Old. Smart. Productive. Voices of Experience," *BusinessWeek* looked at five elders who are still working and excelling, including an amazing lady named Emma Shulman, a social worker who puts in fifty hours a week at the New York University School of Medicine. About Shulman and her long-working peers, writers Peter Coy and Diane Brady have this to say:

> She just might be a harbinger of things to come as the leading edge
> of the 78 million–strong Baby Boom generation approaches its

golden years. Of course, nobody's predicting that Boomers will routinely work into their 90s. But Shulman—and better-known oldsters like investor Kirk Kerkorian, 87, and Federal Reserve Chairman Alan Greenspan, 79—are proof that productive, paying work does not have to end at 55, 60, or even 65. Rather than being an economic deadweight, the next generation of older Americans is likely to make a much bigger contribution to the economy than many of today's forecasts predict. Sure, most people slow down as they get older. But new research suggests that Boomers will have the ability—and the desire—to work productively and innovatively well beyond today's normal retirement age. If society can tap their talents, employers will benefit, living standards will be higher, and the financing problems of Social Security and Medicare will be easier to solve. The logic is so powerful that it is likely to sweep aside many of the legal barriers and corporate practices that today keep older workers from achieving their full productive potential.[6]

Our mission is to explode the conventional wisdom and open your eyes not only to the perils of dependency and traditional retirement but also to the new reality that is available to you. The most thrilling aspect of that reality: *never, ever retire as long as you're able to work.*

Hold on. Put away the tar and feathers. First of all, this is actually not that revolutionary an idea. According to AARP, 72 percent of all workers today plan to work after retirement, and other studies put that number as high as 80 percent.[7] In fact, the Social Security Administration predicts that by 2020, 30 percent of people age sixty-six to seventy and 20 percent of those age seventy to seventy-nine will be employed.[8] The workforce is getting grayer by the minute. We think this is a marvelous step forward; when the Internet boom of the late 1990s (during which you were considered obsolete if you were over forty, much less sixty) collapsed, companies began to rediscover the extraordinary value locked away in the knowledge and experience of workers who had been in their fields for thirty, forty, or even fifty years.

Some of those people will be working out of necessity because they do not have enough assets to live the lifestyle they desire. Others will work out of choice because they want the social interaction and enjoyment. It's not hard to figure out which is better; no one wants to work because they have no other choice. The difference is *time*. What is a choice today can become a harsh necessity in twenty years.

Calculate Your Real Business Assets

You can borrow money. But if you're thinking about starting a business after you leave full-time employment, there are other assets that are more valuable to you. Here's where you figure out what they are. List the assets you have in each area.

Asset #1: Your professional-level skill sets (corporate law, science teaching, etc.):

Asset #2: Your quality professional contacts:

Asset #3: Your personal passions:

Asset #4: Market areas you know well (athletes, doctors, etc.):

Asset #5: Your original business ideas:

Asset #6: Friends who would help you start and run a business:

Our suggestion to you is this: starting today, begin looking for ways you can work in the future that will help you maintain your financial security and give you the lifestyle you've been planning for all these years, but also let you get up in the morning excited about what's to come during the day and expose you to new people and experiences. That way, work is never a necessity, but a choice you make because it benefits you in so many ways. In a nutshell:

Don't retire. Refire.

Refirement means that you exchange working according to someone else's rules for working according to your own. Refirement means you create economic value with your experience, skills, and leadership. Refirement means you quit working at something you like and start working at something you love. Most important of all, refirement means that you work on *your* time, working when you want, stopping when you're ready.

"I think a lot of people are scratching their heads right now and saying, 'Who do I really want to be when I'm older?' says Dychtwald in his interview with us. "Maybe it's not a matter of either working full-time or playing full-time; maybe it's about creating a new balance between work and leisure. More time for family and leisure, but not the end of work. I also think that the Boomer generation, who have just begun to turn sixty, is a very high energy, intellectually vibrant generation, and they look at many of their relatives who have retired and it looks to them to be a wasteland. People are beginning to ask the bigger question, which is, not how fast can I retire, but who do I want to *be* in this next stage of my life? What will be the new balance between contributing to society, working, learning, and playing?"

> *Don't think of retiring from the world until the world will be sorry that you retire. I hate a fellow whom pride or cowardice or laziness drive into a corner, and who does nothing when he is there but sit and growl. Let him come out as I do, and bark.[9]*
>
> —SAMUEL JOHNSON

Don't Quit. Redirect!

When you refire, you retake control of your time. You redefine "work" according to your terms. You don't just go back to a job and say, "Here I am; tell me what to do." You *create* your own working conditions, and they don't even have to be about making money.

Refirement is so simple that it only has four rules.

The Rules of Refirement

1. Only do what you love passionately, and money will take care of itself.
2. Do it on a schedule that lets you do everything else in your life.
3. Give first, and you'll receive more in return.
4. Success is doing what you love with people you love being with.

Does that sound like a great working life? However, the first rule perplexes people—because aren't we talking about working mostly to make money? Not necessarily. If you've saved and invested wisely and you're fortunate enough not to need to work for the income, then refirement is about doing what you love for the mental and spiritual benefit, not for the paycheck. When you refire, your mind and body benefit even if your bank account does not. Of course, the wonderful thing is that when you do something out of love and passion and generosity, financial reward has a way of finding you even if you're not looking for it.

> Two old men had been best friends for years. They both live to their early 90s when one of them falls deathly ill. His friend comes to visit him on his deathbed, and they're reminiscing about their long friendship when the dying man's friend asks, "Listen, when you die, do me a favor. I want to know if there's baseball in heaven."
>
> The dying man said, "We've been friends for years, this I'll do for you." And then he dies.

A couple of days later, his surviving friend is sleeping when he hears his friend's voice. The voice says, "I've got good news and bad news. The good news is that there's baseball in heaven."

"What's the bad news?"

"You're pitching Wednesday."

The Benefits of Refirement

What if instead of being dependent on $3,000 a month from Social Security, you could tap your years of experience and earn $5,000 a month as a speaker to trade groups? There are people out there who do it. Yes, you will risk not being able to collect Social Security benefits if you earn too much money. But let's do the math here:

- *Option 1:* Not working + Social Security = Lack of purpose, moderate income, and dependency on a government administered program
- *Option 2:* Working + no Social Security = Stimulation and challenge, no limit on what you can earn, independence from any government programs

We don't think it's much of a choice. But there are many benefits to refirement beyond earning enough money to not have to worry about finances:

- Earning enough to assist friends who may be in difficult financial straits
- Being able to afford health care or services that improve your quality of life
- Developing new skills or talents
- Building a new network of contacts
- Finding something you and your spouse or your friends can do together

- Building a business you can leave to your heirs
- Inspiring younger adults and children by your example

Refirement is doing the thing you've always wanted to do but never had the time to do before. It doesn't have to be a paying job. Some refired seniors become writers or painters; others volunteer, helping children learn to read or helping beautify city parks. Some take martial arts or cooking classes while others run for school board or city council. Refirement is about turning your time, energy, and enthusiasm to doing something you'd do for free. If you make a living at it, that's a bonus.

Agelessness Secret #4

Eat Red Grapes

Heard of the French Paradox? No, it's not a new car that breaks down every one hundred miles. It's the fact that even though the French eat lots of fats and foods with heavy cream, they suffer from 30 percent less heart disease than Americans. The main reason, researchers think, is that they drink gallons of red wine, which contains a compound that may decrease insulin levels, lower blood pressure, boost good cholesterol, and extend your life span.

The compound, called resveratrol, is a powerful anti-oxidant found in the skins of the red grapes. As you know, antioxidants act to defuse free radicals that can cause cellular damage and hasten the breakdown of the body. But you can also get plenty of antioxidants from eating carrots or sweet potatoes. There's got to be something more to resveratrol.

Apparently there is. Based on work by Harvard researchers in 2003, it appears that resveratrol may stimulate a class of enzymes called sirtuins. The enzymes inhibit some genes, stimulate others, and repair DNA damage, as a result, keeping cells alive and ultimately prolonging life span. So the key compound in those luscious red grapes may not just be great at preventing cell damage, it may actually have the same effect on your aging process as caloric restriction—without actually restricting calories!

As you might imagine, the jury is still out on the magical effects of red wine. Some researchers are not convinced of its effects, and there are even some concerns that it could increase a woman's risk of breast cancer. While resveratrol supplements are available, they don't seem to have the same effect. So if you enjoy eating red grapes, you can receive the benefits of resveratrol directly from the source. *Bon appetit*[10]

Some of the best ideas we've seen for refiring and reentering the workforce come courtesy of *The Boomers' Guide to Good Work—An Introduction to Jobs That Make a Difference*, written by Ellen Freudenheim and published by MetLife Foundation and Civic Ventures:

- Retrain and work full-time in a new field
- Work part-time in the same field you're in now
- Work at a lower salary, perhaps in a nonprofit or educational organization
- Discover an internship opportunity or volunteer job that can lead to paid employment
- Work seasonally or on a project basis[11]

Such options were once the territory of the young, but no longer. Keeping an open mind lets you explore what the report calls "good work" that rewards you in many ways other than monetarily.

THE AGE OF THE "SENIORPRENEUR" IS UPON US

Dan Burrus says in our interview, "Because we have a shortage of young people, we're going to see a lot of thirty- and forty-year-old entrepreneurs hiring sixty- and seventy-year-old bookkeepers and accountants, because where else are they going to get them? I see education as a huge area for the Baby Boomers so they can stay reengaged and continue to be employed. Many of them are going to stay in the field they're in because that's their competency level. Many who have saved money are going to do more reengagement, where they're working in the things that they love to do and are fun to do, turning their avocations into vocations."

Millions of seniors have already discovered what Burrus is talking about. We're already entering the "Golden Age of the Seniorpreneur":

- According to a *USA Today* story from January 2005, 5.6 million workers age fifty and over are self-employed, a 23 percent jump from 1990.[12]
- The rate of self-employment for workers aged fifty and over was 17.2 percent compared with 10.3 percent for the workforce as a whole, according to a RAND Corporation report, "Self-Employment and the 50+ Population."[13]
- An AARP poll from 2003 showed that 16 percent of respondents planned to work for themselves or start their own business in their 70s or beyond.[14]
- James Challenger of the outplacement firm Challenger, Gray and Christmas says that senior entrepreneurs now represent more than 28 percent of all self-employed workers.[15]

At the same time, more retired seniors are "un-retiring" and going back into the job market for economic and personal reasons. AARP reports that 33 percent of all retirees reenter the job market within two years of retirement.[16] Many will go to work for a company, but a growing number will become seniorpreneurs. "Some people are attracted into self-employment for positive reasons, like having more flexible work arrangements or being your own boss," says Lynn Karoly, coresearcher in the RAND study mentioned above, in an interview for this book. "Many employers don't allow the flexibility to gradually decrease your hours or work some weeks and not others, whereas if you're working for yourself you tend to have more of an ability to control that. And for people at older ages, it allows them to pursue interests they might not have been able to when they were younger."

"What is quite interesting is that if you look at the older population that's working at any given time, about one-third of them became self-employed after age fifty," she continues. "It's quite common that people do move into self-employment after a long career as a traditional wage or salary worker."

Are You a Seniorpreneur in the Making?

Not everyone is cut out to be self-employed or run their own business, and that's fine. Some people are just not entrepreneurial, and there's nothing wrong with that. Running your own show comes complete with many risks. You've got to find start-up capital, cover payroll and health-care costs, update your technical skills, handle marketing and sales, and still there's no guarantee of success. If starting a business doesn't appeal to you, there are still many worthwhile ways to work, from volunteerism to community organizing.

But if you possess three important characteristics—physical readiness, the capacity to enjoy taking risks, and a passion for learning new things—then becoming a seniorpreneur could be the most rewarding aspect of your later life. We're not just talking about starting a company where you take on payroll and have an office, or working from your home doing medical transcription or secretarial work. This is your chance to think creatively. What assets do you bring to the table? How could you take what you're best at and make a new career out of it, on your own terms? Even better, how can you take what you love—something you've never made a dime at before—and turn it into a business?

- Become a professional speaker with the help of organizations like Toastmasters and the National Speakers Association.
- Tap your experience to become a contract trainer in your former industry.
- Consult with your old company on *your* schedule.
- If you've spent twenty years painting or writing plays but have never done anything with your creative works, now's the time. Talk to

gallery owners about a show of your paintings, or to a local theater company about performing a piece you've written.

Then there's the Internet. If you don't know much about it, learn. It's easy to take classes at a community college and become familiar with the basics, and it's worth your time. The World Wide Web gives you the unheard of ability to start and run a business; sell products; communicate with customers, workers, and partners; and make a great living from your home. Electronic commerce is an $80 billion business in the United States alone and growing every year. You can sell products directly, use the Web as a marketing and sales center for your speaking or consulting services, even write an online newsletter for your senior community and sell advertising. The Internet is the perfect business tool if your mobility is less than perfect or you just want to minimize your risk. Resources like *Entrepreneur* magazine and Entrepreneur.com can give you even more information.

Another brilliant concept we've run across is seniors teaming with other seniors to start businesses aimed at seniors. It makes perfect sense; you're in their demographic group, and you understand their needs and can connect personally because you share similar life experiences. And while it can be risky to go into business with friends, if you can get past the hurdles, there are many advantages to launching co-op companies with your fellow seniorpreneurs: pooled financial resources, a wider variety of skill sets, more business contacts, and different perspectives. Karen E. Spaeder, writing in *Entrepreneur*, suggests nine ideal senior-to-senior (S2S) businesses:

- Senior care consultant
- Nonmedical home care
- Meal delivery
- Senior clothing and products
- Transportation
- Senior concierge
- Adult day care
- Technology training
- Online dating[17]

Could you start one of these businesses? How about something else? There's nothing stopping you from doing it with some time, work, and planning.

What Kind of Business Should I Start?

It's a critical question, and this test can only help you answer part of it. But you'll at least get some idea of where your interests and abilities are pointing you. Then do what we suggest to everyone: if at all possible, do what you love.

For each question, circle a number from 1–5. 1 means you disagree with the statement completely; 2 means you disagree somewhat; 3 means you're neutral; 4 means you agree somewhat; 5 means you agree completely.

Skills

	Disagree				Agree
1. Technical I am highly skilled with computers and the Internet.	1	2	3	4	5
2. Creative I have well-developed creative skills—writing, drawing, painting, and so on.	1	2	3	4	5
3. Business My strongest skills are in areas like accounting, marketing, or sales.	1	2	3	4	5
4. Hands-on I'm most skilled in things like auto repair, carpentry, house painting, or fixing appliances.	1	2	3	4	5
5. People My strongest areas are my people- and teaching skills.	1	2	3	4	5

Environment & Lifestyle

	Disagree				Agree
6. Workplace I'd like to work in a home office.	1	2	3	4	5

7. Time	Disagree				Agree
I want complete control of my time and to not have to conform to anyone else's schedule.	1	2	3	4	5

8. Teamwork	Disagree				Agree
I like working by myself; I don't really care about working with other people.	1	2	3	4	5

Goals

9. Money	Disagree				Agree
Making a lot of money is the most important thing in my choice of a business to start.	1	2	3	4	5

10. Giving Back	Disagree				Agree
Helping others and giving back to the community is the most important thing in my choice of a business to start.	1	2	3	4	5

11. Novelty	Disagree				Agree
Having the chance to learn new things and to have new experiences is the most important thing.	1	2	3	4	5

12. Risk	Disagree				Agree
I don't mind taking a big risk to start my business.	1	2	3	4	5

SCORING: There's no glib, easy way to score this test. Its goal is to get you to look at the different factors that might influence your business decisions. What picture do your test results paint? If you're an Internet-savvy person who likes working alone, maybe tech support is your game. If you have strong people skills but want control of your time, perhaps you should be a tutor. Look at yourself and start brainstorming.

THINK OUTSIDE THE CASKET

The more creative you are, the more possibilities you'll see. It's amazing what happens when you take what you love to do more than anything else and ask, "How can I turn this into a business?" In an interview for this book, Gary Zelesky, speaker and author of the upcoming book *The Passion Centered Professional,* talks about a woman he counseled about starting a business based on her passion: "I was speaking at a women's conference, and I found myself talking with a woman who appeared to be at her wit's end. I asked her, 'What's your passion?' She said what everyone says: 'It's stupid.' I pressed her. 'What do you love to do?' I insisted. Finally she told me: she loved to go shopping. She loved to shop for clothing, she loved to shop with other women, and she was a smart, savvy shopper."

"I asked her the million-dollar question," Zelesky continues. "'What if you could build a business out of taking women shopping?' Her eyes glowed. I suggested she create a small business in which she would take a group of women shopping in a limousine for X amount of dollars each, and throw in lunch for a little more. I looked up, and we were surrounded by all these excited ladies. The woman began writing down the ideas I had given her, and these other women were talking and giving her more ideas for marketing, sales, services she could offer, and the like. It was one of the most wonderful things I've ever seen. A few months later, I received a business card from the woman. She had started her shopping excursion business and had already taken her first group out."

Seniorpreneurship is a matter of thinking outside the box . . . or, given the dire consequences of retiring and doing nothing, outside the *casket.* Figure out what you love, and then find a way to spend your days doing it. No matter how much money you make, you'll be rich. As Jim McClurg of the Social Enterprise Alliance writes:

> When you're using your business acumen to help people struggling with mental illness, get homeless youth off the street, or work with abused kids, while at the same time providing employment and wages, you may sometimes go home frustrated over work or finance problems. But you never go home wondering why you went to work in the first place; that's front and center all the time.[18]

Money: The Other Side of Work

The King Kong-sized caveat here is, of course, that you can only spend your Second Prime doing what you love if you don't have to take any job just to keep a roof over your head. Even if you have a surefire idea for a business that you can start when you're seventy, there's one element critical to virtually every secure postworking life: saving money and investing wisely. And the sooner the better; thanks to the miracle of compound interest, the more years you have your money in a 401(k), IRA, or SEP IRA, the better you'll do. For example, if you start with $100,000 in your retirement fund at age forty and contribute just $300 per month until you're sixty-five and earn a reasonable return of eight percent, your retirement savings will be worth $948,028 by the time you're ready to refire and leave your job. That's enough to fuel a nice lifestyle and pay for a business on the side.

> To get back my youth I would do anything in the world, except take exercise, get up early, or be respectable.[19]
>
> —Oscar Wilde

The problem, of course, is that far too many Baby Boomers are not practicing disciplined retirement savings. A study by the nonprofit Employee Benefit Research Institute in Washington DC found that half of all workers have saved less than $25,000 for retirement. Workers who invested in company 401(k) plans for at least six years were in better shape, averaging $91,042 in savings at the end of 2004. And the account balances of workers in their 60s averaged $136,400.[20] That sounds like a lot of money, but what if you're used to living high on the hog, spending $5,000 a month on travel, dinners out, expensive gifts, and toys? You're either going to have to cut back in a big way and feel cheated or find some other source of income.

You spend a lot. You've got most of the money, and you're going to be inheriting trillions from your parents between now and 2050—$14 trillion by one estimate. The estimated 76.9 million members of the Baby Boom generation own 67 percent of all personal financial assets but consume $1.7 trillion dollars worth of goods and services annually (JWT Mature Marketing Group).[21] When you crunch all those numbers, you get this result: according to the US Congressional Budget Office, only about 50 percent of Boomer households are on track to accumulate enough wealth to maintain their current standard of living if the chief income earners retire when they plan to. One fourth have their fingers crossed that they will earn high returns on their investments and squeak by. And the final 25 percent, many of them low-income households that haven't managed to save much, will be dependent on programs like Social Security—and we've already made it clear how dependable those are.[22]

If you're a Boomer who hasn't saved much yet and is somehow assuming that another wild stock market balloon will inflate like it did during the Internet boom days and carry you to the land of 20 percent annual returns, we have some sobering information, courtesy of *Fortune* magazine, which ran a story in July 2005, listing the five greatest threats to retirement savings:

1. *Lower stock returns.* Historical market returns since 1926 are 10.4 percent a year, but there's nothing that says that can't drop for the next twenty years.
2. *Inflation.* Inflation figures are misleading, and if the housing bubble doesn't burst, how much is your retirement castle going to cost?
3. *Low interest rates.* Rates on T-bills and bonds are barely outpacing inflation.
4. *Medicare's looming crisis.* Costs are due to rise into the stratosphere, which means Medicare benefits will almost certainly be cut.
5. *Longer lives.* Congratulations, you're living longer! That means you need more money.[23]

What can you do in the face of all this? Don't panic. Plan.

Doing the Numbers

When you read about the financial challenges facing aging Boomers, you find a lot of talk about postponing retirement. There's little or no talk about simply *not* retiring, and that's part of the problem. But another big part of it is that without substantial savings for your postwork life, you don't have the freedom to make the kind of choices that will give you the life you want—the life you've earned.

"Baby Boomers know they haven't saved enough money, haven't accumulated enough assets, and they're starting to get an inkling that they're going to live longer," says Donald Ray Haas, seventy-five, a Michigan-based financial gerontologist and founder of the Center for Financial Gerontology, in an interview for this book. "But they don't realize just how much longer they're going to live. A person age sixty-five, if they live to sixty-five, their life expectancy is in the mid-80s. And for a couple who both live to sixty-five, the mortality tables tell us that the average life expectancy for at least one of that couple is ninety-three."

For Haas' clients and millions of concerned Boomers around the country, their concern is making their money last as long as they do but not reducing their standard of living. The most critical factor in hitting that goal is *time*. If you've started too late or haven't saved enough over the years because of profligate spending or lack of discipline, even if you start now, plowing a large percentage of your income into savings each month, you simply won't have the time for the effects of compounding to make your money grow by the amount it needs to grow to give you the lifestyle you want.

"When you add longevity to the equation with inflation, you need equity investments that are going to grow more than a fixed dollar investment like a bond, savings account, or CD," says Haas. "Long-term statistics show that equity investments—real estate and the stock market—return about ten percent a year. So for the person who is about to retire or a post-retiree, we look at their standard of living and what it costs. Then we go through a calculation to determine how much money they are going to need for the rest of their life to maintain that. We take the first year's retirement income and inflate it each year by the 3- to 3.5-percent of inflation, and I assume each of my clients will live to be a hundred and that they're going to be active. People are more active now, and the Baby Boomers are going to be even more active."

A sixty-year-old man went to a doctor for a check-up. The doctor told him, "You're in terrific shape. There's nothing wrong with you. Why, you might live forever. You have the body of a thirty-five-year-old. By the way, how old was your father when he died?"

The sixty-year-old responded, "Did I say he was dead?" The doctor was surprised and asked, "How old is he, and is he very active?"

The sixty-year-old responded, "Well, he is eighty-two years old, and he still goes skiing three times a season and surfing three times a week during the summer."

The doctor couldn't believe it. So, he asked, "Well, how old was your grandfather when he died?" The sixty-year-old responded again, "Did I say he was dead?"

The doctor was astonished. He said, "You mean to tell me you are sixty years old and both your father and your grandfather are alive? Is your grandfather very active?"

The sixty-year-old said, "He goes skiing at least once a season and surfing once a week during the summer. Not only that," said the patient, "my grandfather is one-hundred-and-six years old, and next week he is getting married again."

The doctor said, "At one-hundred-and-six, why on earth would your grandfather want to get married?"

His patient looked up at the doctor and said, "Did I say he wanted to?"

THE PANIC YEAR

If the numbers don't pan out, and if the soon-to-be retirees don't have enough time to earn more money, then something's got to give. That something is standard of living, the one thing nobody wants to change. If the couple has a few years, they may have to accept higher risks than they would otherwise be comfortable with.

Greater risk is not a dependable foundation on which to build your later life security, so Haas impresses on clients who are in a difficult financial position to manage their spending and try to avoid lowering their standard of living. The numbers are implacable; if your money is projected to run out by the time you're eighty-five, you have no choice but to bite the bullet and make some lifestyle changes.

It's an emotional issue, of course. Haas says that fifty is the "panic year," when people who haven't paid much attention to the need for substantial retirement savings suddenly realize they're nearing their postwork years and they have little or nothing set aside. "That's the wake-up call," he says. "At age fifty they get scared to death. Baby Boomers consistently say they want to retire at fifty-five, but they get to age fifty and they realize that not only are they not going to be able to retire at fifty-five, they may not even be able to retire at sixty-five. And they're willing to go on a crash program, from a zero or negative savings rate up to 20 percent of disposable income. It serves the purpose very well to get them saving."

What Can You Do?

In his interview, Haas points out that there are two basic assumptions wise Boomers must make when it comes to planning for their retirement: "One is that your health-care costs are going to increase, and the other is that you will need a large amount of money, increasing every year, for the rest of your life." But beyond that, what should you be doing now to prepare for a Second Prime where work is a choice, not a necessity? The National Retirement Planning Coalition (www.RetireOnYourTerms.org) has some commonsense suggestions:

- Select a target date for when you want to retire.
- Calculate how much money you need to accumulate by the time you want to retire.
- Find out about your Social Security benefits.
- Maximize your use of tax-advantaged plans such as employer retirement plans, individual retirement accounts, and annuities.
- If your employer doesn't have a pension or retirement plan, ask that one be started.
- Don't touch your savings.

- Diversify your assets.
- Ask questions. Get help. Seek the assistance of a professional financial advisor.
- Start now, set goals.
- Do a retirement plan and monitor your progress.[24]

Of course, we suggest substituting refire for retire, but you get the point. Plan proactively. Don't stick your head in the sand and assume that somehow it will be all right. Take the advice of David Bach, author of *The Automatic Millionaire* and *Finish Rich* books, and automate your savings using your bank's automatic deposit features. Make small sacrifices in your lifestyle now if you have to so you can have a great postwork life later.[25] Visit www.SecondPrime.com to find ideas and tools for starting a business, investing wisely, and using the skills you've spent years developing.

Above all, work. Plan on doing something meaningful and creating some kind of income later in life. "Of the 80 percent of Baby Boomers who plan to work after retirement, 25 percent will work because they have to, indicating that they hate what they're doing. What a terrible way to go through life," says Haas. "The biggest category, 30–40 percent, will continue to work because they want to. I tell my clients to pick something you like and do it, and remember every day you do it, if you don't like it, quit."

Second Prime Strategy—Work and Money

For each of these eight chapters, we're going to help you map out a strategy for creating a marvelous Second Prime. Complete the strategy worksheet as best you can and use it to start building your plan.

1. Things to Do

- Talk to a financial advisor; find one if you don't have one.
- Take stock of your Social Security situation.
- Take the "What Business Should I Start" test and start writing down business ideas.
- Look at your lifestyle and start seeing what you could cut back to live more efficiently.

- Look at ways you might reduce your future health-care costs.
- Take inventory of all your debt and make a schedule for paying it all off by the time you leave your job.
- Talk to your employer about consulting or otherwise continuing to work after you leave.
- Talk to friends about the possibility of partnering on a business after you all retire.

2. Changes You Need to Make in Your Financial Planning or Lifestyle

-
-
-
-
-

3. Your Financial and Work Goals for Your Second Prime

Example: "Earn enough with a small business to travel three months each year."

-
-
-
-

4. Money and Work Resources

- American Institute of Financial Gerontology (www.aifg.org)
- *Entrepreneur* Magazine (www.entrepreneur.com)
- United States Small Business Administration (www.sba.gov)
- Paladin Registry (www.paladinregistry.com)
- Wiser Advisor (www.wiseradvisor.com)
- Startup Bank (www.startupbank.com)
- SCORE (www.score.org)
- Preferred Consumer Small Business Channel (www.preferredconsumer.com/small_business)

Body *or* Never Let Anyone Help You Out of a Chair

Thanks to modern medical advances such as antibiotics, nasal spray, and Diet Coke, it has become routine for people in the civilized world to pass the age of forty, sometimes more than once.[1]

—DAVE BARRY

A person taking stock in middle age is like an artist or composer looking at an unfinished work; but whereas the composer and the painter can erase some of their past efforts, we cannot. We are stuck with what we have lived through. The trick is to finish it with a sense of design and a flourish rather than to patch up the holes or merely to add new patches to it.[2]

—HARRY S. BROUDY

The subtitle alternative for this chapter is "Never let anyone help you out of a chair." That comes from Sophia Loren, but it might as well read, "Never let anyone help you into old age." Your body is a use-it-or-lose-it kind of instrument, and like a guitar or any other instrument, it needs to be kept in tune. You keep it in tune by playing it regularly. If you want to keep your body vital and mobile and fresh and pleasurable, you must keep it moving *without anyone else's help.* You must live independently, always pushing your body to do new things as you age, never giving in to the idea that "I can't do that, I'm too old." Why? As soon as that thought enters your mind, you *become* too old. Dr. R. Buckminster Fuller, Mark's great teacher, took up skiing at seventy-seven years young and was trained by Olympic Gold Medal winner Jean-Claude Killy. Why not be like our ninety-two-year-old friend Jack LaLanne and challenge yourself to break a new record, event, or feat every year?

To remain healthy into your 80s, 90s, and beyond, you must keep everything in motion: your muscles, your capacity to make decisions, your ambitions, your sense of purpose. Keeping your body in tip-top condition into your Second Prime means remaining independent as long as possible, always insisting on doing things for yourself. It means taking control of your health and health care. Because here's a little secret that the folks who have a vested interest in your remaining sick won't tell you:

If you continually move your body and give your biological machine what it needs to run clean and fast, you should not need Medicare.

If Social Security is a car about to lose its right front wheel, Medicare is a train wreck. As we write this book, millions of seniors are trying to sign up for their new 2006 Medicare prescription drug plan at the program Web site: www.medicare.gov. But there are so many options, and they're so confusing, that it's tough for anyone to know what they really need. Yes, this is definitely a government program.

Mix Medicare with the obscenely profitable drug industry, and you don't just have capitalism completely out of control, you have a cabal that professes to care about your health while trying to convince you to dump more powerful drugs into your system. As with so many other aspects of old age, you've been brainwashed into thinking that the only way to deal with the health challenges of age is to take a pill. We know seniors who take thirty, forty, or even fifty prescription medications *a day*. But it doesn't have to be that way. A huge part of this book's mission is to help you understand that you don't need to depend on drug companies for a healthy Second Prime.

How Not to Need Medicare

There are some prescription drugs that do wonderful things and improve lives. Antidepressants like Prozac have changed the lives of tens of thousands of people living with clinical depression. There are beneficial drugs out there. What we find obscene is when pharmaceutical conglomerates use their financial and political clout to create a *lifestyle of medication*, in which everything is handled by popping a pill.

But enough of this pharma-bashing. We're here to talk about *Insteadicare*, where you take control of your own health by keeping yourself well, rather than simply seeking care after you develop a disease. To increase your healthspan, you've got to start taking care of yourself decades before the time when you're "supposed" to break down. You've got to start in your 40s or 50s, or even earlier.

The American health-care system is *prescriptive*, meaning it's all about waiting for disease to develop and then treating it with chemotherapy, surgery, or drugs. "It is no secret that our American health-care system is in trouble," says Cheryl Bartholomew, a certified American Senior Fitness Instructor who serves assisted and independent living, retirement, and active adult communities, and who in December 2005 served as an advocate for senior fitness as a delegate to the White House Conference on Aging (www.whcoa.gov). In an interview for this book, she says, "That is due in large part to our society's focus on 'curative care' rather than 'preventive care.'"

If you tell your doctor you want to work with a trained health-care professional on ways to prevent disease through diet, exercise, and lifestyle choices, you'll probably get a blank stare. You have to sally forth on your own and find an "alternative" practitioner—a dietician, naturopath, chiropractor, acupuncturist, or other professional—to help you develop a healthy lifestyle. Even the word *alternative* rankles Dr. Walter Bortz. "There is no alternative medicine," he says in an interview for this book. "There is only one medicine. I want to practice health medicine, not disease medicine."

The new vision is to make medicine *preventive*, so instead of waiting for disease to rear its ugly head, you're living a holistic lifestyle that's keeping you healthy. Spend twenty years living this way, and you should be fit, mobile, alert, and regularly being told you look fifteen years younger than you are. This is what we call *futurepathic* medicine, an approach built around the many natural, inexpensive things you can do today to ensure a healthy, active, rich, and rewarding tomorrow.

Which Drugs Could You Do Without?

The healthier you keep yourself, the fewer prescription drugs you'll have to depend on. This exercise is designed to get you thinking about the ways you can wean yourself from the pill bottle by making smart lifestyle changes. It works like this:

There are underlying lifestyle choices behind most of the serious diseases seniors suffer from: obesity, poor diet, inactivity, too much stress, smoking, etc. If you can identify the lifestyle choices that have caused or worsened your illnesses, you can make changes that will make a difference. This one might take some research, and when it comes to whether you could reduce or eliminate your drugs, talk to your physician.

Your Condition	Drugs You Take For It	Lifestyle Reasons	What You Could Change	You Could . . .
Example: Hypertension	Coreg	I am 70 pounds over my ideal weight.	• Start walking every morning • Eat low-fat • Lose 3 pounds per month	Cut back my medication in 1 year and discontinue it in 2 years
Your Condition	Drugs You Take For It	Lifestyle Reasons	What You Could Change	You Could . . .
Your Condition	Drugs You Take For It	Lifestyle Reasons	What You Could Change	You Could . . .

The Seven Elements of a Long Healthspan

Inspired? Infuriated? Good—because this all comes down to you and your willingness to quit passively placing your health in the hands of the medical-pharmaceutical complex and to take responsibility for your health. To have a long healthspan, you must explode the "just take a pill" attitude that's so pervasive in this country and make lifestyle changes in the short term to enjoy greater vitality in the long term.

There are eight elements to focus on if you want to have a robust body with few limitations when you're in your 70s and 80s:

1. Getting plenty of the four kinds of movement.
2. Eating a natural diet rich in "super foods."
3. Taking a proper balance of supplements and nutriceuticals.
4. Keeping harmful stress to a minimum.
5. Getting enough sleep and rest.
6. Taking pride in your physical appearance.
7. Continuing to challenge yourself physically.
8. Finding health coverage that recognizes preventive care.

Wholesale lifestyle changes aren't easy. But in them, we're offering a lot in return: a later life where sixty really is the new forty and eighty is the new sixty. There's no time to wait; you lose coordination at a rate of about one percent a year after age thirty.

> *Age is a high price to pay for maturity.*[3]
> —Tom Stoppard

The Four Kinds of Movement

According to Bortz and a broad range of wellness experts, Baby Boomers should be engaging in a combination of four kinds of movement regularly:

- Aerobic exercise—running, cycling, step and elliptical machines, aerobics classes
- Strength training—weight lifting, pulling elastic bands

- Flexibility training—stretching, yoga, Pilates
- Balance training—balancing on one leg, body awareness

Notice that we didn't say "exercise." That's because exercise has a negative connotation for many people. The word implies dragging yourself to the gym, where you'll feel embarrassed in front of fit people, and slogging grimly through boring exercises. But movement is natural. Movement is life.

"When you stop moving, you get old," says Bortz in his interview. There's absolutely nothing wrong with going to the gym four days a week and working out, if you have the time and the desire. However, if gyms just aren't your thing, there is an option. Many specialists in fitness for seniors focus on helping their clients develop *functional fitness*, which is based on getting your body in shape to do the things you do every day. It's "real world" fitness based on natural movement.

"Older adults exercise to remain independent and to perform required activities of daily living: bathing, dressing, carrying trash, caring for and playing with grandchildren, and so on," says Bartholomew in her interview. "To accomplish these goals one should focus on maintaining muscular and core strength, flexibility, range of motion and balance. Exercise also stimulates the creation of neurons, which helps keep the brain responsive. Affecting so many aspects of functionality . . . fitness becomes an important tool for seniors who wish to continue driving into their later years. AAA and AARP now provide an educational program designed for older adult driving safety and comfort, which addresses changes in physique and medical conditions that can adversely affect one's driving ability. For example, without proper strength, flexibility, and range of motion in the shoulders, a person may not react quickly enough to turn the steering wheel and avoid an accident."

Fitness training can take many forms and can be adapted for all levels of ability and special needs. It may include the use of resistance bands, chair-based aerobics, and/or core and balance work combined with stretching. Functional exercise mimics real life situations (chopping wood, lifting suitcases to store in overhead compartments on planes, etc.) and involves simultaneous use and coordination of multiple muscle groups rather than working one muscle group in isolation. Such techniques encourage optimal strength, control, and flexibility, thereby reducing the risk of injury or imbalance.

In their book *Younger Next Year,* Chris Crowley and Dr. Henry S. Lodge recommend a grueling exercise routine: forty-five minutes of intense aerobic work five days a week, one day with *four hours* of intense work (like hiking or cycling), and one day off (gee, thanks). You should never simply jump into that kind of program unless you're already in good shape, but that level of exercise has been shown to reverse your *functional* age (meaning you have the strength, flexibility, or endurance of a younger person) by twenty years or more.[4]

Did you know that weight training is especially important for older adults, who lose 35 to 40 percent of skeletal muscle mass in the years between age twenty and eighty, a process known as *sarcopenia,* which means "vanishing flesh"? However, a person starting weight training even in his or her 90s—as long as the weight training is done with a physician's approval and under the supervision of a specialist in senior fitness—can see huge health benefits and regain a substantial amount of lost muscle mass. Strength training also helps prevent the bone loss that can lead to crippling osteoporosis.

A man's death was mistakenly noted in the local paper's obituary section. The "corpse" hastened to the editor to protest. "I'm awfully sorry," the editor replied. "But it's too late to do much about it. The best thing I can do for you is to put you in the 'Birth Column' tomorrow morning and give you a fresh start."

A BALANCING ACT

These days, there's an equal emphasis on balance in training regimens for older people, for a reason you can probably guess: falls. "The biggest predictor of needing to go to a nursing home is not how old you are or what diseases you have, but how strong your legs are," says Bortz. He recommends balance training be integrated into a training regimen, something like "flamingo stand," where you start by standing on one leg, with one hand on a chair if you need it. "If you can stand on one leg with your eyes shut for half an hour, your balance is intact," he insists.

"When you talk about balance, there are two kinds: static balance and dynamic balance," says Bartholomew. "An example of static balance is when you're standing in line with equal weight distribution on both feet. With some older adults they find they will begin to sway after a few minutes, which may signal a decline in static balance ability. Dynamic balance occurs when one is able to maintain stability while in motion, despite a shift in the center of gravity due to movement."

Balance training, she adds, incorporates body awareness: an understanding of how the body moves and the ability to control and coordinate those movements. "Coordination of movement, proper postural alignment, coordination and muscle strength are all components of balance," Bartholomew says. "Persons who have not fallen may have a false sense of stability and believe that their balance is fine. Many people will mistakenly wait until their balance has been compromised before they seek balance training. A fitness assessment test can best determine one's ability to adequately perform necessary tasks of daily living, within a particular age bracket. It is most beneficial to work on balance before needing a cane or a walker, to slow the process of impairment. If you wait too long, it then becomes a challenge to maintain your current balance status rather than improve it."

Bartholomew adds that the socialization associated with group exercise contributes to making the process more enjoyable and meaningful. For many, the social aspect of classes motivates them to keep their commitment to exercise. Cross-training or varying the kind of exercise performed daily is proven to promote well-rounded conditioning of mind and body. It is important to alternate aerobic, strength, core, and flexibility programs. Rotation of class format also prevents boredom and helps reduce the plateau effect of prolonged repetition of the same routine.

Whatever you choose to do, commit to doing it regularly; thirty minutes or more, most days of the week. The cost of inactivity is steep.

"Preventive care begins with you and me," says Bartholomew. "The focus is currently on obesity, but obesity is the result of inactivity, which is the real culprit. Obesity is merely a symptom of inactivity. More persons die each year from inactivity than obesity." For every year you wait to start engaging in a lifestyle of healthy movement, you increase your chances of developing heart-related problems, cancer, or complications due to obesity (such as diabetes), which potentially threaten your future health.

The good news is no matter when you begin an exercise regimen, you will benefit from it. The earlier you begin, the better your chances for remaining an independently functioning adult who is physically and mentally fit.

Agelessness Secret #5

Eat "Super Foods"

Eating a healthy, well-balanced diet is critical to your continued well-being. But many nutrition experts believe that certain foods offer extraordinary benefits to your body. Eating more of these so-called *super foods* may give you an advantage in avoiding age-related diseases. Courtesy of *Nutrition Action*, a publication of the Centers for Science in the Public Interest, here's a list of ten super foods:

1. Sweet potatoes—One of the best vegetables you can eat, loaded with carotenoids, vitamin C, potassium, and fiber.
2. Grape tomatoes—These sleek, small tomatoes are perfect for snacking and dipping and are packed with vitamins A and C, fiber, and phytochemicals.
3. Fat-free milk—Take away the artery-clogging fat, and you're left with an excellent source of calcium, vitamins, and protein.
4. Blueberries—With a skin rich in pigments called anthocyanins, blueberries are one of the best antioxidant sources you can eat.
5. Wild salmon—Wild salmon are rich in omega-3 fatty

acids that, among other benefits, reduce the risk of sudden death from heart attacks.

6. Crispbreads—Whole grain rye crackers like Wasa and Ry Crisp have a ton of fiber and are usually fat-free.

7. Brown rice—White rice is a waste of time. Brown rice gives you fiber, magnesium, vitamins E and B_6, copper, zinc, and other phytochemicals.

8. Watermelon—It's a low-calorie, great tasting source of vitamin C and carotenoids.

9. Diced butternut squash—You can find this pre-cut, washed, packaged, and ready to cook at many stores. It's filled with fiber and vitamins A and C.

10. Bags of greens—It's easy to buy bags of fresh, organic spinach, kale, broccoli rabe, and other salad greens, all brimming over with nutrients like vitamins A and C, calcium, folate, potassium, and fiber.

11. Broccoli—This is a bonus. Broccoli is one of the healthiest vegetables you can eat, delivering a power punch of beta-carotene, folate, potassium, and a phytochemical called sulforaphane, which reduces cancer risk.[5]

COULD YOU SWIM A MILE AT NINETY-TWO?

It's never too late to start exercising, and if you really work at it, you can see some astonishing results. For proof, look no further than the hordes of athletes in their 60s, 70s, 80s, and 90s competing in track and field, swimming, and other athletic events in the Senior Olympics, state Senior Games, and Masters competitions all over the country.

"I started swimming competitively at sixty-four," says Woody Bowersock, now a lively ninety-three-year-old who still competes regularly and holds twenty-one world records for his age group. Interviewed for this book, he adds, "When I retired, I needed something to fill the time. I used to go jogging after work, but my ankles were bothering me. I used to swim, so I took it back up." Now, at five feet, nine inches tall and 165 pounds,

Bowersock is trim and fit and works out six days a week to keep in swimming shape. He also enjoys being mistaken for a younger man.

Bry Thorne, seventy-nine, didn't start running until he was fifty-four. "I was going through a divorce, and I was upset," he says in an interview we conducted. "I walked up to the local high school track and started jogging around the track. At first, I could hardly do 200 yards. Then I did 400 yards. In six months, a guy asked me to do a 10K. Well, I went out and won my age division. I think my ex-wife did me a favor." Thorne has run marathons in Boston, London, and Los Angeles, completing one in the impressive time of three hours and twenty-five minutes. But one of the greatest benefits of his training and regular competition in Senior Olympics and Masters events came off the track: a complete recovery from prostate cancer.

"Normally, doctors won't operate on you if you're seventy because of the recovery time," he says. "But in my case, the doctor said, 'You're a marathoner, so no problem.' Now I'm completely cancer-free." Thorne doesn't run as fast or far as he used to, but he still competes regularly in 10K races. "My goal is just to hang in there and run until I die," he quips.

> *I have enjoyed greatly the second blooming that comes when you finish the life of the emotions and of personal relations and suddenly find—at the age of fifty, say—that a whole new life has opened before you, filled with things you can think about, study, or read about . . . It is as if a fresh sap of ideas and thoughts was rising in you.*[6]
>
> —Agatha Christie

Few people are more qualified to tout the magic of exercise on an aging body than Jack LaLanne, longtime fitness guru and tireless spokesman for healthy diet and lifestyle. LaLanne, who at ninety-two still works out every morning, holds court on the transformative power of movement. "Old age, you have to work at it," he says in an interview recorded for this book. "Dying is easy. Any stupid person can die. The average American, he works at dying. Exercise is king, nutrition is queen, put them together, you have a kingdom. The only way you hurt the human body is inactivity, sitting on your big fat butt thinking about the good old days. The good old days are right this moment.

"You've got to have goals and challenges," LaLanne continues. "The number one reason some of these older people don't is because they are so physically unfit: they're fat, they've got aches and pains, they're fat, they have arthritis and rheumatism. How did they get those aches and pains? How did they get fat? Did God do it? God helps those who help themselves. Who put the food in my mouth, God? God gives you the power to do it, but you have to do it. Too many old people say, 'Oh, my mother was this, my father was this, I inherited this.' The only thing you inherited from your parents was the color of your hair and eyes. The rest is you."

What's his advice for Baby Boomers who haven't exercised in years? "If you can afford it, you should go to a good gym," he says. "Make sure you get personal supervision. Three to four times a week, you should be doing vigorous exercise. But you've got to make haste slowly, do it one step at a time. Get a physical to make sure you're all right. If you can afford a trainer, great. If not, there are YMCAs, books, and other things. But keep away from hokey stuff like the three-minute abs and the gut master. These things are a bunch of lies. You have 640 muscles in your body, and they all need their share of work. You need strength work, flexibility work, and twelve to seventeen minutes three or four times a week, something nonstop for cardiovascular work. There is no quick fix; you've got to work at it. You've got train like you're training for an athletic event."

The Benefits of Exercise

- *Emotional*—The release of endorphins produced in the brain through physical activity results in positive enhancement of mood.
- *Vocational*—You gain the ability to perform chosen hobbies or tasks of interest (i.e., gardening, needlework, art, woodworking) with less or no pain and greater ease, bringing greater personal satisfaction and direction and purpose to your life.
- *Physical*—Improved ability to function independently promotes a sense of well-being and confidence due to newly discovered strength, increased range of motion, and improved balance/coordination and flexibility. This discourages a sedentary lifestyle.

- *Intellectual*—Physical activity has been proven to stimulate the growth of new brain cells and help maintain alertness and improve mental capacity and mental ability by challenging the mind to focus and learn new movements and to coordinate and process those movements.
- *Social*—Exercise (particularly group fitness) promotes interaction and friendship among the participants. The "buddy" system helps motivate a continued commitment to fitness. Maintaining social interaction has a profoundly positive effect on aging successfully.

In other words, if you want to live, move. Any questions?

Daily Movement Tracker

How much healthy movement do you get every day? The more you move, the more likely you are to keep your weight under control, keep your joints loose and mobile, and retain your strength. Use this worksheet for seven days to track the movement you're getting each day. At the end of the week, look at how much you move and how much more you could move.

Types of Movement—Check each box for each day you do this activity.

	Day 1	Day 2	Day 3	Day 4	Day 5	Day 6	Day 7
Walking							
Walk the dog							
Walk to work							
Walk to the store							
Take the stairs							
Fitness							
Working out at the gym							

	Day 1	Day 2	Day 3	Day 4	Day 5	Day 6	Day 7
Fitness							
Running							
Cycling							
Hiking							
Swimming							
Flexibility Training							
Lifestyle/Sports							
Gardening							
Working around the house							
Dancing							
Tennis							
Golf							
Team Sport							
Playing with grandkids							
Daily Total							

How Much Are You Moving?

- If you're engaging in 13 to 17 of these kinds of movements 4 or more days per week, you're getting a great amount of healthy movement. Don't change a thing.
- If you're engaging in 8 to 12 of these kinds of movements 4 or more days per week, you're doing pretty well. Adding some movement would make you feel even better, though.
- If you're engaging in just 3 to 7 kinds of movements less than 4 days a week, you need to get moving urgently before being sedentary causes serious health problems.
- If you're below 3 types of movements 4 days a week, you're an emergency case. Do whatever you have to do to start moving more.

NATURAL DIET

More from our interview with the redoubtable Mr. LaLanne: "If man makes it, don't eat it. Cakes, pies, candy, ice cream, soda pop, all this canned junk. Some of these cans you can't even read the label. You put this fuel in your body and then you wonder why you're sick and tired and have no energy. You're breaking nature's laws. Every day I get ten pieces of raw vegetables, five pieces of fresh fruit, all the grains I eat are natural whole grains—brown rice, whole wheat, whole oats—and I get my protein from egg whites and fish. And I take thirty to forty supplements each day, just in case it works. You've got to put the right fuel in the human machine if you want the right results."

Note that there's a difference between the vitamins, minerals, and other supplements that Jack LaLanne takes to promote wellness and all the prescription pills many seniors take daily to treat disease. We'll be talking about that difference a little later in this chapter.

There's not much mystery to what kind of diet to eat to promote health. We've all been hearing about what to eat and what not to eat for years. But dental problems, changes in how you taste food, mobility problems, loss of appetite, or depression from being isolated or in poor health can all make it harder to eat healthy. As your body undergoes the changes associated with age, you need to make conscious changes in your eating habits to compensate. But first, the essentials of eating for longevity:

- Eat 5 to 10 servings of fresh fruits and vegetables per day, taken from a variety of colors and types, including red, yellow, and green leafy vegetables.
- Eat plenty of unsalted beans, nuts, and seeds. Increasing evidence suggests that eating raw nuts is beneficial for your heart and brain.
- Eat whole grains.
- Avoid anything "white": white rice, white sugar, white bread. Their simple carbohydrates deliver poor energy and make you fat.
- Get at least 40 grams of fiber per day, divided evenly between soluble and insoluble fiber, preferably from plants and whole grains.

You can also take supplements; go to www.SecondPrime.com for information.

• Watch your fat, cholesterol, and sodium intake. If you're in the habit of adding salt to your food, it's a good habit to break. Your taste buds will make the adjustment in a few weeks. The same with heavy, fat-rich sauces.

• Eat lean meats such as poultry and fish. Keep red meat to a minimum.

• Consume alcohol and sweets in moderation.

Practice what Carolyn C. Armistead, in an article for *Shape* magazine, called "mindful eating," an awareness of everything you eat, rather than just shoveling it down to fill empty space:

Mindfulness means being fully aware within the present moment. When you practice mindful eating, you pay attention to your body's subtle and natural cues, specifically the ones that say "feed me" and "that's enough." It's appealing because it's a mind-set instead of a meal plan. Unlike a diet, there's no self-denial, no counting protein or carb grams, no measuring or weighing your food.[7]

Also, practice the advice many European and Asian families give their children: eat until you're 80 percent full. Ever wonder why Europeans have far lower obesity rates than Americans? Part of the reason is that they understand that it takes fifteen to thirty minutes for the nerves in your digestive tract to tell your brain that you're full. If you eat until you're just beginning to feel full, then stop; in thirty minutes you will feel full. What you won't feel is bloated or guilty.

A pious man who had reached the age of 105 suddenly stopped going to church. Alarmed by the old fellow's absence after so many years of faithful attendance, the pastor went to see him.

He found the man in excellent health, so the pastor asked, "How come after all these years we don't see you at services anymore?"

The old man looked around and lowered his voice. "I'll tell you, Pastor," he whispered. "When I got to be 90, I expected God to take me any day. But then I got to be 95, then 100, then 105. So I figured that God is very busy and must've forgotten about me. And I don't want to remind Him."

DEM BONES

As we said, the basics of healthy eating have been well-documented. But there are age-specific needs you're going to have to deal with if you're going to enjoy a vibrant, thirty-year healthspan and a Second Prime conducted at full sprint. One of them is eating to stave off the terrible condition known as osteoporosis. Osteoporosis is low bone density that affects 28 million Americans, 80 percent of them women, due to bone mass loss related to menopause. Unchecked, the disease can lead to easily broken, brittle bones, loss of mobility, the trademark "hump" you may have seen in some older women (a result of the cervical spine's having lost the ability to hold up the head), and even collapsed vertebrae.

Osteoporosis is a preventable disease. Weight-bearing exercise helps to build new bone mass, and not smoking makes a big difference. But the most important factor is a diet rich in calcium and vitamin D. In her e-book, *Bone Health Guide: Osteoporosis & Thinning Bones*, Joyce Shaffer, PhD, writes that adults over age fifty should consume 1000 to 1500 milligrams of calcium per day, the equivalent of three to five eight-ounce glasses of milk. You can also get ample calcium from calcium-set tofu, kale, broccoli, Chinese cabbage, and other vegetables, in addtion to most types of low-fat dairy products. You can also take calcium supplements, of which calcium citrate malate appears to be the best for absorption, fracture protection, and helping to increase bone mass density. Getting enough of vitamins such as D, beta-carotene, and vitamin C and minerals such as phosphorus, copper, and zinc also shows promise for preventing bone loss.[8]

Senior Achiever

Maurine Kornfeld, 84, Senior Olympian and competitive swimmer

Maurine Kornfeld was in her 60s when she "fell into" swimming. Visiting a nearby YMCA when her Hollywood branch was closed, she asked the swimming coach about joining the aquatic program, and he grilled her about her stroke (she didn't know what he meant) and her experience (none). "He said, 'You can come on Saturday, and I'll look you over,' as if I was a side of beef," she says. "I had never swum with my face in the water."

But some tough tutelage brought out the swimmer in her ("That was Camp LeJeune for my swimming career," she quips.), and she began to compete in meets in some of the roughest parts of greater Los Angeles, much to the chagrin of her family. Two decades later, the former social worker who calls herself a "professional volunteer" works out at 6:30 AM most every day and competes in swimming events on the National Masters circuit as well as the Senior Olympics.

"We had the nationals in August in Mission Viejo, California, and had swimmers from all over," Kornfeld says. "I got three second-place finishes; I was beaten by a woman from the Bay Area. I'm good, but I'm not the best, and I don't care. If I swim my best, it doesn't matter if I won or lost. I really love it!"

Her goals? To improve her butterfly and to compete in the breaststroke without getting disqualified for her kick so often. And what does her family think now? "They don't pay much attention now," she laughs. "My niece thinks I'm a remarkable aunt, but we sometimes question her judgment."

The Diabetes Crisis

A report released in November 2005 by the Yale Schools of Public Health and Medicine predicts that if the health-care system in the United States continues to fail to prevent the increase in diabetes, the number of cases will triple by 2025, making this preventable disease the number one cause of death in the country, surpassing heart disease and cancer.[9]

In his book *Diabetes Danger,* Bortz writes:

> Just a few years ago, in the United States there were fewer than one million diagnosed cases of diabetes. Today there are twenty million, and by 2030, there will be thirty million. A million new cases are diagnosed every year. On average, the diagnosis of diabetes shortens a person's life by fifteen years. Twenty-million cases times fifteen years equals 300-million years of life that will be lost by today's diabetics—a lot of time! Like the rumbles before a volcanic eruption, we recognize that the long interval between the onset of the disease and the occurrence of its catastrophic complications will certainly shorten lives.[10]

The true tragedy is not just the suffering and premature death that result from diabetes but the fact that 99 percent of the new cases will be Type 2 diabetes—a disease caused by lifestyle, a disease that is 100 percent preventable by maintaining a healthy weight and getting a regular dose of strenuous movement.

"There is no magic bullet for diabetes," says Bortz in his interview. "It's really reclaiming our vigorous prehistoric exercise pattern. We used to be born free on the Serengeti, but we're now zoo animals, and zoo animals must be very carefully fed." The bottom line with diabetes is that if you don't become obese, your chances of developing the disease are virtually zero. Thus, Type 2 diabetes joins emphysema and other smoking-caused diseases in the Self-Inflicted Causes of Death Hall of Fame.

Follow the guidelines contained in this chapter and the exercise and diet advice you'll find in a wide range of books and Web sites, and diabetes will not be a concern.

The Bondo Method

Bondo is a filler that car enthusiasts use to repair holes in steel car bodies. You just slap on some Bondo, let it dry, sand it, prime it, paint it, and *voila*! Your car could have been crushed in an accident, but you'd never know it.

The Bondo Method is what too many people of all ages do when it comes to diet: they eat fast food, fats, sweets, and red meat, then pop a bunch of vitamins and supplements and think they're compensating for their terrible eating habits. The supplements are the Bondo camouflaging the body damage done by years of burgers and fries. Living with the Bondo Method is harmful to your body at any age, but when you get past sixty or so, it can be downright catastrophic.

There is really no substitute for eating whole foods, especially fruits, vegetables, grains, nuts, and fish. Supplements can deliver the basic vitamins and minerals, but there are hundreds of beneficial compounds in fresh foods, and scientists think that these compounds may help the body more readily absorb the nutrients in food. When you eat a piece of broccoli, the fiber you consume also helps your body get a greater benefit from the calcium, vitamin C, vitamin A, and folate in the vegetable.

No amount of supplements will counteract the deleterious effects of the saturated fats, sugars, and sodium in processed foods. It's like slapping a coat of primer and a coat of paint on a Ford that's been in a head-on collision. You won't undo the damage; you'll only mask it temporarily.

Fresh Is Best

You should *always* eat food that's as fresh as possible. That means fresh fruits and vegetables and raw nuts and seeds. If you can, eat them raw in a salad; if you must cook them, try steaming or light sautéing. Don't boil them or stick them in a crock pot if you can help it. The fresher and more alive the food, the more vitality it will impart to your body. Of course, some fruits such as the tomato (yes, it's a fruit) are actually more beneficial cooked; cooking tomatoes releases more of the amino acid lycopene, which has been shown to reduce the risk of prostate cancer, among other things. But in general, fresh and raw are the gold standard.

The great thing is that no matter where you are, you probably have access to fresh, organic produce and nuts. Let's start with the supermarket. No, not everything there is organic, and that's okay. It doesn't have to be organic to be healthy. Just be sure to wash your produce to remove pesticides, herbicides, waxes, and other "extras." And in a supermarket, avoid the center aisles where the canned fruits and veggies live. Hit the produce aisle and go crazy.

If you want organic, you have quite a few options, depending on your area:

- Farmers' markets (there are nearly 4,000 certified ones in the United States)
- Private farms
- Roadside produce stands
- Community gardens
- Stores such as Trader Joe's, Whole Foods, and Wild Oats

But the best source of all might be your own garden. If you want to eat better in your Second Prime, consider growing your own food. Not only will you be guaranteed organic produce at a great price, but you'll also get tremendous exercise.

WATER, WATER EVERYWHERE

Your mother was right; drinking enough water is very important for your health. You can follow the traditional guidelines of drinking eight eight-ounce glasses per day, or take your weight, divide it in half, and that's how many ounces of water you need each day. If you can work more water into your day, perhaps by drinking two glasses as soon as you get up, drinking that much water becomes much easier. It's virtually impossible for you to drink too much water.

Water is vital to every aspect of health, especially when you get past age sixty, because dehydration is one of the most common causes of hospitalization among people over sixty. Drinking enough water keeps your liver working properly to flush out fat (helping control your weight), helps insulate you in cold weather, keeps your kidneys and urinary tract clear and working, lubricates your joints, and many other functions. Drinking sufficient water may be the easiest step you can take to ensure long-term health.

Try some tricks to help yourself drink more water, like drinking water with meals instead of liquor or soda or carrying a water bottle with you in your car and at work. And contrary to what some people say, you can get some of your daily hydration needs from milk, juice, and decaffeinated drinks like tea and soda.[11]

Supplements and Nutriceuticals

It's impossible to step into the world of supplements without getting caught up in the war of words over their effectiveness. On one hand, you have the camp that believes taking handfuls of vitamins, herbs, homeopathics, and minerals every day is a great insurance policy against disease. On the other, you have those who believe that it does little more than give you expensive urine.

We come down firmly on the side of the supplement fans. Supplements are not cure-alls; antioxidant supplements don't appear to have much of an effect in reducing the risk of cancer or heart disease, and there's even some evidence that overdosing on certain carotenoids may actually *increase* your risk of lung cancer. But overall, the proof weighs heavily on the side of supplements as necessary components of a healthy, active lifestyle, especially for those at Baby Boomer age and beyond.

Supplements are ways to add vitamins, minerals, enzymes, and other compounds to your body that you are not getting through your diet. Even if you are eating an incredibly well-balanced diet rich in foods like soy, oil-rich fish like salmon or mackerel, and a variety of fresh fruits and vegetables, it's difficult (if not impossible) to get enough of the building blocks that ward off disease. And if you're struggling to change years of dietary habits and eat even a basic healthy diet, taking daily supplements may be the only way your body will get some of the key compounds it needs to remain stable, prevent disease, and stave off tissue breakdown. As we said earlier, supplements are not a substitute for eating a healthy diet, but they're certainly better than doing nothing.

A proper supplement regimen will give you a proper, body-specific dose of the following elements each day:

- Vitamins
- Minerals
- Healthy oils
- Enzymes
- Amino acids
- Phytonutrients (from plants)
- Antioxidants
- Beneficial plant compounds whose effects we can't explain yet

Some Ideas for Supplement Regimens

First comes Dr. Andrew Weil, who, in his new book, *Healthy Aging*, lays out a comprehensive dietary plan that's rich in soy, organic produce, and white, green, and oolong teas.

Weil also suggests a supplement plan heavy on antioxidants such as vitamin C, vitamin E, selenium, and mixed carotenoids (the pigments in carrots and other yellow-orange vegetables), folic acid, calcium citrate, and vitamin D. He also recommends fish oil supplements for their omega-3 fatty acid content, regular consumption of ginger and turmeric, the coenzyme Q-10, and

> *Nature gives you the face you have at 20; it is up to you to merit the face you have at 50.*[12]
>
> —Gabrielle "Coco" Chanel

alpha-lipoic acid for those with metabolism problems. Finally, Weil suggests asking your physician about going on a low-dose aspirin regimen. These are generic suggestions that will not harm anyone, but it's important that you develop an individualized program to meet your specific needs.[13]

But for an example of a complex, very specific personalized supplement plan, we turn again to Barbara Morris, pharmacist and author of *Put Old on Hold*. Her mind-boggling supplement routine, provided to us for use in this book, goes like this:

Supplement	Dose	Comments
Indole-3 carbinol	200 mg	
DMAE	200 mg	
Calcium	2 capsules	*Bone Assure/Life Extension* Product
Ascorbyl palmitate	500 mg	
Melatonin	5 mg	
Mixed tocopherols	1000 iu	
l-Cartinine fumarate	900 mg	
Folic acid	3-5 mg	
Omega-3 fish oil	1000 mg	
Cod-liver oil	1 capsule	
Pycnogenol	5 mg	
Selenium	200 mcg	
Potassium	200 mg	
Beta-carotene	25,000 u	
Lycopene	10 mg	
GTF chromium	100 mcg	
Vitamin D	4000 iu	
CoQ-10	300 mg	
Magnesium	400 mg	
Pantothenic acid	500 mg	
Grape seed extract	2 capsules	
Green tea extract	2 capsules	
Deep Thought	1 tablet	*KAL* product
MSM powder	1 teaspoonful	
Ginko biloba	120 mg	
Taurine	500 mg	
Quercetin	500 mg	
Bromelain	250 g	

Supplement	Dose	Comments
Piracetam	1600 mg	
Super Carnosine	2000 mg	*Life Extension* product
Trimethyl glycine	500 mg	
Vitamin K	10 mg	
Policosanol	10 mg	
Phosphatidylcholine	2000 mg	
Phosphatidylserine	100 mg	
Biotin	5 mg	
a-lipoic acid	600 mg	
n-acetyl cysteine	600 mg	
Acetyl l-carnitine	500 mg	
Ocudyne-II	8 capsules	*Allergy Research Group* product
Vision herbs	2 capsules	
Leg vein capsules	2 capsules	
Glucosamine	1000 mg	
Citrus bioflavonoids	1000 mg	
SAMe	1000 mg	
Ca Ascorbate powder		10 grams
Probiotics	2 capsules	
Salmon oil capsules	4000 mg	
B complex 100	1 capsules	
B_{12}	1000 mcg	
l-arginine	1400 mg	

Prescriptions

Thyroid T3 and T4	Daily	
Progesterone cream	Daily	
Testosterone cream	3 x week	
Human Growth	1 unit 3x week	

Hormone

DHEA	50 mg daily	

According to Morris, she takes about 200 pills per day as part of this routine, washing them down with a whey protein drink. That's a big investment of time and money, but does it work? Well, she's seventy-six, still working, and looks great, so she's not complaining.

"Am I taking too much? Probably, or in some cases, maybe not enough," she writes in explanation of her regimen. "I go by results. I have no typical old age diseases such as high blood pressure, high cholesterol, diabetes, cardiovascular disease, arthritis, memory decline, etc. At work, which requires mental alertness and physical stamina, I am on my feet for ten hours, filling prescriptions, counseling patients, taking phone calls, and constantly making decisions that require focus and precision. I must be doing something right!"

Morris also emphasizes that by no means should anyone simply copy her supplement plan. "I don't advocate that anyone take the supplements and/or quantities that I take," she says. "What I take is based on my experience as a pharmacist and researcher. Everyone must educate himself or herself, in conjunction with a qualified physician or nutritionist, as to what is best for them."

The riders in a race do not stop short when they reach the goal. There is a little finishing canter before coming to a standstill. There is time to hear the kind voice of friends and to say to one's self: The work is done. But just as one says that, the answer comes: "The race is over, but the work never is done while the power to work remains." The canter that brings you to a standstill need not be only coming to rest. It cannot be while you still live. For to live is to function. That is all there is in living.[4]

—OLIVER WENDELL HOLMES

NUTRICEUTICALS: APPROACH WITH SKEPTICISM

Nutriceuticals are combinations of vitamins, minerals, phytonutrients, and other compounds specifically formulated to address a specific health issue such as memory, weight loss, or prostate health. You hear about them all the time—such herbals as saw palmetto, advertised as helping to support prostate health, or gingko biloba for memory and mental function. Since so many grandiose claims are made and so much money is involved and because nutriceuticals are not regulated by the Food and Drug Administration, this is an area where you should exercise extreme caution.

However, some nutriceuticals *are* all they are cracked up to be:

- Research centers such as the University of Arkansas Department of Horticulture are finding numerous benefits in compounds from such plants as spinach and cowpea.
- Turmeric shows promise both as a super antioxidant and in preventing neurological diseases.
- While claims as a brain booster are unproven, ginkgo biloba does improve blood circulation and may provide relief for conditions ranging from Alzheimer's disease to macular degeneration to erectile dysfunction.
- Saw palmetto does reduce the discomfort from a benign enlarged prostate and can prevent the gland from becoming larger.
- Resveratrol is the "secret ingredient" in the skin of red grapes, a phytochemical that is both a potent antioxidant and a powerful anti-inflammatory that can reduce cholesterol levels and heart disease risk.

There are thousands of substances and combinations of substances that could fall into the category of nutriceuticals (you can learn about the individual substances at a great Web site, www.wholehealthmd.com, in the Reference Library), and many do have wonderful benefits. Others are scams. In dealing with nutriceuticals, it's best to follow a few simple rules:

- Do your research
- Be wary of hard sales pitches and big promises
- Talk to a physician or dietician before you take anything

STRESS: THE ALL-PURPOSE DEMON

Stress is to our modern culture what demons were to the people of the Dark Ages: the malevolent cause behind everything that goes wrong. Overweight? Blame stress. Have high blood pressure? It couldn't be that you eat fast food six times a week, don't work out, and pour salt on everything in sight, could it? Nah. Must be stress.

Stress is the most misleading health problem around. So let's get something out of the way right here and now: *there's nothing wrong with stress.* Stress is just your body's physical response to a situation where more physical capacity is needed—the "fight or flight" instinct. When a stressful situation appears, hormones such as cortisol, norepinephrine, and adrenaline get dumped into your system, increasing your heart rate, increasing the flow of blood to your brain, making you feel wired and hyperaware (that's why time appears to slow when you're under stress). It's your body's way of clearing out the unnecessary functions so you can deal with a threat. There are actually three kinds of stress:

- *Eustress*—pleasurable and beneficial stress
- *Stress*—the ordinary demanding stress that is not chronic
- *Distress*—chronic negative stress that can be destructive to health

The stress response is necessary and even beneficial. When you're working on a deadline or dealing with a dangerous situation, your stress response gives you the quickness of mind, agility, and strength to do what you must. In the short term, the stress response can make us perform better and achieve more. It's *chronic distress* that's a problem. The body's fight-or-flight mechanism evolved to deal with threats to life and limb like rival tribes or wild animals; it was never meant to be switched on ten hours a day dealing with the rigors of bumper-to-bumper traffic. When you're under stress constantly, the stress hormones do damage to your body and may actually shrink certain areas of the brain. Sustained distress can also elevate blood pressure and has a deeply negative effect on mood.

Now comes new evidence that chronic distress actually advances the aging process. A 2004 study directed by researchers at the University of California–San Francisco looked at the effects of chronic stress on the genes of mothers caring for chronically ill children. The study revealed that the physiological effects of stress actually damage the *telomeres*, the structures on the end of chromosomes that determine how often cells can divide before they begin to die. Shortened telomeres equal shorter healthy cell life, which leads to tissue breakdowns, muscle failures, hearing loss, reduced brain function, and the other classic maladies of age. This new information would explain why people who suffer from prolonged emotional strain seem to age and become ill before their time.[16]

Dealing with Stress

Obviously, you have a vested interest in reducing the impact of chronic stress on your health. And if you're nearing the age when you'll refire and turn your back on working for someone else, there are numerous ways to do that: Exercise. Find purpose and meaning in your later life. Do what you love with people you love. When you're busy and productive and not worrying about money, you'll find that your stress level barely registers.

Go to Sleep!

According to the *2003 Sleep in America Poll* conducted by the National Sleep Foundation, 26 percent of adults 55 to 64 rated their sleep as fair to poor, as did 21 percent of those 65 to 84. The poll found that while older Americans generally do not get less sleep than their younger counterparts, 37 million do experience frequent sleep problems that can complicate treatment for such conditions as arthritis, diabetes, heart disease, and depression.[16] Stage 4 sleep, the deep sleep during which the body and mind repair themselves, may be altogether absent in some older people. But sleeping poorly and waking up tired are not normal parts of aging. Of course, you may be one of the millions of Americans who has chosen not to get enough sleep. In his interview, Bortz called our obsession with minimizing sleep "a national epidemic."

The average adult needs from seven to nine hours of sleep a day in order to recover from exercise, purge the body of lactic acids and other toxins, and make complete use of nutrients. Whether sleep problems are due to anxiety or inactivity, or just years of habitually not getting enough sleep, if you're to have a healthy, active Second Prime, you've got to build sleep into your lifestyle.

"The importance of sleep to healthy aging is often overlooked in the medical community, but it's becoming increasingly apparent that good sleep could be a new vital sign," said Robert N. Butler, MD, president and CEO of the International Longevity Center USA (ILC), in a November 2005 news release. "Poor sleep is a condition that needs to be addressed, diagnosed and treated—it could be as important as nutrition, exercise, and social engagement to the health of older adults."[17] But how do you address it safely? A 2005 Gallup survey released by the ILC showed that 77 percent of older adults expressed concerns about the long-term effects of prescription sleep aids, with addiction being the obvious greatest concern. But drugs are quick fixes for problems that can be solved safely and naturally with some changes in lifestyle.[18]

In *Dare to Be 100*, Bortz suggests changing the typical time you fall asleep by doing things like taking a warm bath two hours before the time you want to go to sleep. Eating later will have the same effect, lowering body temperature to bring on sleepiness faster. He adds that many things can help improve sleep habits:

- Creating a sleep environment that is quiet, dark, and warm.
- Dealing with worrisome things early in the day, rather than late. (The ILC survey showed that worry over caring for aging parents was one of the most common factors in Baby Boomers' ability to sleep.)
- Avoiding stimulants like coffee late in the day.
- Eating foods that promote regularity.
- Going to sleep with your mate.
- Exercising to produce fatigue and relaxation.[19]

Another excellent way to get more sleep is to create a routine around going to bed: go to bed at the same time every night, engage in the same preparatory activities, light candles, put on relaxing music, meditate. Engaging in the same activities as a precursor to sleep helps signal your body that it's time to stand down and begin relaxing. Reading in bed also seems to help many people fall asleep, but if you fall asleep in the sack while reading this book, please don't tell us. It would hurt our feelings.

A reporter was interviewing a 104-year-old woman: "And what do you think is the best thing about being 104?" the reporter asked.

She replied: "No peer pressure."

You're So Vain . . . Good!

To us, there are two kinds of vanity. First, there's the bad vanity, the kind that keeps you from using hearing aids and eyeglasses and other technologies that can enhance your life, that drives you back to the cosmetic surgeon for one expensive surgery after another, that leads to self-loathing and depression when you finally realize that the youthful, clear-skinned person you once were is gone forever. That's the type of vanity that hardens older people, turns them bitter and angry.

Then there's the positive vanity, also called "healthy body image." It's the vanity in which you accept that yes, you're changing as you age, but you're going to do whatever you must to look the best you can in your 70s, 80s, and 90s. What's more, you refuse to be a frumpy old codger—you're going to dress well; keep your hair, beard, and nails neat; keep your teeth healthy; and always look your best when you go out or entertain at home. The first kind of vanity denies that with the passage of time come changes that can't be avoided; the second accepts that those changes will come, but resolves to make the most of them. The first is born of fear, the second of pride. We'd rather live proud than afraid.

Pride in how you look makes you exercise more, eat better, and dress more attractively. Knowing you look good gives you confidence and enhances your sex drive. It also gives you the élan to flaunt your age, not hide it. If you look good and feel good, you'll take pride in your wrinkles. You'll enjoy the stares you get from men or women twenty years your junior as they watch you pass. You'll get a kick out of confounding the expectation of what an "old person" is supposed to dress like, walk like, or look like.

Think Prevention, Not Cure

To lengthen your healthspan, you have to quit thinking about being disease-reactive and starting thinking about becoming *disease-deflective* so that disease and physical breakdown pass you by, looking for easier targets. Fitness, great diet, supplements, and rest are your Kevlar body armor against illness. You're a hard target, so disease goes elsewhere for easier prey. You make yourself disease-deflective by doing all the things we've talked about in this chapter. You also work with a team of health-care practitioners who work with you to keep you well—whatever you need to help you live the long, healthy life you covet.

There is, of course, a place for conventional medicine. We're strong believers in screenings such as colonoscopies, mammograms for women, and prostate screenings for men. Certainly it makes abundant sense to have an annual physical so you can catch any problems at their earliest stages. But beyond that, running to your primary care physician and being handed another pill bottle at the slightest sign of an ache or pain? That's crazy. But how do you create a health-care support system that's disease-deflective when health insurance companies are so focused on conventional medicine? Answer: you swim out of the mainstream.

Antidotes to Conventional Health Coverage

"The new movement is called consumer-directed health care or CDH," says Paul Zane Pilzer, economist, entrepreneur, and author of *The New Health Insurance Solution*, in an interview for this book. "The average large company health-care plan today in America costs $14,000 per family each year. Companies are now allowed to say to employees, 'We've been spending $14,000 for your family. Here's $14,000 a year, tax-free. You must buy health insurance with the money, and whatever you don't spend, let it roll forward to next year.' Now, every time you pick up a prescription at the doctor, you're going to ask, "Is there a generic available? Is there something in the same category that will do the same thing for half the money? Because every dollar I don't spend on health care, I get to keep."

> *Experience is the name every one gives to their mistakes.*[20]
> —Oscar Wilde

Pilzer says consumer-directed oversight of the cost of health care will alter the landscape completely. "It changes everything overnight," he says. "All of a sudden, the health-care industry, which is currently $2 trillion, or one-sixth of our economy, joins the rest of our economy. When someone delivers good health care at a good price, you'll run over there, and when someone delivers bad health care at a bad price, you won't go back. People can direct that money into wellness and prevention programs instead of just treatment of symptoms programs, and of course they'll accumulate hundreds of thousands of dollars in health savings accounts for their future health care and retirement, when they're no longer working."

If you're in the Baby Boom generation, chances are you're still working and may have access to this kind of HSA or health savings account. According to Pilzer, four million Americans are covered by such an arrangement, and he expects hundreds of millions more to be covered in the next twenty years. "We will look back on the era from 1945 to 2005 as the dark ages for American health care, when the only way to get decent health care is through your employer," he says.

OTHER OPTIONS

But what if you're already retired from a full-time job and moved on to your retirement, something that doesn't give you the option of an HSA? There are other options for you:

- Convenient storefront clinics, located in consumer shopping meccas like Wal-Mart and Target stores. Going by brand names like Redi-Clinic and Mini-Clinic, these clinics offer services at a much lower price than hospitals and deliver more respect for your time. Show up at a busy time, for example, and they might hand you a pager and invite you to go and shop, and they'll page you when the doctor or nurse can see you.

- You can get your own family health insurance policy and open a Health Savings Account, which will allow you to save up to $5,450 per year tax-free toward covering your medical expenses. But get such coverage early, before you or someone in your family develops preexisting conditions.

- Concierge health plans. These plans, which you arrange with private personal physicians, are in addition to the premium and deductible of major medical, prescription, or catastrophic coverage you might have. Here's how it works: to see an internist or general practitioner who offers concierge service, you must first join his or her practice by paying an annual premium, ranging from $2,000 a year at the low end to as much as $20,000 at the high end. In return, you get a personal physical each year where you'll discuss sleep habits, nutrition, medical history, and so on; same-day appointments, and sometimes even private Web pages with your complete updated medical history. For those patients who can afford it, concierge care is like a return to old-fashioned small town doctoring. Find out more at www.conciergephysicians.org.

"People need to change their health insurance to a program that rewards them for being healthy," says Pilzer in his interview, "that lets them save each year tax-free what they don't spend on current health care, that automatically gives them and their family members the incentive to make the proper health choices, because the proper health choices are also going to save you money. You don't need health insurance to pay for things you're never going to use."

Deterioration Is Not Normal . . . It's Up to You

When you look at how your body ages as a product of the choices you make, age-related decline ceases to be an inevitability. "A lot of people unconsciously assume that they will get-old-and-die: one phrase, almost one word, and certainly one seamless concept," write Chris Crowley and Henry S. Lodge, MD in their book *Younger Next Year*:

> [They assume] that when they get old and infirm, they will die soon after, so a deteriorating quality of life does not matter. That is a deeply mistaken idea and a dangerous premise for planning your life. In fact, you will probably get-old-and-live. You can get decrepit if you like, but you are not likely to die; you are likely to live like that for a long, long time. Most Americans today will live into their mid-eighties, whether they're in great shape or shuffling around on walkers . . . good reason to make the Last Third of your life terrific—and not a dreary panoply of obesity, sore joints, and apathy. "Normal aging" is intolerable and avoidable. You can skip most of it and grow old, not just gracefully but with real joy.[21]

Senior fitness instructor Bartholomew gets the final word. In response to our questions, she writes: "Physical deterioration and its resulting psychological consequences may be typical, but they are not normal! It occurs when personal health loses status as a priority . . . until it is lost. The good news is that many conditions brought on by a sedentary lifestyle can be eliminated, delayed, or improved. The future of this country and its elderly is not in 'sickness care.' Rather, it depends upon healthy lifestyle choices."

Second Prime Strategy—Body

1. Things to Do
• Map out the exercise you get each week and find ways to add more.
• Talk to a personal trainer or sign up at a gym.

- Track your diet and find ways to add more fresh fruits and vegetables, whole grains, and raw nuts.
- Adjust your schedule to get more sleep.
- Talk to your physician about a personalized supplement program.
- Drink at least eight glasses of water daily.
- Look into ways to lower stress such as quiet time, walks in nature, prayer, deep breathing.
- If you don't already, start scheduling annual checkups and regular dental visits.
- Catalog the ways in which you would like to improve your appearance.
- Start doing online research into alternative health insurance.

2. Changes You Need to Make to Improve Your Health

-
-
-
-
-

3. Your Body Goals for Your Second Prime

Example: "Get down to my college weight in 12 months."

-
-
-
-
-

4. Body Resources

General Health

- Eternal Health (www.eternalhealth.org)
- National Institute on Aging (www.nia.nih.gov)
- Alliance for Aging Research (www.agingresearch.org)
- Infoaging.org (www.infoaging.org)
- The Okinawa Centenarian Study (www.okinawaprogram.com)
- American Academy of Anti-Aging Medicine (www.worldhealth.net)
- Mayo Clinic (www.mayoclinic.com)
- Medline Plus (www.nlm.nih.gov/medlineplus)

Movement
- National Senior Games Association (www.nsga.com)
- *Geezerjock* magazine (www.geezerjock.com)
- International Council on Active Aging Fitness Facility Locator (www.icaa.cc/facilitylocator.htm)
- Fifty Plus (www.50plus.org)
- Senior Fitness.com (www.senior-fitness.com)
- About.com (http://exercise.about.com/od/exerciseforseniors)
- Helpguide.org (www.helpguide.org)

Diet
- The World's Healthiest Foods (www.whfoods.com)
- Diabetes Danger (www.diabetesdanger.com)
- Nutrition Action Healthletter (www.cspinet.org/nah)
- WholeHealth MD (www.wholehealthmd.com)

Supplements
- Office of Dietary Supplements (http://ods.od.nih.gov)
- US Food and Drug Administration (www.cfsan.fda.gov/~dms/supplmnt.html)
- NatureMade (www.naturemade.com)

Sleep
- National Sleep Foundation (www.sleepfoundation.org)
- Sleepnet (www.sleepnet.com)
- The Better Sleep Council (www.bettersleep.org)

Health Insurance
- The New Health Insurance Solution (www.tnhis.com)
- Extend Benefits (www.extendbenefits.com)
- eHealthInsurance (www.ehealthinsurance.com)
- Alternative Health Insurance Services (www.alternativeinsurance.com)
- Society for Innovative Medical Practice Design (www.conciergephysicians.org)
- Fitness and Wellness Insurance Agency (www.fitnessandwellness.com)

Books
- *121 Ways to Live 121 Years and More!* by Dr. Ronald Klatz, president,

American Academy of Anti-Aging Medicine, and Dr. Robert Goldman, chairman, American Academy of Anti-Aging Medicine
- *The New Health Insurance Solution* by Paul Zane Pilzer
- *Dare to Be 100* by Walter M. Bortz II, MD
- *Younger Next Year* by Chris Crowley & Henry S. Lodge, MD
- *Merchants of Immortality* by Stephen S. Hall
- *Aging Well* by Andrew Weil, MD

Mind *or* Are You "Sageing" or Aging?

Wisdom doesn't automatically come with old age. Nothing does—except wrinkles. It's true, some wines improve with age. But only if the grapes were good in the first place.[1]

—Abigail Van Buren

Of all the self-fulfilling prophecies in our culture, the assumption that aging means decline and poor health is probably the deadliest.[2]

—Marilyn Ferguson

A person who is "sageing" is becoming a "sage," accumulating wisdom through long life experience. Consider Jeanne Louise Calment, the Frenchwoman who lived to the oldest reliably documented age, 122. Though mostly blind and deaf by her 120th birthday, her mind was still intact as was her sense of humor. She famously joked, "I have one wrinkle on my body, and I'm sitting on it." She also claimed that she had lived so long because she had quit smoking when she was 117.[3] You've got to love that. However, the examples of Madame Calment and other super-centenarians bring up one of the most critical questions of aging: how can you hang onto the memory, wit, and capacity for thought that make you who you are?

First, you can't remember where you put your keys. Then, you can't remember why you wanted your keys. Then you can't remember where you were driving in the first place. Sound familiar? It is if you watch the news. Part of our "make them afraid, then sell them the cure" culture has been to tell us all the ways that, day by day, our marbles are rolling away. The result is a generation for whom every forgotten name and "Why did I come into this room?" moment breeds a bit of existential terror expressed in the cold thought, "Am I losing my mind?"

The fear is understandable. After all, we are our brains. Everything that we are—our passions, talents, relationships, skills, histories, lessons, heartaches, and triumphs—exists in those billions of neural connections residing within our cranial bones. Apart from belief in the soul, the mind is everything. It's the seat of our reason and our humanity. So when we think we see the beginning of an inevitable decline from sharp, agile thinking to confusion, loss of independence, and loss of identity, the response is terror, understandably.

That's led to yet another pernicious cultural stereotype: everyone over sixty is a senile fool who must be addressed in the cadences of a clueless English speaker trying to make himself understood in a foreign country by talking LOUDER and s-l-o-w-e-r. People assume getting old means an inevitable plummet into dementia, being condescended to by family, ignored by corporate America, and ripped off by scam artists. It's a slander that is painful, damaging, and fundamentally false. Since the best way to go about shredding stereotypes is by flinging facts, here are a few facts about the mind in your Second Prime.

> *What a man knows at 50 that he did not know at 20 is, for the most part, incommunicable. The knowledge he has acquired with age is not the knowledge of formulas, or forms of words, but of people, places, actions—a knowledge gained not by words but by touch, sight, sound, victories, failures, sleeplessness, devotion, love—the human experiences and emotions of this earth and of oneself and other men; and perhaps, too, a little faith, a little reverence for things you cannot see.[4]*
>
> —ADLAI STEVENSON

Brain Aging Is Inevitable; Dementia Is Not

Let's start with a few names:

- Brooke Astor, 103 at this writing, New York superstar philanthropist
- Ray Bradbury, 85, writing legend
- John Wooden, 95, legendary basketball coach and motivational speaker
- Buck O'Neil, 94, former Negro Leaguer and ambassador for the Negro League Museum in Kansas City, Missouri
- Arthur C. Clarke, 87, writer and author of *2001: A Space Odyssey*
- Helen Thomas, 85, doyenne of the White House Press Corps for thirty years
- Studs Terkel, 93, oral historian
- Daniel Schorr, 89, journalist and National Public Radio commentator
- Lena Horne, 88, spectacular jazz and blues vocalist
- Oral Roberts, 87, evangelist and founder of Oral Roberts University

And how about Art Linkletter, ninety-four, who travels 150,000 miles a year to speak, writes books, is a top philanthropist and a leading investor in clean energy? The world is brimming over with men and women in their 70s, 80s, and 90s who are writing, creating, innovating, and inspiring at astonishingly high levels (by the way, if you doubt that these folks are still with us, visit a fascinating Web site, www.deadoraliveinfo.com). They are all living refutations of the idea that with age comes breakdown. That said, some changes do inevitably come with age.

"Most people will agree that by age fifty or so about half of the population has what we might call 'age associated memory impairment,'" says Dr. Gary Small, director of the UCLA Center on Aging and author of *The Memory Prescription*, during an interview we did with him for our book. "What does that mean? It's not really impairment, but if you have these people perform standardized memory tests, you find that on average they do not perform as well as a group of twenty-year-olds. There's a noticeable change, and they will report to you that they know there's a change. However, that does not usually go on to more serious forms of memory loss like dementia.

"As we get older, what now is termed mild cognitive impairment becomes more prevalent. This is a more serious form of memory loss, but people are still functioning independently. They don't have Alzheimer's disease, which is when the problem becomes so severe that they can't handle things on their own. Alzheimer's disease or severe dementia—which includes several types of senility caused by vascular disease, strokes, or any number of conditions—affects 5 to 10 percent of people sixty-five or older, and by the time you get to age eighty-five, the prevalence ranges anywhere from 30 to 50 percent."

Hmm. There are a lot of terms floating around in this discussion. Let's establish a clear etymology. A brief glossary:

Mild cognitive impairment or age associated memory impairment. This is the relatively benign "I can't remember the name of that person I just met" kind of impairment that often becomes noticeable as early as the late 30s. This is generally a result of normal aging processes in the brain and should be nothing more than an annoyance, a loss of what we call "agility of thought"—you don't think as quickly, you lose focus more easily, you forget what you were thinking about ten seconds earlier, and so on.

Dementia. This is the term applied to any kind of progressive brain dysfunction that leads to the increasing restriction of normal lifestyle activities. Dementia can be brought on by a variety of traumas or diseases and can be a precursor to the more serious symptoms of Alzheimer's disease. Dementia can even be produced by a bad reaction to some medications. Some dementia is reversible through the normal healing processes; other dementia is permanent.

Senility. An outdated term for dementia.

Alzheimer's disease. The shadow of self-annihilation that hangs over every senior experiencing memory problems. Alzheimer's is an incurable, progressive brain disorder that gradually destroys a person's memory and ability to learn, reason, and communicate. Alzheimer's patients often experience personality changes, paranoia, and delusions, as well as a heartbreaking loss of self-recognition or identity. Perhaps the most famous Alzheimer's sufferer was former president Ronald Reagan.

Agelessness Secret #6

Do the Crossword Puzzle

Keeping your mind fit, just as keeping your body fit, is a matter of consistent work over time. Challenging your brain to think in new ways can actually create new nerve connections, many scientists believe, and help minimize loss of memory and mental agility as you age. But how can you give your mind a daily workout? Try the crossword puzzle in your daily newspaper.

Crosswords, brain teasers, and other puzzlers are very effective ways to challenge and extend your thinking regularly, even daily. They can increase your vocabulary, encourage you to research questions, and spark interest in new subjects. Novelty is powerful; everything you do that works rarely used areas of your brain equals a healthier brain.

Some of the ways you can work your mind regularly:

- Solving daily crossword and other puzzles
- Reading puzzle books and Web sites
- Listening to radio puzzles such as "The Puzzlemaster" with Will Shortz on National Public Radio
- Learning a new word each day
- Setting out to discover a new fact each day
- Attending classes, lectures, and group discussions

A blend of all these activities will help you develop your intellect and curiosity and open new horizons of inquiry to you. Most important, they will help keep your brain firing on all cylinders.

Your Mind Determines Your Future

Every thought you've ever had, every memory of your children or grandchildren, every emotion you've ever experienced, they all occur in your mind. Your mind is the wellspring of your creativity where lines of iambic pentameter begin, where you process color and taste and sound, and where you talk to God. The mind is *everything.*

As you stand on the cusp of your Second Prime, you have the power to determine what those years will look like. Will they be dependent or independent? Sick or robust? Short or long? Your future is a fabric of choices, and it's your mind that will make those choices. Your mind has the power to reshape your world but only if it retains the capacity to choose. If you do not do everything in your power to keep your mind agile and sharp and active, you risk one day losing the ability to determine your own future. As Dr. Andrew Weil says, the goal is to live and love long and healthy and have a rapid decline right before the end. To achieve that goal, you not only have to keep your body fit but your mind as well.[5] Here's another way to look at it:

You should be "sageing," not aging.

More on the concept of sageing later on. Right now, let's talk about the brain. It's the most extraordinary construct in nature, a remarkable organ that even now science is just beginning to understand. It's made up of approximately 100 billion neurons, nerve cells that conduct bio-electrical impulses along an incredibly complex neural network to control every aspect of your body's function.

With a machine this complicated, many things can go wrong. In *The Memory Prescription*, Small writes:

The scientific evidence is clear: brain aging begins as early as our twenties. Therefore it is never too early, and probably never too late, to fight off brain aging. Data show that as our neurons age and die, the actual overall size of the brain shrinks or atrophies. Also, aging brains accumulate lesions known as *amyloid plaques* and *neurofibrillary tangles*. This decayed material, resulting from cell death and degeneration of brain tissue, collects mainly in areas involved in memory and is believed to be responsible for Alzheimer's disease.[6]

In his book, Small states that brain scans show brain decay in people in their 20s and 30s while people in middle age can show brain activity similar to Alzheimer's without any memory problems. A computer will, over time, accumulate viruses, fragmented software, corrupted files, and damage to its hard disk until it cannot function properly. Our brains operate in the same manner. Over time, debris accumulates, and the organ becomes slack. The final result is a loss of function. But you can buy a new computer. You've got to dance with the brain what brung you.

OTHER CAUSES OF MEMORY LOSS

So we have the slow loss of brain cells, and we have the slow buildup of the cellular equivalent of plastic grocery bags and Styrofoam fast food boxes in the landfills of our brains. But there are other factors that can produce memory loss:

- *Stroke or another circulatory event that interrupts the flow of blood to the brain.* When a blood clot or other obstruction prevents the circulatory system from feeding the brain with oxygen, for each minute the brain's blood supply is restricted, millions more brain cells perish. If treatment is not fast enough, serious mental impairment can result. Brain tumors can also impair memory.
- *Free radicals.* In his scientific report, *Boosting Memory, Preventing Brain Aging*, Dr. Michael Elstein, the Australian antiaging researcher

and author of *Eternal Health*, writes that these molecular toxins can destroy the cellular structures that provide energy to our brains. Since our brains use 20 percent of our body's energy, the results can be devastating to brain health.[7]

- *Drug side effects.* All powerful drugs have side effects, and some popular classes of drugs, especially statins (taken to lower cholesterol) and SSRs (taken for depression) have been linked to memory loss in some users.
- *Head injuries.* Sudden trauma to the brain due to a car accident or fall, for example, can cause memory loss. The effects can be overcome, assuming the damage is not too great to begin with.
- *Inflammation.* Increasingly, inflammation, a natural part of the body's immune response, is being seen as a possible cause for a wide range of diseases. Prolonged inflammation in the brain, as a response to abnormal protein deposits for example, can damage healthy brain tissue. Anti-inflammatory drugs are now being tested to prevent Alzheimer's disease.
- *Nutritional deficiencies.* Older people who do not eat a healthy diet can lack critical nutrients needed for brain health.
- *Stress.* Elstein writes, "There is clear evidence that stress which is unresolved and constant impairs learning and memory."[8]
- *Deficiency of fatty acids.* The brain is composed largely of fatty acids (such as the commonly known omega-3, found in oily fish like salmon and mackerel), which most people do not consume enough of.
- *Hormonal imbalances.* Diseases of the endocrine system can cause the body to lack normal levels of important hormones like DHEA, estrogen, and testosterone, all of which are vital to brain health.

That's quite a litany of potential demons threatening your mental health. But that's the negative perspective; the positive angle is that as time passes, science and medicine are regarding mental impairment not as a "that's just part of getting old" condition (which it was seen as for many centuries) but as something with a set of specific causes, some preventable and curable, some not.

"People thought (dementia) was just a normal part of aging," says Small in an interview for this book. "Now we see it as a disease, as a condition, and we need to deal with it and research it, and we're doing that. Now we find that it may be an inevitable result if people live long enough, but in many situations we can intervene early and stave it off. That's our approach now. We're testing drugs in people with mild cognitive impairment. We find that these drugs may delay the onset of Alzheimer's disease. I think the key here will be identifying the problems early, intervening early, and heading it off. I don't mind getting Alzheimer's disease as long as I'm 120 and I have lived a long and fulfilling life."

The Difference Between Annoying and Terrifying

We all have what are known as "senior moments," when we forget something we know we should remember or can't recall why we came into a room. Most of the time we slap ourselves on the head and poke fun at ourselves, knowing that such moments are usually the product of a distracted mind, a busy schedule, or the disease known as multitasking. But when should we not be so cavalier? When does a senior moment cross the line into the kind of memory loss we should actually worry about?

First, it's important to know what not to worry about. You shouldn't worry about every memory lapse; they happen to everyone at every age, not just people over fifty-five. If you know a word but can't recall it, for instance, you'll remember it later. Temporarily forgetting words, forgetting where you left things, and forgetting the names of people to whom you were just introduced are often signs of distraction, a restless mind, or anxiety in a social situation. Unless they prevent you from functioning in your daily life, they are nothing to worry about.

When memory lapses become continual and interfere with your ability to function in your daily life, that's when it's time to worry. The most serious issue is when you have a change in your recent memory. People with Alzheimer's disease will often remember details of their distant past with great clarity but forget conversations they had two days before. Again, forgetting such things once in a while is no big deal; forgetting them chronically may be a sign of a much more serious problem. Other warning signs to watch for include the following:

- You have trouble learning new things.
- You forget routine things constantly.
- You have a hard time remembering how to do things you've done a thousand times in the past.
- You have a hard time keeping track of the events of the day and in what order they occurred.
- You find yourself using the same phrases or repeating stories in conversation.
- You have difficulty managing your finances or making decisions.

If you find that you or someone you know are having these kinds of problems, don't panic. These symptoms aren't necessarily a harbinger of Alzheimer's. Don't speculate; get checked out by your physician.

An elderly man is in to see his doctor. The doctor runs his tests, then tells the man, "I have good news and bad news."

"What's the bad news?" asks the man.

"You have terminal cancer," says the doctor.

"Oh, no," says the man, devastated. After a moment to gather himself, he asks, "What's the good news?"

The doctor says, "You also have Alzheimer's. In six months you won't remember you have cancer."

The "A" Word

Alzheimer's disease may be the most dreaded affliction among older Americans because, unlike cancer or heart disease, Alzheimer's steals not just your health but your identity. The disease affects more than 4.5 million Americans today, according to the Alzheimer's Association, twice as many as in 1980. The association also estimates that because of the nation's aging population, the number of people with the disease will grow in coming years to from 11.3 million to 16 million cases by 2050.

You know the litany of Alzheimer's effects. Progressively, it destroys the patient's ability to reason, learn, make judgments, and participate in even the most routine aspects of daily life. In the late stages of the disease, patients' personalities can change, they can experience frightful hallucinations, and they may forget the identities of those closest to them. There is no cure. Drugs can delay the onset of symptoms for years, but the decline is inevitable. Alzheimer's is well on its way to taking its place at the top of the hideous hit parade of maladies that kill most Americans along with heart disease, cancer, stroke, and diabetes.

What's frustrating is that researchers don't know exactly what causes the disease. There are many possible causal factors, as we've listed here, but no magic bullet. One of the leading theories is that a protein fragment called beta-amyloid may be largely responsible for the neural damage that leads to the disease. According to this theory, beta-amyloid, which is part of a larger protein, can accumulate in the brain when the larger protein is "cut" into smaller pieces to perform various tasks. The beta-amyloid fragments become plaques that clump onto brain cells, disrupting cell-to-cell communication and triggering an immune system response that results in inflammation, eventually killing the affected brain cells.

If the beta-amyloid theory proves correct, drugs could be developed to counter its effects. But that's years off. What we know now is what Alzheimer's does to the brain. Whatever sets the disease in motion begins injuring the brain years before symptoms appear. By the time obvious symptoms begin to appear, neurons have already begun to degenerate and die.[9]

WHAT'S GOOD FOR THE BODY IS GOOD FOR THE MIND

Art Linkletter is chairman of the board of directors of the John Douglas French Foundation for Alzheimer's Disease (www.jdfaf.org), so he knows that while work continues on finding the causes and treatments, the best we can do at this point is practice prevention and catch signs of cognitive impairment at their earliest stages. Upon detecting possible signs of the memory impairment that could presage the early stages of Alzheimer's, visit your physician. A battery of screenings—including a CT or PET scan (which can check for the telltale signs of plaques that damage brain function) as well as memory, reasoning, and balance tests—can usually indicate with 90 percent accuracy if you have the early signs of Alzheimer's.

Early detection is crucial. According to the 1998 article, "Projections of Alzheimer's Disease in the United States and the Public Health Impact of Delaying Disease Onset" by Brookmeyer, Gray, and Kawas in the *American Journal of Public Health*, finding a treatment that could delay onset by five years could reduce the number of individuals with Alzheimer's disease by nearly 50 percent after fifty years.[10]

Some key signs to consider in someone close to you:

- Does the person have a family history of dementia or Alzheimer's disease?
- Watch for sudden mood swings, agitation, or depression. People in the early stages of the disease can lose control of their emotions.
- Notice how the person moves. Does he or she lack normal balance and coordination? It is not unusual for a person developing Alzheimer's to change his or her walk.
- Monitor for signs of confusion such as getting lost on familiar streets, losing the train of a conversation, or forgetting the names of common objects.
- Does the person suddenly have a short or nonexistent attention span or behave inappropriately around other people?
- Be sure to eliminate drug reactions or hearing and vision impairment as the causes of problems. Responses to medications can cause memory loss, while the loss of a sense can bring about both anger and confusion.

Even with all that good advice, prevention seems like a better way to go. As with almost all the other physical breakdowns that afflict us as we age, Alzheimer's is only partially caused by genetics. Researchers in Seattle have identified a single defect on chromosome 14 that may be a major risk factor in early-onset Alzheimer's, which affects people under age sixty-five. Late-onset Alzheimer's, which represents the majority of cases and appears after sixty-five, can be partially traced to a gene found on chromosome 19.[11] However, the work is still in its early stages, and most scientists agree that there is no one identifiable cause of the disease. That's cause for hope because if the presence of an "Alzheimer's gene" simply increases your risk of developing the disease, then your lifestyle choices put you in control of whether you develop it or not. Remember, lifestyle is 70 to 75 percent of longevity!

"We've done studies on identical twins," says Small in his interview. "One twin gets Alzheimer's. The other does not. If you look at their lifestyle, who got the Alzheimer's? The twin who liked to party, who smoked and drank and had a bad diet. The other twin didn't. We don't have all of the lifestyle factors down yet. For example, there are studies suggesting that anti-inflammatory drugs protect the brain. We're not sure yet. Part of my job is to try to get the information out to people so they can make informed decisions on how to conduct their lives to protect their brains tomorrow."

Evidence suggests that the best way to prevent Alzheimer's disease is to do all the things that you would otherwise be doing to live a long, healthy life. By living a healthy lifestyle—exercising; eating lots of fresh, nutritious foods; keeping your weight under control; reducing stress; challenging your mind; staying active and purposeful; and maintaining rich, rewarding relationships—you keep your entire body, including your brain, healthy. Lifestyle choices may be your most effective weapon at avoiding not just Alzheimer's, but all kinds of dementia.

"I call them the big four," says Small. "Mental activity, that's one. Physical conditioning is two. Reducing stress is three. Number four is a healthy brain diet."

Barbara Morris, pharmacist and author of *Put Old on Hold*, insists that science holds the key right now to preventing Alzheimer's disease. She writes in response to our questions: "Yes, we do know how to prevent

Alzheimer's. An extensive amount of existing research indicates that specific nutrients and antioxidants have the potential to help prevent this dreaded disease. However, the medical establishment—the pharmaceutical industry, the government, and assorted corporate entities with financial interests to protect—ignore the results of credible, prevention-oriented research."

Dr. Lester Packer has been a professor and member of the Department of Molecular and Cell Biology at the University of California at Berkeley and is in charge of the Packer Laboratory, one of the world's leading antioxidant research centers. In his book, *The Antioxidant Miracle*, Packer says, "We have performed numerous experiments in my laboratory that demonstrate that vitamin E (along with Coenzyme Q-10, the other fat soluble antioxidant) can reduce lipid peroxidation in the brain. What's even more exciting is that a recent multi-institution, double-blind, placebo-controlled study conducted by the Alzheimer's Disease Cooperative Study showed that vitamin E worked even better than standard drug therapy in treating Alzheimer's patients."

Packer believes that "Based on the growing number of studies that show vitamin E and other antioxidants can protect against so-called brain aging, vitamin E may prove to be useful in delaying the onset of Alzheimer's disease, or in some cases, even preventing it from occurring in the first place by protecting brain tissue against oxidative damage." [12]

> *Life is not stationary. Seconds, minutes, hours, days, weeks, months, and years all tick away at the same clip for everyone. No age group can be isolated. None of us can settle into infancy, youth, middle age, or old age. We all grow older, and, incidentally, it is an exciting thought if the accent is on growing. "Though our outward man perish," said Paul, "yet the inward man is renewed day by day" (2 Cor. 4:16).* [13]
>
> —Hugh W. Pinnock

We believe in reducing your risk factors through means that you can control. So let's leave behind the sad specter of Alzheimer's and take a look at the many ways you can keep your mind dazzling and keep away not just Alzheimer's but all the other types of dementia as well.

Brain Food: A Lot More Than Fish

Some cognitive impairment as you age is probably unavoidable, but with the right lifestyle choices and an active effort to maintain your brain health starting as early as possible, you can stay sharp and mentally agile to the end of your days.

Some recent research suggests that the age-related slowdown in thought may be reversible. Studies in 2003 on monkeys at the University of Utah School of Medicine revealed that a neurotransmitter called GABA, which helps the neural connections in the brain respond to specific stimuli, may be depleted with age, resulting in brain impairment. Tests have yet to be conducted on humans, but in the monkey subjects, drugs that boost the activity of GABA in the brain appear to reverse the effects, restoring brain function. If this holds true in humans and can be done safely, it's possible that some kinds of mental decline could be reversed. GABA-enhancing drugs are used now to treat epilepsy.[14]

Beyond miracle cures, however, lie commonsense miracles that hold out just as much hope for keeping the brain healthy into old age. Elstein says that adults should adopt a variety of methods for keeping the brain healthy into old age:

- Maintaining optimal nutrition, especially with essential fats found in nuts, seeds, oils, and small fish and the essential amino acids found in eggs, beans, lean meats, nuts, and seeds, is important.
- Supplements of vitamin B_{12} and folic acid have been demonstrated to reduce the risk of Alzheimer's disease by almost 60 percent.
- Hormones are important for preserving memory. Research indicates that estrogen is beneficial for women while testosterone helps men. DHEA, thyroid hormones, and pregnenolone might also help. Maintaining optimal levels of DHEA will reduce the harmful effects that cortisol, the stress hormone, has on the memory center based in the hippocampus. Meditation will also help in this regard. Having good levels of

thyroid hormone also prevents the brain from becoming sluggish.

- Exercising the brain and remaining gainfully employed is vital. The old slogan "use it or lose it" absolutely applies to the brain.
- Reducing toxicity from heavy metals such as mercury, lead, and aluminum can protect health.
- Managing food allergies—including those to wheat and gluten, dairy, and yeast—can be beneficial.
- Taking herbal tonics such as gingko biloba, brahmi, and withania has been shown scientifically to boost memory. Other nutrients such as phosphatidylserine, alpha-lipoic acid and acetyl-L-carnitine have benefits as far as memory is concerned.
- Blueberries have also been shown to boost memory.
- Exercising and being less of a couch potato is important.
- Nutrients such as vitamins C and E, magnesium and choline—which makes acetylcholine, the brain chemical responsible for memory— will also assist with the augmenting of higher mental powers.

We've mentioned blueberries, but there are other great brain foods:

- *Cruciferous vegetables such as broccoli and cauliflower.* Harvard scientists have reported that a diet rich in such vegetables seemed to stop age-related declines in thinking.
- *Green leafy vegetables like spinach and kale.* They are rich sources of folate, which appears to play a major role in preventing stroke and also may help the body break down the amino acid homocysteine, which is toxic to brain cells.
- *Nuts and oils.* The brain is 60 percent fat, and raw nuts give you plenty of healthy fats that lower cholesterol and fight inflammation. Olive, canola, and other monounsaturated oils also appear to reduce Alzheimer's risk.
- *Fish like salmon and tuna.* Mom was right: fish is brain food, at least oil-rich varieties that give your brain more of those important healthy fats.

Staying "Quizzically Fit"

But perhaps the simplest, greatest advice comes from AARP's Staying Sharp public information program, presented by NRTA: AARP's Educator Community along with the Dana Alliance for Brain Initiatives. These recommendations treat the brain as a muscle, which, like any other muscle in the body, must be worked to remain fit and strong. But instead of becoming physically fit, you can use these ideas to train your brain to become what we call "quizzically fit"—that is, challenging yourself with new questions, new puzzles, new stimuli, and new tasks that give your brain and mind a great workout. Some marvelous suggestions from Staying Sharp:

- *Switch sides.* If you're right handed, use your other hand for such activities as brushing your teeth or using the computer mouse. This activates areas of your brain that get little use.
- *Change the scenery.* Rearrange the décor in a room or your whole house, or try taking a new route to work. This remaps the visual and spatial networks in your brain.
- *Use the sign language alphabet.* Learning to spell the manual alphabet, twenty-six hand positions that coincide to the twenty-six letters, works both the visual and motor areas of your brain.
- *Do things blindfolded.* Try eating blueberries, sorting coins, or other tasks without using your eyes. Blueberries contain compounds that bridge the gap between aging nerve cells.
- *Do puzzles.* Crossword puzzles are great for language and reasoning, while jigsaw puzzles work your spatial intelligence and are more likely to activate new pathways in your brain.
- *Tell stories.* Take turns reading a book aloud with your spouse or a friend. Reading and listening stimulate your brain's left and right hemispheres to work together.
- *Stimulate your sense of smell.* Smell is the only sense connected to the limbic system, a primitive part of the brain associated with memory and emotion. That's why a scent can send you tumbling back to your childhood. Try listening to music while burning

aromatic firewood or cooking something fragrant, and you'll
build brain connections by combining two senses that don't
normally work together.

- *Be a reporter.* When you describe things to others, you improve
  your visual memory and your attention span.
- *Walk.* Aerobic exercise increases levels of a chemical called BDNF,
  for brain-derived neurotrophic factor, which protects nerve cells
  from free radical damage. Older adults who start a walking
  program show substantial improvement in planning, scheduling,
  and task coordination.[15]

New concerns for the Boomer generation

➤ *Then*: Long hair
   Now: Longing for hair
➤ *Then*: A keg
   Now: An EKG
➤ *Then*: Acid rock
   Now: Acid reflux
➤ *Then*: Moving to California because it's cool.
   Now: Moving to California because it's hot.
➤ *Then*: Watching John Glenn's historic flight with your
         parents
   Now: Watching John Glenn's historic flight with your kids
➤ *Then*: Trying to look like Marlon Brando or Elizabeth
         Taylor
   Now: Trying not to look like Marlon Brando or
         Elizabeth Taylor
➤ *Then*: Paar
   Now: AARP
➤ *Then*: Hoping for a BMW
   Now: Hoping for a BM
➤ *Then*: Getting out to a new, hip joint
   Now: Getting a new hip joint

THE 14-DAY MEMORY PRESCRIPTION

However, no solution is as comprehensive as Small's 14-day Memory Prescription, developed in cooperation with the UCLA Center on Aging. "Some people said to me, 'Doc, tell me exactly what to do,'" says Small in his interview. "And that's what I did. I said, 'Get up, do this exercise, eat this.'"

Small's fourteen-day program begins with candid assessments of your mental and physical condition, as described in his book, *The Memory Prescription*. What follows is a two-week whole body, whole mind regimen that addresses the "big four" factors related to memory and brain function: exercise, healthy diet, mental challenge, and stress management. Stress in particular, Small insists, is a potent but often-ignored contributor to memory loss. "There have been studies showing that animals under stress have smaller memory centers in the brain," he says. "People with psychological proneness to stress have an increased risk for getting Alzheimer's disease. Study volunteers who were injected with stress hormones like cortisol can't remember and can't learn new information. Fortunately, it's temporary. If you take the stress hormone away, their memory function improves."

On Small's fourteen-day prescription, patients follow a strict dietary plan, exercise, employ stress-reduction techniques, and do "mental aerobics" designed to challenge memory and reasoning and develop memory improvement skills. In his book, Small offers in-depth information about the types of exercise that offer the most cognition benefits; dozens of advanced mental exercises that challenge the brain, develop memory skills, and promote the creation of new neural pathways; antioxidant-rich, brain-healthy foods as well as foods harmful to mental function; numerous ways to reduce stress such as massage and developing proper sleep habits; and even insight into the truths and myths about supplements and hormones.

Can just two weeks on such a program make a difference? "We studied (the program) at UCLA and had dramatic results," says Small. "When we did brain scans on people who did this two-week program, including the big four I mentioned, we saw there was a significant change in their brain efficiency. They were much more efficient after just two weeks in the memory centers of the brain. And they felt better. When people start eating right and relaxing and exercising, they sleep better, they feel more positive, and they feel empowered because their memory abilities have improved.

We've seen a lot of people who jump-started a healthy lifestyle, which in the long run will help them live better longer."

Small believes a key goal is to get people to make the two-week regimen a permanent part of their lifestyle. "I think one agenda would be to have an advanced course—longer-term courses," he says. "I've been working with groups outside of UCLA (to do that). I think that a lot of people will want to come in each week and keep using memory boosters to keep their minds sharp."

> *Have regular hours for work and play; make each day both useful and pleasant, and prove that you understand the worth of time by employing it well. Then youth will be delightful, old age will bring few regrets, and life will become a beautiful success.*[16]
> —LOUISA MAY ALCOTT

A FEW CHANGES GO A LONG WAY

There is much you can do to take control of your brain and ensure that your mind is sharp and agile well into your Second Prime. That's hopeful. But what about the mild cognitive impairment that often comes with age even if you're stuffing yourself with antioxidants and working out at the gym?

Age-related slowdown in thought doesn't have to be something you live with. Humans are remarkable for their ability to adapt to changing conditions. You can adapt to a slowdown in your faculties, so you may not notice much of a change. For instance, what appears at first glance to be a thinking problem can be a problem with sight or hearing. Perhaps your vision has deteriorated a bit and you require better light to read by, or your hearing has lost some of its acuity, so you need the volume higher on a radio or a microphone to hear properly. Or you don't concentrate as well, so you need a quieter, less distracting environment in order to learn. There's nothing wrong with your noodle; it's your sensory equipment that needs a bit of help. Learn to compensate.

Old Jokes by J.L. Kuntz

Jokes and stories about old age fill my e-mail as friends and relatives feel inclined to send them along. Countless jokes and cartoons lampooning senior citizens. They are of a common theme and parody, failing hearing and failing eyesight. Memory also is a favorite target. Since a majority, if not all, of these jokes originate with senior citizens, they cannot be called politically incorrect. Some are truly funny while others can only be characterized as mean-spirited. No subject nor body part is sacred, and it seems that at some indeterminate age, certainly beginning some time in the late 50s, they are discussed or depicted with wild abandon. Thus are depicted toothless, paunchy, flatfooted individuals who look on life with bewilderment; women whose breasts hang to their knees and men with bellies so big they no longer can see their feet, let alone their manhood. You know the ones, you have seen and laughed at some yourself on occasion. It is, it appears, a time of self-mockery. No other age group parodies itself with such vigor. I find it depressing.

I have heard various talking heads speak of this self-ridicule in a positive light; implying that we have accepted and are coping well with the aging process. I beg to disagree. The jokes and cartoons avoid the reality of aging and the permanence of its end. I find it all so annoying since I know that I have slowed, know that my eyesight is not what it should be. Yet, in my heart, I know I can't be that old. My thoughts tend to younger things. And I remember. Remembering, I know what I miss.

I miss the passion. I miss the passion of waking in the middle of the night and coupling with an intensity often lacking when both are fully awake. I miss the spontaneity of grabbing hands and running until breathless for no earthly reason. I miss the immortality of younger days.

I resent the fact that I have become cautious on a ladder. I used to climb to the roof without a thought. Now I make that journey only when absolutely necessary and fear lurks at the corners of my mind, especially if I have to work along the eaves. The fear may be justified. A sliding ladder and dangling half on, half off the roof awaiting ignominious rescue tends to give one a healthy respect in such matters. As a result, some tasks are long delayed as I use the excuse of not having enough time.

I used to think thirty-five the perfect age. At thirty-five, you are old enough to be pretty well established in who you are and what you are doing. At the same time, you have come to realize that you actually were pretty stupid in your younger years. You now understand that you really don't know it all. At thirty-five, if you are wise, you are in reasonable physical shape and you can still consider yourself immortal.

I miss, I miss . . . the list could be as endless as those plaints of old age which intrude on my days. But even in this passing regret, there is an inner peace not possible in youth. There is the quiet joy of being with friends, of being with her, of becoming lost still in the scent of her hair, the same scent from days when time was new. There is the renewed satisfaction of reading a good book or of being curious enough to still want to learn new disciplines. There also still is the joy of running, the satisfaction of meeting self-set goals. As for climbing ladders, perhaps it is time to cede that task to someone else. Although it would give me distress, if someone must fall off the roof, I would prefer that it would be someone else's body that plummets past the window. Realizing this, I often press the delete button without regret, knowing that the same joke, or one similar, will reappear in my e-mail queue.

As I set off on my morning run, I promise myself that I will not go quietly into that dark night.[17]

You can also adopt habits that make remembering things easier:

- Make to-do lists.
- Keep a personal calendar. Use computer-based ones that send you e-mail alerts to remind you of upcoming commitments.
- Keep important items like car keys in the same place.
- Follow a daily routine.
- When you meet someone new, repeat his name back to him after you're introduced. "Tom? Nice to meet you, Tom."
- Write yourself notes reminding you to do certain tasks and leave them where you're sure to find them.

One of the best ways to keep your brain forming new connections and remaining active and agile as you age is to go back to school. Find ways to learn new skills or learn about new subjects. You can attend a community college, audit courses at a university, go to classes at a community recreation program, attend courses through a private company like The Learning Annex, or even attend "distance learning" classes on the Internet for everything from computer certification to foreign languages. More and more universities and schools are embracing the concept of lifelong learning, in which learning does not stop with an undergraduate or graduate degree at twenty-one or twenty-five, but continues throughout life.

That spirit is sending Baby Boomers back to school in record numbers. The range of educational choices is as varied as the people seeking them: some folks go for advanced degrees in scholarly subjects, others seek vocational skills to pursue hobbies of longtime interest such as woodworking and computer use, and still others are just out to learn something fun, from flower arranging to tango dancing. After all, an AARP study showed that 73 percent of Baby Boomers polled expected to have a hobby or special interest in their retirement.[18] That translates to a lot of learning to be done.

Nothing is healthier for the mind than the seeking of knowledge. As philosopher John Dewey said, "Education must be reconceived, not as merely a preparation for maturity (whence our absurd idea that it should stop after adolescence) but as a continuous growth of the mind and a continuous illumination of life."[19]

Sageing, Not Aging

A Rush University study of 1,000 priests, nuns, and brothers of religious orders has shown that the mental abilities of older people do not change much from year to year unless they develop a debilitating illness such as Alzheimer's.[20] Think about that: if you practice what we preach in this chapter, you have an excellent chance of enjoying decades of clear, creative thought and memory. Like so much else, it's your choice. Research shows that when people buy into the cultural stereotype of old age as a time when your mind goes to pot, they're more likely to lose more of their cognitive function. A positive attitude about the mind and old age goes a long way to preserving brain health. Pessimists please take note.

Whether you breeze into your 90s with a mind as sharp as a tack or forget a few names and faces as the decades pass, age gives you many delightful gifts to compensate. You've gained an immense store of wisdom, what Duke University researcher Lawrence Katz, PhD calls "a dense and rich network of associations developed through a lifetime of experiences."[21] Wisdom is a commodity that cannot be bought. It must be earned.

With age, you're gaining foresight, understanding, and perception that younger people simply don't have. It's like being able to see the future; you can assess a situation based on your experience, look at the people involved based on what you know about people (and the fact that they never change), and predict what will happen with remarkable accuracy. If younger folks don't listen to you, that's their problem.

But when you're growing in wisdom and knowledge and insight— and when you're sharing those qualities with younger people who need guidance, mentoring and guiding people who need what you know— you're not aging. You're *sageing*. You're turning one of the most profound aspects of age into an asset for yourself and others. And maybe, just maybe, you're learning something as well. We should all strive to sage, not just age. The world would be a better, wiser place.

Second Prime Strategy—Mind

1. Things to Do

- Assess your memory and that of your spouse for any signs of impairment.
- Pick up a copy of *The Memory Prescription* by Dr. Gary Small.
- Stop paying attention to negative stereotypes about age and lost marbles.
- Start doing things to reduce stress and get more rest.
- Look into classes at your local college, university, or community center.
- Pick five challenging books and start reading.
- Pick a new skill you want to learn in the next year.
- Begin eating more brain-healthy foods.

2. Changes You Need to Make for a Healthier Mind

-
-
-
-
-

3. Your Mind Goals for Your Second Prime

Example: "Learn to speak Italian in the next twelve months."

-
-
-
-
-

4. Mind Resources

- SeniorNet (www.seniornet.org)
- UCLA Center on Aging (www.aging.ucla.edu)
- John Douglas French Alzheimer's Foundation (www.jdfaf.org)
- Alzheimer's Association (www.alz.org)
- Alzheimer's Disease Education and Referral Center (www.alzheimers.org)
- Family Doctor.org (www.familydoctor.org)

- Dementia.com (www.dementia.com)
- Neurology Channel (www.neurologychannel.com)
- Internet Mental Health (www.mentalhealth.com)
- The Human Brain (www.fi.edu/brain)
- Elder Wisdom Circle (www.elderwisdomcircle.org)
- Mentoring (www.mentoring.org)

chapter seven

Sex *or* Still Enjoying It While Everybody Else Is Just Talking About It

There is a brief time for sex, and a long time when sex is out of place. But when it is out of place as an activity there still should be the large and quiet space in the consciousness where it lives quiescent. Old people can have a lovely quiescent sort of sex, like apples, leaving the young quite free for their sort.[1]

—D. H. LAWRENCE

My father told me all about the birds and the bees, the liar. I went steady with a woodpecker till I was twenty-one.[2]

—BOB HOPE

A nd now, a few words about sex. Sex. Sex, sex, sex. After all, it's one of our favorite subjects; we can talk about it for hours. If you listed our culture's favorite subjects, sex would appear at the top of the list. There's nothing we love to talk about and gossip about more, and for good reason, because sex is life. Unfortunately, too many seniors are just talking about it and nothing more, and that's a shame. Because it doesn't have to be that way.

Of all the societal stereotypes surrounding age, the idea that seniors and sex don't mix is perhaps the strongest. If you're buying into that myth, wake up; there's a lot more sex going on among the elderly than you realized. Good thing, too, since sexual activity is one of the best ways around to reduce stress, improve attitude, and keep relationships strong as the decades accumulate.

A Few More Sexual Myths

Myth: Impotence afflicts every man in old age. In reality, though many men take longer to achieve an erection when they're older, men who continue to be sexually active into their 50s and beyond tend to retain their potency.

Myth: Sex can be hazardous to your health if you're over fifty-five. Not so, say experts. Sure, if you have a heart problem, it's best to take it easy, but the idea that a healthy sixty-five-year-old man is going to suddenly drop dead during the act is something out of a bad Hollywood movie.

Myth: The sex drive gradually drops for men and women as the years advance. Horsefeathers. Extensive research has shown that those who continue to become more intimate and active as they age retain as much of their interest in sex as they had when they were younger even if they may not engage in intercourse as often.

Myth: Old people can't be sexy. Nothing could be more ludicrous. Apart from the fact that in today's society, people in their 60s and 70s are considered middle-aged, the idea that experienced, confident people who have taken care of themselves can't be sexy is absurd.

We mythologize sex in our culture, and that doesn't change when we talk about sex among seniors. But where the myths tend to be positive when the subject is younger people, as with so many other stereotypes, the talk turns negative when we look at folks over retirement age. That's why it's so important to speak up and contest such myths and misconceptions.

Use It or Lose It

As years of workouts keep your body able to bend and stretch into your 70s, years of sexual activity in your middle age will help keep you active into your later years. Men who stop having regular sex in their 50s and 60s increase their chances of becoming impotent later on. Women also risk losing their sex drive.

What's just as important, says Sallie Foley, a social worker, sex therapist, and author of *Sex and Love for Grownups: A No-Nonsense Guide to a Life of Passion*, is that sex remains just as enjoyable for people even into their 90s. In an interview for this book, she says, "Women's confidence in their sexuality increases as they get older because they're no longer tethered to stereotypes. It's as if women are saying 'Look, I've dealt with the body image stereotypes. I'm not living by anybody's stereotypes. I set my own pace now.' People who are past their 50s or 60s, if they're sexually active, tend to say that their pleasure in sex has increased as they've gotten older."

If you follow health news, it's not difficult to see a regular flow of new research being released about the sex lives of people over fifty. For example, a 2004 AARP study, "Sexuality at Midlife and Beyond," looked at more than 1,700 men and women over forty-five and discovered some surprising new realities about sex among the senior set:

- 22 percent of men report using some kind of drug or treatment to treat sexual performance problems
- 60 percent of respondents agree that sexual activity is a critical part of a good relationship
- 63 percent of men and women described themselves as extremely satisfied or somewhat satisfied with their sex lives

The general picture suggests that older people are more willing to discuss sex as a health and a quality of life issue. At the same time, more physicians and health-care providers are looking at sexual activity as a marker of health and a predictor of serious conditions such as heart disease. "We know that healthy and physically active respondents are generally more satisfied with their sex lives than those with a medical condition," wrote Linda Fisher, research director at AARP, in an article on SeniorJournal.com. "Thirty-one percent of men said better health for themselves would increase their satisfaction with their sex life, and 23 percent said better health for their partner would increase their satisfaction. [3]

Women appear to be the greatest beneficiaries of the senior sexual revolution. As they age, women generally suffer from fewer problems with sexual performance than men and retain the same sex drive and desires. The result is a boost in sexual confidence among Baby Boomer women. A 2005 survey revealed that 82 percent of them consider themselves very or somewhat confident sexually. What's interesting is that in the younger groups of women surveyed, the confidence level was lower. This suggests that as women age, they are less concerned about what other people think and more aware of their own sexual knowledge and ability. The study backs this up—62 percent of female Boomers said they had a greater sense of what satisfied their sexual needs, and two-thirds said that having good sex was a priority in their lives.[4]

Agelessness Secret #7

Attitude

Optimistic, purposeful, stubborn people tend to live longer. We've heard stories for years and years about how a positive attitude lengthens your life, helps you fight off disease, and so on. Well, now it appears those stories were true.

According to research brought to the general public by *Time* magazine in 2004, people who test at the top of the scale for happiness and a positive state of mind produce about 50 percent more antibodies in response to the flu vaccine. Optimism boosts your immune system.

That's not all. Other research into positive emotions has shown that feelings like optimism and hopefulness reduce the risk or severity of cardiovascular disease, high blood pressure, pulmonary disease, diabetes, and even respiratory infections. A Dutch study even showed that elderly patients with positive, optimistic outlooks had a 50 percent reduced risk of death over the nine-year term of the study.

The whys of this effect are less clear. Some scientists think that emotion affects the body's biochemistry, reducing the levels of immune-depressing stress hormones like cortisol. But that's not enough to account for the dramatic improvements in health and longevity attributed to wearing your frown upside down. So what's at work here?

The truth is, it doesn't matter. It may be that being habitually happy means you're more likely to exercise and eat right, proven ways of staying healthy into old age. Or there may be some unknown neurological effect of optimism that prevents disease. The simple fact is that a positive state of mind is beneficial to your health and life.

That's why seniors volunteer, work at polls, tutor, work with charities, sit on school boards, and so on. Being involved in things, having a cause to work for, is invigorating. Just as invigorating are the personal relationships you develop through that kind of work. According to Senior Care Management, seniors who are connected to the community, who maintain a diverse circle of relationships, and who attend organizational meetings are more likely to have good health.[5]

So brighten up. It really will make you feel better.

THE PHYSICAL SIDE OF SEX

The growing body of research and surveys suggests that great senior sex is not wishful thinking but fact. The simplest reason is health. Older Americans are healthier today: exercising, eating better, quitting smoking, staying purposeful and busy. And with greater health and vitality comes greater sexual desire. If you feel alive and vibrant, you're more likely to enjoy making love with your mate; if you feel exhausted all the time, you're going to have no interest in the bedroom.

What's becoming clear is this: *sex is good for you*. Since living a full, brilliant Second Prime means doing all you can to ensure that body and mind remain full of energy, sex is one of the keys not just to a happy old age but to a healthy one as well. Look at some of the physiological benefits of an active sex life cited in a 1997 study from Queens

University in Belfast, Northern Ireland, correlating overall health with sexual frequency:

- *Reduced risk of heart disease.* A 2001 follow-up study to the Queens University work found that men who had sex three or more times per week reduced their risk of heart attack or stroke by half.[6]
- *Weight loss.* A typical sexual episode burns about 200 calories, about the same as doing fifteen minutes on an exercise bike. The pulse rate can rise as high as 150, which is prime fat burning level for most folks. And muscular contractions actually work the buttocks, pelvis, thighs, neck, and abdomen. Sex also boosts the production of testosterone in men and women, leading to stronger bones and better muscle development.
- *Pain relief.* Just before orgasm, levels of the hormone oxytocin rise to 500 percent of their normal levels, releasing endorphins that can relieve pain from arthritis, migraines, and more.
- *Improved sense of smell.* It appears that the act increases production of the hormone prolactin, which in turn causes the brain to develop new neurons in the brain's smell center.[7]
- *Improved immune system.* According to a study conducted by Wilkes University in Pennsylvania, people who have sex about two times per week produce 30 percent more immunoglobulin A, a main component of the immune system. Caveat: the test was performed largely on people in their early 20s.[8]
- *A healthier prostate.* Some researchers have seen a connection between men who have infrequent sex and greater risk of prostate cancer. This implies that more frequent sex could help remove impurities through the semen that might otherwise cause prostate problems later on.[9]
- *Healthier teeth.* Board Certified Sexologist and licensed psychotherapist Marcy Dater Weiss, PhD, LCSW, CAP, SAP, says in an interview for this book that kissing, which is usually a part of sex, encourages the production of saliva, which lowers mouth

acidity and washes the mouth clean of food particles. (Hey, we didn't say this information would be pretty.)
- *Better skin*. Dr. Weiss also suggests that the increased perspiration that comes with rigorous sexual activity can cleanse the pores.

But in the end, these are all just bonuses. Do we really need a reason to enjoy sex? We just know that we do. Sex is an integral part of being human, vital, and alive. The great thing about frequent sex is, practice makes perfect. "The more you do it, the better you get," says Dr. Weiss. "If you are a golfer, you practice your swing. A tennis player practices his serve to get better. Why not practice making love?"

THE CHOREOGRAPHY OF LOVEMAKING

We've established that sex is good for you, whatever age you are. Now we're going to wreck another misconception that seniors don't enjoy sex as much as younger people do. All the evidence suggests just the opposite: people over fifty-five enjoy sex as much or more than their younger counterparts.

How is that possible? Let's begin with the obvious: no kids and fewer distractions. Unlike when you're younger and have to deal with the demands of children, the stresses of your job, and all the other myriad comings and goings of life, when you're older you have more control of your time. You can make love when and where you like. That freedom is conducive to passion and spontaneity.

But also, when you're older, you're better at sex. You know what you want, and what's more, you each know just what pleases the other. "Younger people don't really know about the choreography of lovemaking," says Foley in her interview. "It develops over time, with communication, assisted by the natural process of aging for men, which tends to delay orgasm a little bit. So for men as they get older—if you think about the sexual response cycle as being desire, arousal, orgasm—their sexual response cycle slows a little bit, and women's is slower in general. The sexual response cycles for men and women match up better, and they tend to focus more on the eroticism of their sexuality, not just the 'home run' of an orgasm. Couples in their 60s actually talk about feeling like they're more in sync now in terms of their sexual activity."

A couple's unbreakable emotional bond is another reason sex is often better in the Second Prime of life. You are more intimate. You know about the small touches, mood creators, and the anticipation of sex that leads to greater arousal and an experience that can last for hours. At the same time, you know each other's signals, so you know when he or she might not be in the mood for a long, slow evening of seduction. Sex should be *fun*, and the more you know about what makes each other swoon, the more fun it is.

When Being Bad Isn't Any Good

One of the most common reasons seniors do not have frequent sex is simply that they suffer from poor health. They may not have taken care of their bodies over the years, they may be overweight and have little energy, or they may suffer from a broad range of medical problems from arthritis to high blood pressure that make them afraid to have sex for fear it will be a danger to their health.

If you're in pain, lethargic, under stress, or simply don't feel healthy and well, sex will not be very much on your mind. Problems such as an enlarged prostate or treatment for prostate cancer can produce impotence in men though new treatments such as radioactive "seed" implantation have been developed in recent years that specifically reduce the risk of sexual side effects—a sign that the medical community is finally recognizing the importance of sex in the senior years.

Another reason some older Americans suffer from poor sex lives is that they are on medication that inhibits their sexual drive. "A lot of times, people will come in and say to me, 'Things don't work like they used to,'" says Dr. Weiss. "One of the first things I do is have them medically checked to make sure everything is in working order. Once we see if there are any medications they're on that are affecting their sexual performance, we can go on from there." Medications for high blood pressure and antidepressants are known to reduce libido as well as erectile function. In fact, about 25 percent of cases of erectile dysfunction (ED) are due to medication. Other types of medication that can inhibit sex include:

- Antipsychotics like chlorpromazine and thioridazine
- Cholesterol lowering medications, including statins
- Medications for anxiety and sleeplessness[10]

If you're experiencing sexual problems and you're taking prescription medication, ask your physician if what you're taking can inhibit sexual drive or arousal. Then you can take the proper action.

Sometimes the causes of a poor sex life are more subtle. Couples may suffer from a poor body image, comparing their older, less-toned and less-muscular bodies with the young, sleek bodies they see all over the media these days. It's enough to make them feel inadequate, and if they're ashamed of how their bodies look, they are not going to want to shed their clothes. Unfortunately, the bodies we see in the media are unrealistic—models and actors who have personal trainers, makeup artists, and all the time in the world to get in shape; after all, they're paid to look good.

If you're buying into the myth that everyone but you looks perfect, it's time to ask yourself why. Do you really think you're the only one who's gotten older? Do you really think the changes in your body have gone unnoticed by your loved

> *Men reach their sexual peak at eighteen. Women reach theirs at forty-five. Do you get the feeling God is playing a practical joke?"*
>
> —RITA RUDNER

one? In the end, if you're exercising, eating right, and taking care of your fitness and grooming, you're going to look as good as you can look, and that breeds confidence. And as any mature person will tell you, confidence is sexy. If you haven't taken care of yourself and are self-conscious about your body because of it, you know what to do. Get to the gym, start eating better, and develop a lifestyle around losing weight, moving, and being fit. You'll find your confidence—and sexual energy—rushing back.

IT'S THE RELATIONSHIP, STUPID

A few pages back, we mentioned that women said relationship was a critical part of their enjoyable sex life. The same is true for men, especially as the ardor of youth turns into the more deliberate, seductive sex of older age. The relationship matters.

"What we see come up in the literature is that women say, 'I don't care if my husband takes Viagra or not, I'm still not interested in sex with him because he's been a jerk for years,'" says Foley. "Viagra isn't going to settle that problem." She says that one of the biggest problems the couples she sees have—couples who should otherwise not have sexual difficulties—is that they don't communicate about sex. They don't discuss their relationship, love, or sex. In an article for SeniorJournal.com, she says, "They use euphemisms rather than communicating honestly with each other. Some older adults also don't know where to obtain relationship information specific to their situation. When they do find this information—a magazine article about sex, for example—they do not know how to broach the subject with their partners."[12]

It's virtually impossible to become aroused by someone, regardless of how good they look, when you feel alienated, resentful, or shut out. On the other hand, Second Prime couples who enjoy great sex, says Weiss, "have a very young, positive, optimistic attitude."

In her book, *Sex & Love for Grownups: A No-Nonsense Guide to a Life of Passion*, Foley offers some additional advice about keeping the fires of passion burning in the years when they're waning for many couples:

- *Live a life of connections.* Even if a perfect love eludes you, making sure that you have a wallet full of photos of family and friends will give meaning to your life.
- *Don't be afraid to try something new.* If you continue to see yourself as an adventurer, or if you've never taken a risk to try new things, now's the time.

- *Expect your relationships to be like your car.* No matter how much time and care you devote to your vehicle, it still occasionally breaks down and always needs maintenance. Relationships are like that too.
- *Abandon either/or thinking.* Life is complex, and thinking in rigid yes-or-no categories will often fail you. In order to respond to relationships and their complexity, think of diversity, plurality, and many possible solutions to a problem.
- *Take time to celebrate.* Ask people what they love about life and they'll tell you it's the very ordinariness of life that is spectacular about living. After a crisis, what really counts is the restoration of normalcy.
- *Love.* Relinquish the need for perfection and focus on what's real.[13]

GETTING YOUR GROOVE BACK

If the relationship is great, but the sex isn't, what can you do? Start with your health and fitness. Everything begins there. Dr. Weiss points out that everything you should be doing for a vital, lively Second Prime in general will also enhance your sex life. "Seniors with healthy sex lives exercise regularly, do things for their minds, get lots of sleep, and eat right," she says. "Men make sure their prostate is healthy, they take vitamins. They have a really healthy lifestyle and a positive, healthy attitude."

Foley also emphasizes that for men who have lost some sexual function, PDE5 inhibitors (we won't state any brand names, but you know one of the drugs as a little blue pill) are godsends. "They're wonderful medications," she says. "For years as a sex therapist, people would come in with erectile dysfunction, and I would basically have to say, 'We don't really have anything for you to do, except just live with this.' So people are saying, 'Why should I live with erectile dysfunction when these drugs can help me?' They've really helped lots of couples." There are, as you probably know, some health concerns for men in taking such drugs, especially men who are taking nitrates for heart problems. But don't let fear condemn you to living with ED. Talk to a physician and find out if these drugs can help you.

Another step Boomers can take now to ensure better sex later is to practice Kegels (named after its creator), an exercise that works the pubococcygens or PC muscle. "That helps to strengthen orgasmic response for women," Foley says. She explains how the exercise works for both men and women: "The Kegel works the muscle that stops and starts the flow of urine. You know the muscle. There are two kinds of Kegels. One kind is what we call the 'blinker Kegel.' Meaning, you could sit at a long, left-turn light with your car blinker on and tense and relax your muscle in time with the blinker on the car. You might do fifty of those a day.

"Then we say to do about twenty to thirty of the other kind of Kegel," Foley continues, "which would be tense-hold-2-3-4-5, relax-2-3-4-5. Do those on top of your blinker Kegels, and you get a really good muscle work-out. For women, this can prevent urinary incontinence and improve the flow of blood to the vagina to keep the vagina healthy and more supple. For men, they have striated muscles that hold the penis in place and help the penis stay steady when it is engorged with blood. Those striated muscles are actually exercised by doing Kegels."

A seventy-year-old man has never been married. One day he meets a beautiful seventeen-year-old girl, and it is love at first sight. They get married and go to Florida for their honeymoon. When they get back, his friend says to him, "So, tell me, how was it?"

"Oh, it was beautiful," says the man. "The sun, the surf, we made love almost every night, we . . ."

His friend interrupts him. "A man your age! How did you make love almost every night?"

"Oh," says the man, "we almost made love Monday, we almost made love Tuesday . . ."

What Can You Do to Make Things Sexier?

Sex is in the mind as much as the body—if the mind doesn't get aroused, the body usually doesn't follow. So if you want a healthy, active sex life in your Second Prime, you've got to work on creating an entire lifestyle that's more conducive to sex, arousal, and romance. For each of the areas below, write down some of the things you and your spouse could do to make life sexier.

Meals
Do you eat out every night? When you cook at home, do you both cook? If you do, do you enjoy music while you cook, or is it all business? What could you change?

Attire
How do you dress for each other? Do you always go casual? Could you dress up or dress sexier?

Home Atmosphere
What does your home look like? Is it sterile or inviting? Do you have music, soft lighting, and cozy spaces? What emotions does your home provoke in you?

Bedroom Environment

Robes, candles, music, fragrance . . . they can all turn a bedroom into a haven of romance and desire. What touches could you add to your boudoir?

Conversation

How do you speak to each other? Do you listen and look into each other's eyes or nod and stare into space? Teasing, witty, seductive conversation is key to great sex.

Entertainment

When you go out, what do you do? Dinner with the same people? What about dancing or a weekend at a secluded B&B? Be creative.

Be Open Minded

Let's do the math: 78 million Baby Boomers will be entering their Second Prime in the next twenty years. Women tend to outlive men in this country by about seven years. That means in twenty-five to thirty years, there will be millions of widows looking for companionship.

"I think that in the years to come, you're going to see the emergence of friendship networks," says author and aging expert Ken Dychtwald in his interview for this book. "At the end of the day, the Noah's ark model works best, where there's one boy for every girl. Unfortunately, because women are biologically superior to men, as we age as a society, there will be a lot more women than men. So some of what we've thought of as being the attraction between couples as being sexually based I think will be as much based on companionship and friendship."

Second Prime Strategy—Sex

1. Things to Do
• Talk to your spouse about your sex life.
• If you're not already working out and eating right, start.
• Talk to a physician about any sexual problems you may have.
• If your relationship needs work, find a sex therapist you can talk to.
• Begin turning your bedroom into a warm, seductive space.
• Look at any medications that could be inhibiting your sex drive.
• Talk to a specialist about lubricants or other sex aids.

2. Changes You Need to Make for a Better Sex Life
•

•

•

3. Your Sexual Goals for Your Second Prime
Example: "Have more instances of closeness, touching, and romance every week, even if some don't lead to sex."
•

•

•

4. Sexual Life Resources
• Sallie Foley (www.salliefoley.com)
• His and Her Health (www.hisandherhealth.com)
• The all-in-one Christian Web Site Community (www.praize.com)
• eHarmony (www.eharmony.com)

chapter eight

Spirituality *or* Plugging Into a Higher Power

From his cradle to his grave a man never does a single thing which has any first and foremost object but one—to secure peace of mind, spiritual comfort, for himself.[1]

—MARK TWAIN

Man doth not live by bread only.

—DEUTERONOMY 8:3

In *How to Make the Rest of Your Life the Best of Your Life,* we have deliberately made an effort to cast our net beyond the usual topics of health, fitness, and diet to look at aspects of successful aging that can't be easily measured in a laboratory. And whatever your beliefs, the world of the spirit has a real affect on how long and how well we live . . . and perhaps as important, how we die.

Psychiatrist Dr. Elizabeth Targ devoted her career to something that most scientists wouldn't touch with a ten-foot pole: the study of the healing effects of prayer. In 1995 and 1996 at the University of California–San Francisco, she set up the most precise studies of prayer healing ever conducted: randomized, double-blind scenarios in which AIDS patients had a fifty/fifty chance of being specifically prayed for by a group of people whom they would never meet, some hundreds or even thousands of miles away from the subjects, and who were from varied spiritual backgrounds.

In both the initial study and the 1996 follow-up (in which prayer was offered for one hour a day for six straight days, rotating weekly for ten weeks so each test-group patient received distant prayer from ten people), the results seemed to defy logic. In the first study, four of the ten AIDS patients who had not been prayed for had died. None of the ten who had been prayed for had died. In the second, larger study, the results showed that the control group (who were not prayed for) spent a total of sixty-eight days in the hospital for thirty-five AIDS-related illnesses while the group receiving the healing prayers spent only ten days in the hospital for thirteen illnesses. The chances of this happening randomly are a mere *5 percent*.

> *Look at the lives of those [who] gave themselves to Scripture reading and prayer and various other forms of self-examination and spiritual exercises. They believed in the culture and the discipline of the spiritual life and it was because they did so that God rewarded them by giving them these gracious manifestations of himself and these mighty experiences which warmed their hearts.* [2]
>
> —D. Martyn Lloyd-Jones

Case closed, right? Not so fast. In what can only be seen as a ghastly irony, Targ herself developed a fast-growing glioblastoma—a brain tumor—in mid-2002. Surgery could not remove the tumor, which had buried spidery tentacles deep into her brain tissue. Prayer therapy, unfortunately, did not work for Targ. She died less than four months after her diagnosis. Questions remain about Targ's work, but the study had one profound effect—scientists readily concluded that more study should be done! [3]

Spirituality and Longevity

For many, scientific studies are a moot point. If you believe that the power of Jesus can heal the sick, you're going to believe it even if one hundred Stanford laboratory studies say otherwise. Such is the resilience of faith. And if you think prayer does nothing more than offer comfort, you're going to continue to believe that, at least until there is concrete evidence of the contrary staring you in the face. And for the most part, it doesn't matter. Even if we don't have scientific proof of the power of prayer to heal, we don't need science to know that prayer and spirituality exert enormous influence over our lives.

There is more than a little anecdotal evidence to support the idea that having some sort of strong spiritual belief helps us live longer. There's no question that it helps us live better. Belief gives us strength, reminds us we're not alone in hard times, sets our moral compass, encourages us to help and forgive others, and gives us hope. Our faith can lend an additional dimension to life at a time when leaving work behind leaves us feeling rudderless and at sea, not sure why we're still hanging around this world.

True spirituality manifests itself in certain dominant desires.

1. First is the desire to be holy rather than happy.

2. A man may be considered spiritual when he wants to see the honor of God advanced through his life even if it means that he himself must suffer temporary dishonor or loss.

3. The spiritual man wants to carry his cross.

4. Again, a Christian is spiritual when he sees everything from God's viewpoint.

5. Another desire of the spiritual man is to die right rather than to live wrong.

6. The desire to see others advance at his expense.

7. The spiritual man habitually makes eternity-judgments instead of time-judgments.[4]

—A. W. TOZER

"Creating a spiritual retirement deals a lot with who you are as a spiritual being," says Molly Srode, a former nun and hospital chaplain who currently lectures on spirituality and is author of *Creating a Spiritual Retirement* and coauthor (with her husband, Bernie Srode) of *Keeping Spiritual Balance as We Grow Older.* Interviewed for this book, she says, "It's about finding out who you are, finding purpose with who you are and not what you do. I talk to retirees who were CEOs, sales managers, and the like, and they say, 'I'm nobody now.'

"My husband and I are campers," Srode continues, "and I met this man while we were walking our dogs at a campground. He said, 'I just retired, and since then, this little dog is all I have in my life.' Then he toddled down the lane and got into his $150,000 motor home. I thought, *How sad.* What is really valuable in our lives? Driving a fancy car, being a CEO, being young and beautiful? There is more to life than what we *were.*"

WHERE SCIENCE MEETS SCRIPTURE

Scientists are often spiritual beings, too, despite the common misperception that anyone devoted to the discovery of the hidden clockwork of nature must be, by definition, an atheist. So there have been plenty of people who have explored the question of faith and longevity in a systematic and scientific way. Their findings are interesting and promising:

- In 1997, a Duke University study showed that older people who attend religious services regularly had lower levels of the protein interleukin-6, which is linked to immune system diseases such as lupus, rheumatoid arthritis, and B-cell lymphoma.[5]
- A 1995 study from Dartmouth Medical School found that patients with an active social life and a strong religious faith were less likely to die in the six months after heart surgery than those without either one.[6]
- A 1989 study in Georgia of 400 people showed that those who believed religion was important had lower diastolic blood pressure than those without an interest in religion.[7]
- A 1997 inquiry published in the *American Journal of Public Health* concluded that frequent churchgoers were more likely to live longer than people who did not attend services frequently.[8]
- A 2005 study conducted at Bowling Green University suggests that test subjects who repeated such statements as "God is love" or "God is peace" experienced reduced pain and discomfort. "It is . . . likely that there is something uniquely inherent in the practice of spiritual meditation that cannot be completely conveyed through secular meditation and relaxation," said Amy Wachholtz, a PhD student who conducted the study.[9]

- A 2001 study from Duke University revealed that hospital patients who were struggling with their religious faith or who harbored such feelings as "being abandoned by God" or "believing the Devil caused their illness" were 19 to 28 percent more likely to die during the two-year follow-up period after their hospital stay.[10]

Perhaps most persuasive is a study by sociologist Terrence Hill and researchers at the University of Texas–Austin. Published in the *Journal of Gerontology* in 2005, the study found that among people sixty-five and older who attended church once per week, the mortality rate was 32 percent lower than those people who did not attend church.[11] "We controlled for health, behavior, and cognitive impairment, and the link didn't go away," said Hill in an article for Sage Crossroads.[12] On the heels of a 2003 study of longevity and religion that found a 25 percent reduction in mortality among regular churchgoers, this study was seen as confirmation that an active spiritual life does help you live longer.[13]

But why? What's at work here? The most obvious answer is that the hallmarks of a religious lifestyle are good for your health. People who shun smoking, drinking, and sexual promiscuity and promote work can claim to have health advantages. It's been documented repeatedly, for example, that Seventh-day Adventists, who promote this kind of healthy lifestyle, including a vegetarian diet, enjoy greater longevity than the average American. In most cases, God is good . . . for your body.

Write Yourself a "Prayscription"

However, for many of the faithful, belief in God and going to church don't translate into five-days-a-week gym sessions and a vegetarian diet. So what's behind the greater life span of the spiritual? Many researchers suggest that the social networks that form in religious congregations offer valuable support for their members. Regular attendance at religious services gives people a place to both lend support and receive it, helping them cope better with such stresses as financial hard times, disease, or the loss of a loved one.

The benefits of spiritual beliefs may go even deeper than the social connections, suggests Harold Koenig, the psychiatrist who led the Duke study listed earlier. He believes that faith gives the elderly a sense of meaning to their lives, a sense that the changes in their bodies and the deaths of those they care about are part of a greater plan. Life does not seem meaningless or random; seniors can get a feeling of control at a time when so much of their control seems to be slipping away from them. At the same time, the positive message of many religious traditions, as well as the opportunity to be actively involved in the activities of a faith community, helps many seniors stay upbeat and optimistic while filling useful, productive roles in the community.[14]

Finally, spiritual beliefs often imbue older individuals with hope and peace that can keep them optimistic, relieve stress, and prevent depression. Strong beliefs help seniors cope with mortality while helping them develop acceptance of the events that later life brings. Such people usually remain the type of caring, giving, forward-looking folks who live long, purposeful lives. "I find that seniors who are in touch with faith or who are aware of the presence of spirit are more contented, at peace, and more creative," says Molly Srode. "They live one day at a time, in the present."

So if you're seeking a longer, happier, healthier life, it might be smart to practice spiritual wellness—to write yourself a *prayscription*.

How Are You Spiritual?

There are many ways to express your spiritual side—in church, in your actions, in your thoughts. Write down the different ways you are spiritual in your life. What do you do? What moral, ethical, personal, or religious belief does each act reflect? What would you add or subtract?

Religious Services

Contemplation and Reflection

Acts Toward Family and Friends

Acts Toward the Greater Community, Nation, or World

LIVING WHAT THE PROPHETS PREACHED

If you take to heart the teachings of Jesus, who spoke so movingly and eloquently of compassion and healing, then you also understand the other, perhaps greater benefit of faith. Rather than simply giving you peace or hope, a spiritual foundation also enables you to give to others.

Srode says in her interview that those who understand that they are spiritual beings as well as physical beings "sense the presence of the divine in their lives. There are qualities of spirit, and when we can see them in our life, we can see that spirit. If I have been generous today, that's my spirit. If I have been compassionate, patient, loving, creative— that's my sense of the divine coming through in those qualities." Even people who consider themselves "generally spiritual" tend to have great respect for life, acts of caring and compassion for others, justice, peace over violence, and selflessness. Those who have given compassion, good- will, love, and trust to others in abundance are far more likely to get those same gifts back later in life. "I think having a strong spiritual life," says Srode. ". . . helps people live the life they were supposed to live."

Having a strong faith also helps people who are dealing with the wrenching changes that aging can bring to feel that something about them has not changed. Their bodies have gotten slower and achier, and friends and family have passed away, but the essence of who they are— their morals and values and love—are the same as they were at eighteen and forty-eight. There's a beauty to that continuity, a real sense that who we truly are transcends the temporary changes in our bodies.

PRACTICAL SPIRITUALITY

For many of us, what may have been a vague sense of "I believe in God" can become a far more urgent call to faith when we feel our bodies slowing down. Or perhaps, as you enter your Second Prime, you feel your beliefs craving a new outlet, a new mode of expression. That's healthy. Your faith should no more remain idle and static than your body should; you should always be seeking new ways to express your faith. That's what Srode calls "practical spirituality."

For most of us, practicing our spirituality means going to church. That's the most obvious, tangible expression of something larger than ourselves—a community of fellow voyagers who care for and about us and each other. For

Everybody prays whether [you think] of it as praying or not. The odd silence you fall into when something very beautiful is happening or something very good or very bad.

The ah-h-h-h! that sometimes floats up out of you as out of a Fourth of July crowd when the skyrocket bursts over the water. The stammer of pain at somebody else's pain. The stammer of joy at somebody else's joy. Whatever words or sounds you use for sighing with over your own life. These are all prayers in their way. These are all spoken not just to yourself but to something even more familiar than yourself and even more strange than the world.[5]

—FREDERICK BUECHNER

some, being part of a congregation is the ultimate expression of fellowship, belonging, and love, and the collective strength of that family is what empowers them to make a difference in their community. But faith should also manifest in other ways. So spend time to quiet your mind and touch the invisible, but then get thee to a homeless shelter. Or a museum. Or an after-school program. When you give of yourself, living with purpose, without thought of personal gain, you're touching the best of yourself. As any person of faith knows, it's not only your words that reflect your beliefs, but your actions.

Some of the most beautiful words in the Bible are surely these: "It is more blessed to give than to receive" (Acts 20:35). When we give generously of ourselves, we reap generously. And what can we give? These words from an unknown author in times past give advice that can't be beat:

> *Give strength, give thought, give deeds, give wealth;*
> *Give love, give tears, and give thyself.*
> *Give, give, be always giving.*
> *Who gives not is not living:*
> *The more you give, the more you live.*

Ask yourself, "What would Jesus do?" The answer may very well be: He'd be on the street helping people. In all likelihood, the more you seek to give yourself away, the more you will find that you have to give and desire to give.

Finally, you can seek to see the spiritual life in the ordinary chores and routines that, on the surface, may seem anything but spiritual. Every act of life has a spiritual side to it, which we often overlook. Thomas Merton once wrote: "It is in the ordinary duties and labors of life that the Christian can and should develop his spiritual union with God."[16] Begin to see what is happening around you as an opportunity to express your spiritual beliefs and love.

Agelessness Secret #8

Keep Your Balance

When you're in your 80s or 90s, a fall is a serious matter. In fact, falls are the cause of 87 percent of all fractures in people over sixty-five. And as of 1995, falls were fatal to

8,000 Americans over sixty-five. The scary truth is, the average senior only lives one year after breaking a hip.

Why? Most likely it's depression at the loss of mobility and at the sudden feeling of being "old." For an eighty-year-old who has been robust and healthy all her life to suddenly break a hip, something that "only happens to old people," can bring on negative feelings and a sense of giving up on life. If mobility is severely restricted after an injury, the loss of independence for a proudly independent person can be devastating.

What to do? Aside from keeping yourself in prime physical condition, hone and perfect your balance. Having a strong sense of balance and body awareness will help you avoid falls in your later years. It will also help you avoid having to use such devices as walkers or canes, which can also drive home the idea of being old.

Seniors should add balance exercises to their workout program. Such exercises can include standing on one leg, walking heel to toe, and taking rapid steps forward and backward. Use two hands on the back of a chair to support yourself initially then, as you progress, use one hand and then no hands. As you become very proficient at balancing, try closing your eyes when doing your exercises.

When you want to become more advanced, systems like *tai chi* and yoga are excellent for developing strong balance and strong, muscular cores. *Tai chi*'s slow, precise movements build a body awareness and body control while yoga's poses require strong muscles, especially in the lower legs and abdomen. In both cases, be sure to work with a trained, experienced instructor so you can proceed at a pace that's safe and comfortable for you.

Also, some prescription medications have been linked to a greater incidence of falls in the elderly, including benzodiazepines, anticoagulants, and drugs that cause orthostatic hypotension, or low blood pressure upon standing. If you're taking such drugs, ask your pharmacist about alternatives.[17]

THE CENTER OF OUR LIVES

Strip away the trappings of religion and ritual and you get to the essence of what faith in God means to the person in the latter third of life: a center of calm and right in a life where so much is relative. We don't always have that when we're younger; we tend to chase financial, material, and career rewards, thinking they will satisfy. But the material is, by its nature, evanescent; it fades. So we're always moving, dodging, and weaving toward the next possible source of enlightenment, peace, and harmony.

That's because the things that last never come from what's *outside* of us, only from what is *inside*: hope, honor, and most of all, love. Name a raise that meant as much to you as holding your child. Name a possession you wouldn't surrender to have a lost parent back for a day. In the end, the things that God grants us are the only ones that should occupy a place at the center of our lives. Sure, we continue to pursue material goals and try to make money in our Second Prime, but the reasons we do so should be intangible: passion, a desire to give, creativity. Those qualities can only be found when we give ourselves fully to what cannot be seen, bought, or taken, but given and felt.

On the first day, God created the cow. God said, "You must go to the field with the farmer all day long, suffer under the sun, have calves, and give milk to support the farmer. I will give you a life span of sixty years."

The cow said, "That's kind of a tough life you want me to live for sixty years. Let me have twenty years, and I'll give back the other forty." And God agreed.

On the second day, God created the dog. God said, "Sit all day by the door of your house and bark at anyone who comes in or walks past. I will give you a life span of twenty years."

The dog said, "That's too long to be barking. Give me ten years, and I'll give back the other ten." So God agreed.

On the third day, God created the monkey. God said,

"Entertain people, do monkey tricks, make them laugh. I'll give you a twenty-year life span."

The monkey said, "Monkey tricks for twenty years? I don't think so. Dog gave you back ten, so that's what I'll do, too, ok?" And God agreed again.

On the fourth day, God created man. God said, "Eat, sleep, play, have sex, enjoy. Do nothing, just enjoy, enjoy. I'll give you twenty years."

Man said, "What? Only twenty years? No way, man. Tell you what, I'll take my twenty, and the forty the cow gave back, and the ten the dog gave back, and the ten the monkey gave back. That makes eighty, okay?"

"Okay," said God. "You've got a deal."

That is why for the first twenty years we eat, sleep, play, have sex, enjoy, and do nothing; for the next forty years, we slave in the sun to support our family; for the next ten years, we do monkey tricks to entertain our grandchildren; and for the last ten years, we sit in front of the house and bark at everybody.

LIVE IN THE MOMENT

"Living in the moment is a spiritual thing," says Srode in her interview. "That's where we're with God. I think with aging, that's important. Your body does begin to go, and I see signs that it's coming. There are so many questions that aging people ask: 'What if I run out of money before I die? What if I go blind? What if I go deaf?' These are very real concerns for people moving beyond retirement to aging. If we sat around and worried about these things, we'd have no quality of life. You can't see the beautiful autumn leaves if you're worried."

Even the antiseptic world of medicine is warming to the notion that spirituality and faith may need to become part of the healing process. To be sure, there's plenty of skepticism. But the question being asked more and more in the medical community is, how might faith factor into the healing process? According to one national survey, nearly thirty US medical schools offer courses on spirituality and health, while 99 percent of the physicians at a 1999 meeting of the American Academy of Family Physicians said they believed that religious beliefs aid healing. Some doctors are even starting to take "religious histories" during office visits as well as health histories.[18]

Does this mean these trained empiricists think prayer heals from across the globe? Certainly not, though some might. It means they acknowledge that, for whatever one of the many reasons faith works, it works. It helps people stay healthier and live longer.

Senior Achiever

Ebby Halliday, 95, founder, Ebby Halliday Realtors

Ebby Halliday started her Dallas, Texas–based real estate company in 1945, and today it boasts more than twenty-eight offices, more than 1,600 independent contractors and employees, and is one of the top twenty privately-owned residential firms in the country. That's a long way from the one-woman show she began more than sixty years ago.

Her first job was working in a basement Kansas City millinery store for $10 a week in the depths of the Depression. She had little luck selling luxury items like hats at a time when people's biggest concern was where their next meal was coming from, but she learned to sell, she says. In 1938 she was transferred to Dallas. "I stepped off that train and thought I'd died and gone to heaven. It was still in the aura of the 1936 Centennial," she says.

Halliday still goes to work every day. "Work isn't work unless there's something you'd rather do," she says. "I developed my work ethic in the midst of the Depression. Everybody had to work if they wanted to eat, and you developed a habit of working. I've kept that habit all my life."

The company Halliday ("Ebby" to practically everyone) built is now a major charitable donor to the Dallas–Fort Worth community and also has its own mortgage and insurance companies as well as a relocation arm that helps people find homes in new parts of the country. Halliday herself gives plenty of pep talks to her people and keeps them motivated and is the company's face in the community and local politics.

Halliday says she's motivated to keep going because of her innate competitiveness and because she wants to leave her company in the best shape possible. "I want to leave it at the top of the game to the people who have helped me build it: my employees."

The End

Naturally, we can't have a conversation about old age and faith without talking about death. For believers, death is not the end but the beginning of a new life in heaven. Faith can give us peace and hope in the face of what, for others, is a frightening mystery.

The later years of life are not simply a time of physical and emotional crisis; they are also a time of existential crisis. Why are we here? What is the meaning of life? What are we supposed to do to make the most of our time? These questions grow in importance as we age, and not addressing them seems to us to ignore an essential element of successful aging. As Canadian psychologist and researcher Paul T. P. Wong, PhD, writes:

> The worst fear is not death, but the discovery that we have never really lived when the time comes for us to die. We all have the urge, the desire to live fully, to do something significant, to make a difference, so that we don't have to dread the death-bed realization that we have squandered away our precious life.[19]

Amen. That is the true value of spirituality in your Second Prime. It allows you to pursue your life with passion and purpose and love, to really *live* while taking comfort in knowing that whatever happens tomorrow, it will be part of a larger plan that leaves nothing to chance. And that, friends, is a blessing in any creed.

A grandfather and his grandson were out for a walk one evening when the boy asked one of those questions that children seem to spring upon their elders without warning, "Gramps, what is dying like?"

The grandfather pointed toward the lights that were starting to come on in various houses along the street.

"I think it's like this," he said. "We're out on a walk with God one evening, and when we reach the street corner, He turns to us and says, 'Why don't you spend the night at my house tonight?' And we do."

Second Prime Strategy—Spirituality

1. Things to Do

- Learn about your family's spiritual traditions.
- Look at your own values, morals, and ethics.
- Write down the things that give your life meaning.
- Find out about opportunities for service in your congregation.
- List your spiritual beliefs.
- List your spiritual doubts.
- Talk to your attorney about an ethical will.
- Seek out opportunities for spiritual growth in your congregation.

2. Changes You Need to Make for a Better Spiritual Life

3. Your Spiritual Goals for Your Second Prime

Example: "Be more active in my spiritual community, volunteer more often."

4. Spirituality Resources

- Christian Community Health Fellowship (www.cchf.org)
- The Intersection of Faith & Life (www.crosswalk.com)
- *Christianity Today* (www.christianitytoday.com)
- Elder Hope (www.elderhope.com)
- Christian Answers (www.christiananswers.net)

Attitude *or* Be Regretless

A man's liberal and conservative phases seem to follow each other in a succession of waves from the time he is born. Children are radicals. Youths are conservatives, with a dash of criminal negligence. Men in their prime are liberals (as long as their digestion keeps pace with their intellect). The middle-aged . . . run to shelter: they insure their life, draft a will, accumulate mementos and occasional tables, and hope for security. And then comes old age, which repeats childhood—a time full of humors and sadness, but often full of courage and even prophecy.[1]

—E. B. WHITE

Old wood best to burn, old wine to drink, old friends to trust, and old authors to read.[2]

—FRANCIS BACON

Backward or forward? That's your choice. You can choose to look backward and relive the past's failures, injuries, and missed opportunities. Or you can choose to learn from the past and look ahead to the adventures and possibilities that lie in your future. Which you choose to do will have a great deal to do with whether you spend your Second Prime active, vigorous, and hopeful or bitter, angry, and frail.

If age is a coat of many colors, attitude is what determines the color the coat will be. A positive attitude is the color of life: vibrant magenta, rich vermillion, emerald green. A negative attitude drapes you in the hues of death and loneliness: black, ash gray, muddy brown. Your attitude is nothing more or less than how you respond to and explain the multitudinous events, people, and turns of fortune that life throws your way every day. Earlier, we looked at Martin Seligman's concept of "learned helplessness," in which each of us chooses how to explain our failures—either internalized and due to personal shortcomings we are doomed to suffer with or externalized and due to circumstances that we can change. Attitude in general is based on the same concept: how you choose to explain the events of life determines your attitude toward life and, in turn, the quality of that life.

For example, you're an old person living in a retirement community. One day you notice that a small piece of statuary that stands outside your charming house is gone. You react to this by:

a. Concluding that some young vandals must have gotten into your gated Nirvana and stolen your statue, and calling down angry damnation on everyone under twenty-five for the rest of your days.

b. Chalking it up to some person or persons and harrumphing that it's just one more example of how messed up the world is.

c. Scratching your head and thinking, "Hmm, that's funny," and starting an investigation. Eventually, you realize that you removed the statue because your late mother-in-law gave it to you and your wife, and you always thought it was ugly. You put it in the garage and, because you're an Old Geezer whose mind is going, forgot about it. Case solved.

The point (other than that you need a new statue and a trip to the Home Depot is in order) is that the way you choose to explain the things that happen to you determines your attitude. Attitude is a habit. You either choose to perceive yourself as a victim of a specific target ("young people are all punks"), a victim of the whole world ("the whole world is going to hell in a handbasket"), or as the recipient, not of any specific malice, but of random chance or even misunderstanding. It's easy to see how the first two choices would lead you to develop a bunker mentality in which everyone else is the enemy. With the third choice, you simply have a "stuff happens" mentality in which you shrug and let the problem go or figure there must be a sensible reason behind it and set out to find it.

The Senility Prayer

God, grant me the Senility
To forget the people
I never liked anyway,
The good fortune
To run into the ones I do,
And the eyesight
To tell the difference.

HOPE TRAINING

Even the way you regard positive occurrences becomes a habit. Some people, as the bumper stickers say, expect a miracle. They know that if they do good, good comes back to them. When positive things happen, they're not surprised. Others assume that good fortune is a fluke and that fate will turn around and bite them as payback for having something good happen. These are the kinds of folks who, if they won the lottery, would say, "Sure, and I bet I get run down by a bus next week."

Do you know people like this? Tiring, aren't they? You want to shake their eyes open so they'll see their blessings. In the end, some people have trained themselves for *hope* while others have trained themselves for *despair*. You can sense them a mile off; they have their own body language, their own aura. We call the hope-trained "mailbox watchers" because they're like the kids who, once upon a time, would wait for the mailman to deliver the new *Saturday Evening Post* or *Collier's* magazine, certain that something good was on the way every day. They're relentlessly positive and powerful, always expecting good things, confident that even though things might not look so great now, they're sure to get better. Frequently, they're people of very deep faith who draw a sense that "something better is coming" from their beliefs. The funny thing is, it's not uncommon for such people to be poor, live in the worst areas, or suffer from debilitating physical conditions. And yet they achieve great things.

The late Christopher Reeve was such a hope-trained individual. Here was a man who, due to a terrible accident, had gone from being physically unstoppable to being a quadriplegic. If any man had a right to be furious at God and fate, it was this man. But he made a choice to train for hope, and that hope carried him not only back to acting and directing but also to becoming a global spokesman for research into treating spinal cord injury. We throw the word *hero* around pretty blithely these days, but Chris Reeve was the genuine article.

At the same time, it's not hard to find people who seem to have everything—money, power, position—who are trained in despair. They are the people we call "duck and covers" because they're always expecting disaster. They might drive a beautiful car and live in a huge house, but they're always convinced someone is about to mount an assault on what they have. They regard much of the world—especially people who are not exactly like them—with suspicion, distrust, and fear.

It's like the two boys who were each placed in a room. One boy was put in a room with a pony, and he spent all his time crying, worried that someone would take the pony away. The other boy was put in a room with a pile of horse manure, and he immediately dove into the pile and started digging, crowing, "There's got to be a pony in here somewhere!"

As you move into your old age—as you decide how you will be old— you must choose whether you will look forward or look back. As we'll talk about in this chapter, everything comes down to a single word: *regret*.

Agelessness Secret #9

See Your Dentist

Nobody likes going to the dentist, but if you want to keep your teeth well into old age, you go anyway. But there's evidence that going regularly might do a lot more than help you avoid dentures and implants.

In a 2004 journal report, the American Heart Association revealed that numerous studies had shown that oral health was a more reliable predictor of coronary disease than many other markers. In short, your oral health affects your risk for coronary disease.

Researchers identified five types of oral disease that are now thought to produce the inflammation associated with cardiac disease. And inflammation is now thought to be one of the major causes for many of the deadliest diseases that kill older Americans. There isn't a firm link yet that says that oral disease causes heart disease, but the two definitely appear to be linked.

Still not enough to get you in for a cleaning every six months? Well, there's more. Research now also shows that Caucasians with periodontal disease (bone loss due to infection) have a 15 to 18 percent greater stroke risk than those with healthy teeth. Scientists think this is due to the high risk of infection so close to the brain. Think about it; bacteria only need to travel a few inches from your jawbone to the blood vessels in your brain, which can lead to clots and eventually stroke.

Most dentists and dental researchers agree that poor oral hygiene is a health risk because it introduces infection into the body on a daily basis. So it becomes more important than you thought to see your dentist regularly for a thorough cleaning. And there's one more factor linked to good oral health: people with poor oral hygiene—and thus, poor teeth—tend not to get the proper nutrition that their body, especially their heart, needs. If you can't eat a balanced diet becaused your mouth hurts, you're going to lack some nutrients.[3]

If you've been going like clockwork to the dentist for years, congratulations. Good for you. If you don't go anymore, maybe it's time to ask for a referral.

REGRET IS A TIME MACHINE

Physicists and experts in relativity will tell you that there is no such thing as time travel. Nonsense. Time travel is real; it exists in our minds. We choose to live forward or backward, in the future or the past, all while our bodies continue to exist in the present.

Regret, or the lack of it, is the only real time machine. Regret is the fuel behind the dark negative clouds that some older people seem to live under. These are the people who live out the unfortunate stereotype of old people as cranky, resentful, fearful, and cynical. Nobody gets to seventy and says, "Well, I'm going to be a nasty, unpleasant humbug without a kind word to say to anyone because darned if that won't make my golden years more enjoyable!" No, such people are assembled one grudge at a time, over decades. These are the curmudgeons who can't seem to get their heads out of the past; if they're not dwelling on a hurt that happened thirty years ago, they're approaching the affairs of today as though the same hurt is waiting to pounce on them again.

We feel regret over missed opportunities, risks not taken, loves lost. When we fail to embrace life, chase our passions, and try to live our dreams, we build an armor of regrets. In the end, that armor keeps out the rest of the world, separating us from those who might bring hope and love into our lives. Worst of all, regret makes us despise those who *have* lived their dreams because in them, we see our own failures. A senior living a life filled with regret is living in the past, traveling back in time every day to relive decisions that might have been made a different way but cannot be. It's the time travel paradox: you might be able to travel to the past, but you can't change it.

One more thing about regret: it's a mistake reminding you to learn. Don't relive your regrets, but learn from them. If a decision caused you pain in the past, don't make the same mistake again. That's how you turn past pain into future joy.

Old Folks' Party Games

- Musical Recliners
- Spin the Bottle of Mylanta
- Simon Says Something Incoherent
- Doc, Doc Goose
- Red Rover, Red Rover, the Nurse Says Bend Over

- Kick the Bucket
- Twenty Questions Shouted into Your Good Ear
- Pin the Toupee on the Bald Guy
- Sag, You're It!

Don't Regret. Re-Great!

A life built on regret is a tragedy. But that's not the only choice. You can choose to live with the opposite of regret, which we call *re-great*. That means every day you're looking forward to a future of optimism and possibility. You've made peace with the choices of your past, and while you've gained wisdom from them, you don't dwell on them. The past is done. The future is ahead of you, and the possibilities are without limit. Every day is a revival of hope and potential.

Living with re-great is also time travel, but in this case you're traveling into the future, imagining what can be. This is what Dr. Norman Vincent Peale called "positive thinking." Peale was a true visionary, the man who inspired Art Linkletter to turn his life toward preventing drug abuse after the drug-related suicide of Art's daughter. Dr. Peale taught that you can condition your mind to think positively. In doing so, you create your own reality. Where regret leads you to see the world with suspicion and fear, re-great leads you to regard life as a canvas waiting for you to create your masterpiece.

This is the power of attitude in determining whether you get old or grow old:

No matter what money or abilities you bring to your plan for
your old age, your attitude will determine its outcome.

Think about that. You could be a multimillionaire, but if you enter your later years with a negative, defeatist attitude full of resentments and grudges, you will not have a Second Prime. You will rot away in a dark room. Your attitude toward life shapes your ability to shape the future. A positive attitude attracts people to you, energizes you to make changes, inspires you to "color outside the lines." A negative attitude drives people away, makes you quit at the first sign of difficulty, convinces you that things are beyond your abilities. *Attitude affects the outcome.*

Regret chains you to the past, both its injuries and its failures, and takes energy from you. Positive thinking or *re-great* makes peace with the past, points you to the possibilities of a hopeful future, and gives you more energy.

ATTITUDE AFFECTS YOUR HEALTH

All right, so a positive attitude is motivating and empowering. No surprise there. But what if we told you that rejecting regret and living with re-great is actually good for your health and longevity?

It's part of our collective wisdom—along with eating your vegetables and getting a good night's sleep—that keeping a positive outlook is good for our health. But in the rush to give our genetics credit or blame for everything that happens to our bodies, that bit of wisdom was forgotten. Now with the new knowledge that lifestyle is 70 to 75 percent of our longevity, we're starting

> *The process of maturing is an art to be learned, an effort to be sustained. By the age of fifty you have made yourself what you are, and if it is good, it is better than your youth.*[4]
>
> —MARYA MANNES

to accept that where the mind goes, the body follows. And there's scientific evidence that a positive attitude does equal living longer.

A 2002 Yale University study of 338 men and 322 women in the same small Ohio town looked at how the subjects responded to certain statements about aging such as, "As you get older, you are less useful." The responses allowed the researchers to categorize the people according to their self-perceptions about age and age-related stereotypes. Then they waited. The results were shocking: the test subjects with a positive self-image lived seven-and-a-half years longer than those with a negative self-image—a greater benefit than is gained by maintaining a healthy weight, exercising regularly, or not smoking! Even after taking into account factors such as age, gender, socioeconomic status, self-reported health, and level of social interaction, those people with a sunny outlook out-lived the others.

The researchers found that people acquire stereotypes about aging decades before they themselves become old, and thus are preconditioned to think about age in a certain way that they never question. If they see old people as wise, they will think themselves wise in their old age, whereas if they are conditioned to think of seniors as senile, that will become their self-fulfilling self-perception. The researchers also wrote something that validates the mission of this book: "The negative self-perceptions of aging reported in this study may reflect a societally sanc-tioned denigration of the aged, and . . . ideally an effort will be made to counter these views and actions directed at the elderly."[5]

Remember the Ten Myths? That's precisely what we're talking about: the stereotypes of the old as frail, flatulent, and feeble. It's absolutely critical that you and all Baby Boomers learn to defy and refute those debilitating ideas because they do become self-fulfilling prophecies. Writing about the Yale study, public health specialist Amy Scholten says the researchers suggest a variety of approaches to combat negative soci-etal stereotypes of aging:

- Emphasizing positive stereotypes of aging among young people by promoting more interaction and activities between the generations
- Encouraging older people to become more aware of the negative stereotypes about aging that they receive from others
- Helping older people become aware of the ways in which they target themselves with negative stereotypes about aging
- Increasing awareness of the negative impact of stigmatization[6]

We'd like to add one more: making sure you pass your copy of *How to Make the Rest of Your Life the Best of Your Life* on to at least three other people. At long last, we've outlived and outlasted the timeworn stereotypes.

As Archie Bunker Would Say, "Laugh, Dingbat!"

Author and Georgetown University Medical School professor Dr. Candace Pert states in her book, *The Molecules of Emotion*, that the messages of the emotions we experience are stored in our bodies—and particularly our brains—as chemical messages. These chemical messages influence how easily we get sick and how well our bodies' natural defense systems respond to disease. Maintain a positive attitude and a sense of humor, she says, and your chemical messages are more likely to work for you, rather than against you.[7]

But you've always known that laughter and humor feel great. Physiologists and physicians have known for years that the act of laughing has real cardiovascular benefits. Laughter lowers stress, reduces blood pressure, and even enhances the body's immune system. Beyond the laboratory benefits, humor just feels great. When you have a terrific sense of humor, you attract others to you, handle the ups and downs of life more easily, and walk around in a much better mood. Think about grandparents or other elders you've known in your life, and think about how much you enjoyed the ones who always seemed to have jokes to tell and always had a twinkle in their eye. Humor and shared pleasure with others improve life.

In the central place of every heart there is a recording chamber. So long as it receives a message of beauty, hope, cheer, and courage—so long are you young. When the wires are all down and our heart is covered with the snow of pessimism and the ice of cynicism, then, and only then, are you grown old indeed![8]

—Samuel Ullman

One man who knows that intimately is television legend Norman Lear, who created such landmark programs as *All in the Family* and *Maude*, and who, along with luminaries like Sid Caesar, Neil Simon, and Mel Brooks, is often credited with inventing modern television comedy. Lear, a spry eighty-three, still has a wicked sense of humor, but after becoming a father again late in life, this former hard-driving TV writer who loved eating dinners alone with his thoughts is revitalized by time with his family. In our interview, Lear says, "My ambition is to be the best that I can be in every moment, whatever that moment happens to be about. This morning I woke up at 6:15, woke up one daughter who had an early medical appointment, woke up the other daughter a little bit later, made breakfast for both, then woke up my son. Those moments were as important to me as receiving an award or picking up the newspaper and reading my name. They're the moments that are really what success is all about. Robert Louis Stevenson said it is a better thing to travel hopefully than to arrive. That says it all too."

Senior Achiever

Richard Hankins, 76, American Airlines mechanic

Dick Hankins started working as an aircraft mechanic at TWA when the Korean War was raging and air travel was an adventure. Fifty-five years later, he still works a full week at American Airlines (which merged with TWA in 2001) doing nondestructive testing on aircraft, looking for flaws that might damage a plane in flight. A Christian, fit grandfather of two who still plays beach volleyball at family reunions, he relishes the fact that his work plays such an important role in safety.

"You don't wait until something's broken; you try to anticipate," he says. "A plane is not like a taxicab where you can pull it over to the curb when something goes wrong. There's only one place for that aircraft to go, and that's down."

For his long service, Hankins earned the prestigious Charles Taylor Master Mechanic Award in 2001. The honor is named for the bicycle mechanic who, working with the Wright Brothers, became the first aviation mechanic in powered flight. "It's an elite group, because you've been drawing Social Security for some time before you're even eligible," says Hankins. "It's hard to find people who have been working continuously that long."

But Hankins has discovered other passions as well. Late in life, he has become a lay humanitarian activist, having visited South Africa during a world peace conference, helped ferry supplies to the poor in Haiti, and now is planning a trip to Jordan to talk about aviation careers. There's the possibility of even more travel as he considers turning to a consulting role as his fifty-fifth anniversary in aviation looms. But, he insists, he will always work.

"In the words of my longtime friend Bessie Baldwin, 'I'd rather wear out than rust out,'" he says. "I work because there's work to do."

LIVING REGRETLESS

Here's the difficult part: If you've reached fifty, fifty-five, or sixty with a negative outlook on life, a cargo of regret on your shoulders, or no sense of humor, how do you develop positive thinking habits? Like most of us, you know from experience that it's very difficult to change the habits of years or decades. So how do you live without regret?

Like all things in this book, you make a choice. That choice has four aspects to it:

1. *Close the book of past pains.* If you constantly dwell on the slights, injuries, heartbreaks, and failures of your past, the first step to living regretless is to stop dwelling on them. Haul them out into the light, have one last long look at them, and let them go. Close those chapters of your life that make you feel like sitting in a dark room and fingering worry beads. Of course, letting go of a painful past is more than just a matter of saying, "I let it go." But you have to start somewhere, and that means one day standing up and saying, "I will no longer be haunted by the past," then reaffirming that again and again until you develop a new set of mental habits that look forward, not back. That's training for hope.

2. *Set goals for the future.* Goal setting is a proven aspect of any self-improvement program. To get where you want to go, you need to have some idea of where you're going. Living without regret means living with purpose and passion, and both demand that you strive toward

something. That means setting specific goals for yourself. Goals give you something to look forward to, get you moving and keep you moving, and help you formulate defined plans. Without goals, life is ill-defined and hazy. With goals, life sharpens. The unimportant drops away, and the important comes into focus. Look at setting goals in different areas:

- Career
- Art
- Health
- Relationships
- Travel
- Money

3. Do what you've always wanted to do. This is the most important aspect of the regretless lifestyle. Many of life's harshest regrets are of the "I wish I had" school. We believe there's no greater sadness than someone on his deathbed saying, "I wish I had . . ." So to live regretless, give yourself permission to do the things you've always wanted to do. Was there something you wanted to do in your 30s but didn't? Do it now. Is there something you want to do now but have been saying, "Maybe next year . . ."? Forget next year. Do it now. The beauty of doing what you've always wanted is that you're following your passion, and there's nothing more energizing and revivifying than that.

4. Affirm your new view every day. Affirmations have tremendous power. Simply speaking an idea increases the chances of it coming to pass. Each day when you wake up, repeat to yourself a mantra that represents your new view of your past and your future. Try such positive statements as:

- "The events of my past are finished and have no power over me."
- "I am a force for positive change and I am moving ahead to do great things."
- "My past failures are only lessons that I apply in gaining wisdom."
- "There is no limit to what I can achieve in the next twenty years."
- "I am vital and powerful, and I am living my dreams each day."

These phrases and others like them will help you retrain your mind for hope, optimism, and positive action. A life-affirming attitude—just like smoking, exercise, or watching a certain TV program—can become a habit. With discipline you will rewire your brain and transform your thought process until thinking positively is as natural as breathing.

Try the Live Regretless exercise to begin your journey toward a life without regret and full of promise and purpose.

Live Regretless!

Based on the four steps to living regretless, complete this exercise. This will become your blueprint toward a daily retraining of your mind toward a positive, "the possibilities are endless" attitude.

1. Close the Book on Past Pains
What hurts or regrets from your past still haunt you today? Write down each one, including the reason it still darkens your life. Once you have admitted to yourself what is holding you back, you can take steps to rid yourself of the regret.

Pain #1:

Pain #2:

Pain #3:

2. Set Goals for the Future
Part of looking ahead is having ambitions for the years to come. Write down the three goals you would most like to achieve in the next five to ten years, including when you would like to achieve that goal and, most important, the first steps you need to take to make that goal a reality.

Goal #1:

To be achieved by:

Steps to take to achieve the goal:
1)
2)
3)

Goal #2:

To be achieved by:

Steps to take to achieve the goal:
1)
2)
3)

Goal #3:

To be achieved by:

Steps to take to achieve the goal:
1)
2)
3)

---

3. Do What You've Always Wanted to Do

Write down the things you've always wanted to do but haven't . . . yet.
Then for each, write down the first step you'll take toward finally doing it.

I've always wanted to:
First step:

I've always wanted to:
First step:

I've always wanted to:
First step:

---

4. Affirmations
Write down three to five affirmations you can say to yourself every day to retrain your mind.

Affirmation #1: Example: "I am healthy, happy, and excited to be alive and contributing greatly to everyone I meet."

Affirmation #2: Example: "I am a genius and use my genius in every way to make the world better."

Affirmation #3:

Affirmation #4:

Affirmation #5:

LIVE AT FULL VOLUME, IN FULL COLOR

Have you always wanted to have adventures? Live in the lap of luxury for a time if you can afford it? Climb a mountain? If you're financially secure and in good health, why aren't you doing what you've always wanted to? It's not uncommon for older people to get so set in their ways that they set up barriers for themselves in which any act that lies outside their narrow experience is reflexively rejected. Financial gerontologist Donald Haas told us about clients of his who have always wanted to fly first class or buy a flashy new car, and have the cash to do so, but won't let themselves do it. They still think like financially constrained people, or they tell themselves that pleasure is somehow unseemly.

Don't buy it! Living with pleasure and joy is one of the purposes of living at all! When you live your life with the maximum delight and accomplishment, you're honoring creation. You're living as you were intended to. Have adventures. Give yourself permission to do things you've never done before. Remember, your Second Prime is a new era of your life. Travel on your own, without a tour group, relying on your mind and instincts to navigate the medina of Marrakech or the tracks of the Australian outback. Work with organizations like Earthwatch to get your hands dirty in scientific projects around the globe, tagging sea turtles or digging for Etruscan artifacts. Write a book and get it published. Run your first marathon. Read the collected works of Dickens, Hemingway, and Swift. Make your life a masterpiece.

Second Prime Strategy—Attitude

1. Things to Do

- Examine past failures or hurts and identify the ones that hold you back.
- Resolve to close the book on your past, relying on it only for wisdom.
- Develop daily affirmations that train your mind to think about the future.
- Find the things you had always wanted to do in your younger days and do them.
- Develop a list of a few things you want to do now and do them.
- Set goals for five, ten, and twenty years hence.
- Associate with people who are positive.

2. Changes You Need to Make to Develop a Regretless Attitude

-
-
-
-
-

3. Your Attitude Goals for Your Second Prime

Example: "Meet ten new people who have a relentlessly positive outlook on life."

-
-
-
-
-

4. Attitude Resources

- AARP (www.aarp.org)
- Time Goes By (www.timegoesby.net)
- Fearless Aging (www.fearless-aging.com)
- Positive Attitude Institute (www.positiveinstitute.com)
- Dr. Wayne Dyer (www.drwaynedyer.com)

Creativity *or* What's Grandma Moses Got That You Ain't Got?

> One of the few graces of getting old—and God knows there are
> few graces—is that if you've worked hard and kept your nose
> to the grindstone, something happens: the body gets old but
> the creative mechanism is refreshed, smoothed and oiled
> and honed. That is the grace. That is what's happening to me.[1]
>
> —MAURICE SENDAK

> Whoever undertakes to create soon finds himself engaged in
> creating himself. Self-transformation and the transforma-
> tion of others have constituted the radical interest of our
> century, whether in painting, psychiatry, or political action.[2]
>
> —HAROLD ROSENBERG

I t's a full house, filled with that low susurration of hundreds of people when they're whispering to each other in anticipation. The lights go down and silence falls. Then . . . wow! The small stage is filled with dapper men in tuxedos and spats and lovely ladies in magnificent ornate costumes that look like they belong at the Moulin Rouge. Together they tap, soft shoe, kick impossibly high, sing, and for more than three hours project enough joy, sex appeal, and confidence to light up the city of Palm Springs, California, where this spectacle takes place.

The catch? You've probably got it figured out. Every one of these high-stepping performers is old enough to get the senior citizen discount at a movie theater. This is the Fabulous Palm Springs Follies, a world-famous musical revue and vaudeville-style extravaganza that's been packing the house in this desert city since 1990. And if you think we're talking about cute little tap dancing grandmas like you'd see in your local assisted living center's annual Christmas variety show, think again. This is professional song and dance, and the performers are all seasoned professionals with decades of experience on the Broadway stage.

CREATIVITY IS LIKE CHEESE

We'll get back to the Follies performers in short order. But first, let's talk about creativity. In this book, we've looked at a lot of aspects of growing old, and with many of them—body, mind, sex, attitude—you're simply trying to stave off the ravages of time and keep what you had when you were in your 30s and 40s, right? But creativity is different. The beauty of having a creative element to your Second Prime is that creativity is one of the few things that actually *get better as you age*. Operatic sopranos don't begin to reach their peak until they reach their mid-30s; Placido Domingo is still singing Wagner at sixty-five. Actor Eli Wallach, ninety, just published his autobiography, *The Good, the Bad and Me: In My Anecdotage*. Woody Allen continues to churn out intellectually rich films at seventy. Choreographer Twyla Tharp continues to bring musicals to Broadway at sixty-four. Little Richard is still playing concerts at seventy-three. Rita Moreno dances and is still appearing in films at seventy-four.

B. B. King reigns as king of the blues at seventy-six. Jazz icon Dave Brubeck is still "taking five" at eighty-five. Dick Francis continues to turn out mysteries about the world of horse racing after eight-and-a-half decades. At eighty-four, comedienne and actress Betty White has become an activist for animal rights. Painter David Hockney, sixty-eight, goes on working and mentoring younger artists. Legendary folk singer and activist Pete Seeger plays before packed houses at eighty-six. Madeleine L'Engle, author of the beloved *A Wrinkle in Time*, recently published her latest book of poems, *Many Waters*, at eighty-seven. Quincy Jones carries on writing brilliant film scores and making music at seventy-three. At seventy-six, Stephen Sondheim continues to revolutionize American musical theatre. Poet and historian Maya Angelou is considered a national treasure at seventy-eight. Norman Mailer carries on with his stunning, muscular, classically American prose at eighty-three.

We could go on. And on. And on. But by now the message should be clear: creativity is hardly the bailiwick of the young. In fact, the opposite almost seems to be true: people's creative powers—writing, design, music, composition, choreography, architecture, painting, sculpture, and so on—seem to be enhanced by time, experience, and a deeper understanding of life's joys, sorrows, and lessons. Even if physical abilities wane, the compensatory deepening of skills and insight allow great artists to explore new dimensions of their abilities. So the dancer becomes teacher or choreographer while the concert pianist takes up the baton. If art resides in the mind and spirit, and age only makes both more sublime and complex, then age and art grow together in beauty.

How Can You Make a Living with Your Creativity?

Maybe you don't care about making money with your creative work. That's fine. But if you do, you've got to figure out how. Complete this exercise, and you'll be on your way.

1. What do you do?
What's your creative pursuit? Be specific. Don't just write, "I paint." Write "I paint desert landscapes with watercolor."

My creative work:

2. Who Might Buy Your Creative Work?
Here you're speculating about markets, people who might pay for the creativity you can offer. For example, if you're a professional storyteller, your possible audiences might be schools, cultural festivals, community centers, private parties, and even churches. List all you can think of.

Possible market #1:

Possible market #2:

Possible market #3:

Possible market #4:

Possible market #5:

---

3. How Will You Reach Your Markets?

It might be enough to take your photographs to gallery owners. Then again, it might not. Do you need to advertise? Get a story written about you in the local paper? Sell on the Internet? Time to think like an entrepreneur?

---

4. What Are Your Goals?

Set specific goals for your first year.

- Do I want to earn a living doing this?
- How much do I want to earn per month?
- How much time per month do I want to spend marketing my work?
- How much time do I want to have per month to be creative?

CREATIVITY MAKES EACH DAY NEW

The years that come after you quit working for someone else can be the most creative of your life. You have more time to pursue your creative work, more experience with what does and doesn't produce the best results, and hopefully a more profound sense of what inspires you. For seniors, developing a creative facet to life—or if you already have one, expanding it and turning it into something greater—not only can add joy and fulfillment to life but also can help you live longer and better.

Keep in mind, we're not just talking about writing, painting, acting, making short films, or singing. Woodcarving, quilting, building furniture, flower arranging, speaking, landscaping—dozens of pursuits can be considered creative. What matters is that you're tapping your imagination and skills to bring something into being that didn't exist before you started. In fact, creativity doesn't have to have anything to do with the physical act of creation; it's a state of mind.

"Creativity is by no means limited to artists," write Nohl Martin Fouroohi and Ellen Liu Kellor of My New Friend, life care consultants offering specialized services and support for elders, people with special needs, and their families:

> It is something that all of us can draw upon to refresh, invigorate, heal, and connect. There is a multitude of ways to be creative in our lives. It may involve paint or canvas, storytelling, choosing our clothes, gift giving during the holidays, or even the way we arrange our home. Creativity and its many forms are boundless. For seniors, using art to communicate and to process the complex events in their life opens a new window to the world. Artistic endeavors help seniors stay engaged in life, bringing happy memories alive, bridging the past with the present, and offering choice and control. Writing life stories, making memory books, and organizing photo albums can connect those in someone's life today with those from their past, helping to keep alive a part of themselves. Identity-loss or change may be experienced due to a loss of a spouse, family members, retirement, or a move, which may lead to depression. Creative activity has been shown to reduce depression and isolation [by] offering the power of choice and decisions, two aspects that seniors may feel they are losing. Simple choices such as whether to have a plant in one's room, the arrangement of furniture, picking the time and night of the movie, and which vegetable to eat had a profound impact on the health and well-being of the elderly in a nursing home . . . Choice and creativity go hand in hand with optimizing health and longevity.[3]

The power of creativity dovetails beautifully with the other non-physical aspects of healthy aging that we've discussed. The creative act is a mental workout demanding that decisions be made about composition, materials, sound, light, people, everything under the sun. Thus, it's a challenge for the mind, which needs challenges to stave off cognitive impairment. The creative act is always changing; writers talk about their characters taking over the story while sculptors remark that the stone shows them the shape that's inside it. Every creative endeavor is filled with surprises and stimulation; tedium is impossible. The creative act is an act of control. You as the creator are entirely responsible for what appears on the stage, the screen, or the canvas. At a time of life when many people feel they have little control, creation grants them complete control over the life and death of an idea. If something isn't working, you don't have to tolerate it. You reject it and begin again.

Perhaps most important, creativity is purpose. We'll talk more about purpose in the next chapter, but suffice it to say this: without purpose and meaning, there is no life. The creative individual has purpose; every day is filled with it. Every day comes complete with new brainstorms, frustrations, conundrums, and flashes of brilliance. No wonder the truly creative never retire. Who would want to?

"Oh, I sure am glad to see you," the little boy said to his maternal grandmother. "Now Daddy will do the trick he's been promising us."

The grandmother was curious. "What trick is that?" she asked.

"He told Mommy that he'd climb the walls if you came to visit," answered the boy.

THE CREATIVE AGE

Even better, there is a growing body of evidence that suggests creativity actually improves brain health. At the forefront of this work is Gene

D. Cohen, MD, PhD, director and professor of health-care sciences and psychiatry at the Center on Aging, Health & Humanities at George Washington University and the author of *The Creative Age: Awakening Human Potential in the Second Half of Life*. Cohen has led a twenty-five-year study looking at creativity and aging in 200-plus seniors. In his book, Cohen states that lengthy research shows creative endeavors actually improve memory and brain function by reinforcing connections between cells, especially those linked to memory. He says that being creative improves morale and mood to help prevent depression and feelings of isolation, helps seniors respond to problems in healthier ways, improves sleep by challenging the brain, and even improves the immune system by fostering an overall more positive outlook on life. Writes Cohen in his book:

> Creativity strengthens our morale in later life. Creativity allows us to alter our experience of problems, and sometimes to transcend them, in later life. Part of the nature of creativity is its engaging and sustaining quality—no matter what our actual physical condition, we *feel better* when we are able to view our circumstances with fresh perspective and express ourselves with some creativity. Creativity makes us more emotionally resilient and better able to cope with life's adversity and losses. Just as exercise improves our muscle tone, when we are creatively engaged, our emotional tone is elevated.

Cohen also waxes eloquent on the health benefits of creative work:

> Creativity contributes to physical health as we age. Increasing numbers of findings from psychoneuroimmunological studies—research that examines the interaction of our emotions, our brain function, and our immune system—suggest that a positive outlook and a sense of well-being have a beneficial effect on the function of our immune system and our overall health. These findings are particularly strong among older persons.

Creative expression typically fosters feelings that can improve outlook and a sense of well-being. Just as chronic unrelieved stress has a detrimental effect on the immune system, continuing creativity, by promoting the expression of emotions, promotes an immune system boost.[4]

Such findings have fueled the development of a new approach to mind and brain exercise called *neurobics*. Cocreated by Dr. Lawrence C. Katz, PhD, a neurobiologist at Duke University Medical Center, neurobics confirms what we talked about in the mind chapter: an active and creative mind is a healthy mind. Katz and cocreator Manning Rubin, in their neurobics book, *Keep Your Brain Alive*, state that by using the five senses and the emotions to shake up your everyday routines and challenge your brain to think in new ways, you stimulate the brain to produce natural growth factors called *neurotrophins*, which fight the effects of mental aging. In essence, the more new ways you find to use your mind, the younger your mind will remain.[6] And since creativity is all about using your mind to bring something new and unexpected into being, having a strong creative life in your later years would seem to be the perfect prescription for keeping your brain not only alive but also dancing the tango.

> *The faster you blurt, the more swiftly you write, the more honest you are. In hesitation is thought. In delay comes the effort for a style, instead of leaping upon truth which is the only style worth dead-falling or tiger-trapping. In between the scurries and flights, what? Be a chameleon, ink-blend, chromosome change with the landscape. Be a pet rock, lie with the dust, rest in the rainwater in the filled barrel by the drain spout outside your grandparents' window long ago.*[5]
>
> —RAY BRADBURY

THE SHOW—AND LIFE—MUST GO ON

Now let's return to the Follies performers. To see a performance of the Fabulous Palm Springs Follies is to be amazed by the acrobatic dancing and vocal talents of men and women who are old enough to have performed on Broadway during World War II; to meet them in person is to be still more amazed by their energy, humor, and incredible vitality. In a postshow interview, they all said essentially the same thing: the show is what keeps them really, truly alive.

"If you're going to think old, you're going to be old," says Dorothy Kloss, the oldest performer in the show at eighty-two and, like her compatriots, a stylish, fit, vivacious professional. "Everyone in the Follies, none of us feel that we're old. When we hit that stage, it's like dynamite." A room of Follies performers—all of whom have spent most or all of their lives performing on the professional stage—radiates good humor, positive energy, and confidence, and why not? These are people who are dancing, singing, and acting at a very high level at a time when most of their contemporaries are in assisted living. There's a connection, and it's not just physical, though a lifetime of staying in shape for the stage doesn't hurt.

"I started in the business when I was eight years old, and I'm seventy-six now," says Dick France. "I just had a heart attack last year, I had quadruple bypass surgery, and I'm still in it." Did he ever think about not coming back? Briefly. But boredom overcame any fears he had about his health.

"I was born and raised in this business," he says. "I love this business, it makes me want to get up in the morning. It inspires me. And these are my friends. We're still a society all our own, we have our own sense of humor, we dress a certain way, and when you're not in your group of people, you're lonely."

Anyone who has spent years in the arts knows that after a while performers become family—supporting each other, sharing their joys and sorrows, and insulting each other in the way that only people who love each other can. Hank Brunjes, seventy-three, and Leila Burgess, seventy (who wears many hats as performer, company dance manager, and creative consultant), went to the same high school, and that bond between performers stayed strong over the years, so much so that in 2000, when Brunjes was grieving over the loss of his parents and doubtful about auditioning for the Follies, calls from Burgess and many other cast members finally convinced him to make the trip.

"He came out to the audition, and he looked awful," says Burgess to roars of laughter. "When we were in high school, I had a crush on him. But here he is, and he auditions, and he's a nervous wreck."

The producers hired him, but Brunjes was still dubious about performing. Burgess didn't let him mope for long. "She said to me, 'Why don't you go down to the nursing home down the street and you can drool with the rest of them,'" he says. "Then she hung up on me. And I stood there in my kitchen by myself, thinking, *Leila, I'm coming!* And that was it. I realize now that I'm really a big ham, and I'm enjoying it more and more. As you get older it's like, 'Wow, the energy I'm getting!'"

One of the central tenets of creativity is that it gives not only to those who create but also to those who witness. That's certainly true, say the Follies performers, of the people who come to see the show. The comment they hear most often from audience members? "That we inspire them," says France. "They say, 'If they can do it, we can do more than we're doing. Not dance, but live.'"

Burgess agrees. "There are people in the audience who have nothing to do with show business who look up and say, 'I'm that age. I'm going to join the Follies,'" she says.

Time Has Touched Them Lightly

More than anything else for these men and women, the Follies is about love: love of fellow performers, love of the art and craft of the stage, and love of life. It's that love that keeps these extraordinary artists not just going but driving themselves, and each other, to improve. Burgess had been a dance teacher when she saw the show, auditioned, and became dance captain. Over time, she came to know so well what the others looked best in and what they needed that she kept getting more and more responsibility. Now she's involved in casting, costuming, sets, and more, challenging her to learn new skills at an age when what most of her contemporaries are learning is a new golf swing. "All I ever wanted to do was dance and have a good time, and now, here I am with all these people under me," she says. "I'm involved in every aspect, and it's very exciting for me. Of course I get tired, but I wouldn't change it for the world."

"The show is on such a high level," says Brunjes, "and I have a right to say that because I've done a lot of Broadway shows. For us at this age, to be on this level, it really feeds our ego (and we all need actors' egos) to the point where the audience just feels happy. The audience actually feels they're part of us."

France agrees. "Because it is at such a high level, it keeps us at a high level," he says. "This is what it's all about for all of us: the love of each other and the understanding of each other." The cast is family, and like any good family, they push each other to be better and remain at that high level, and that improves not only the audience's experience but their own.

In the end, the show is *life*—positive, affirming, and energizing. "I was on a fishing trip this year, at a very swanky fishing camp, and I'm eating breakfast with four CEOs," says Brunjes. "I came in for the third day, and I said, 'Hi, everyone, how you doing?' And this guy says, 'Why are you always so happy?' And I said, 'Maybe it's because I'm not a CEO.'"

"That's that magic of show business," says Kloss. "You're around extremely happy people 95 percent of the time. Where else can you be surrounded by music, comedy . . . the most serious point is when you get your check and go to the bank. To be young and now to relive all that and to still be able to do it—why shouldn't we be happy?"

Purpose, positive attitude, rewarding work—the gentlemen and ladies of the Follies have them all, and that's what keeps them young. As they say, when they're on the stage, age doesn't matter. "You keep working and you keep living," says France. "Being positive keeps us going forward, forward, forward all the time instead of backward."

Brunjes takes it a step further. "Movement is life," he says. "That's why most people like to work out; they don't even know why. Because if you're not moving, like I was on Long Island when Leila called me, you're slowly giving up your life."

Kloss seems to sum it all up. "This man came up one day, and he said, 'You know, Dorothy, I've been coming to this show for many years, and I've been watching you every year, and time has touched you lightly.'

That was the nicest compliment I've ever had," she says. "If you still have an interest in yourself, in how you look and how you feel . . . the good thing is we get out there; we get out in the world. The Follies is the first show that has given older people a chance to say, 'Hey look me over, here I am again!'"

Agelessness Secret #10

Eat Less

Caloric restriction, which means cutting one-third of a person's daily caloric intake, is the only method scientists have found that reliably increases life span and, so far, only in cold-blooded animals. But many who work in fields of longevity research believe that caloric restriction may actually slow down the aging process and enable humans to live longer and remain healthier.

Though controversial, "undernutrition without malnutrition" has extended the life spans of many simpler creatures, from worms and insects to mice. One of the possibilities is that since the metabolism of food into fuel produces free radicals that can damage the body's cells, consuming less food means fewer free radicals, leading to less cellular damage.

In addition, several scientists have found that consuming fewer calories may actually slow the effects of aging on the nervous system, reproductive system, and the endocrine system, which produces the body's hormones. This may help the body retain its sensitivity to insulin, the hormone that regulates blood sugar levels, reducing the risk of diabetes and related damage. It's also thought that caloric restriction may improve the immune system and ward off some age-related cancers.

Though the cellular effects of caloric restriction are still speculative in primates like man, the other health benefits of eating a low-calorie diet are obvious: it prevents obesity and leads to lower cholesterol, lower blood pressure, and a general avoidance of the conditions that lead to deadly lifestyle-related illnesses such as heart disease and stroke. However, eating a calorie-restricted diet is work; if you're a normal male going from 2,500 calories per day to 1,700, you've got to plan each meal to make sure you're getting all the nutrients your body needs. And of course, those guilty pleasure foods are gone forever.[7]

Is living an extra twenty years worth giving up pastries, chocolate, or prime rib? That's a quantity-versus-quality of life question, and it's for you to decide. But caloric restriction certainly offers the possibility of a longer, healthier life. You can learn more at www.calorierestriction.org.

GALLERIES, GARDENERS, AND ENRICHING THE WORLD

It's not just individual seniors who are catching on to creativity's power to transform life. The wider culture has started to realize that creative seniors are a marvelous untapped resource for uniting communities and opening the eyes of children and adults alike to beauty, mystery, and provocative thought. Programs to identify, nurture, and share the creative gifts of older Americans are popping up everywhere. One example is Eldergivers (www.eldergivers.org), which promotes and celebrates work by seniors in the visual and literary arts and encourages intergenerational relationships. Programs like Art With Elders place professional artists in elder care facilities to teach seniors to bring out their own artistic gifts while Elder Arts Celebrations organizes juried art shows in the galleries of art school campuses. One of the organization's main goals: to make age visible to a society that tends to turn away from the very old. Organizations like Eldergivers reminds us that seniors are as vital and creative as anyone else.

A different approach can be found in New York City. That's where you'll find The House of Elder Artists (THEA), a group of artists and activists working with the Women's Housing and Economic Development Corporation to build a not-for-profit residence in Manhattan where seniors in the arts would "retire"—not to stop working but to continue to engage in a creative relationship with the city and its people. The space would feature public readings, master classes, performances, lectures, art show-ings, and much more while providing affordable housing for New York's population of visionary elder artists.

Another kind of art receiving wide public acclaim can be found on two-and-a-half acres in Boat Canyon in Laguna Beach, California. Here, Hortense Miller, ninety-seven, began cultivating an extraordinary gar-den in 1959 on the hillsides below her 1950s Moderne-style house. Today the Hortense Miller Garden, which features a vast variety of plants from the California coastal zone, is considered a landmark for gardeners worldwide. Miller herself has become a local treasure, known for her encyclopedic knowledge of local flora and fauna, her delightful wit, and her poetic musings on gardening, nature, and the cosmos, collected in a marvelous book, *A Garden in Laguna: The Garden Essays of Hortense Miller*. Both house and garden reflect her exceptional creativity and love of integrating the organic and inorganic in ways that delight the senses. If you travel to Laguna Beach, her garden is a must-see.

No less remarkable is Aminah Robinson, sixty-four, a Columbus, Ohio, folk artist who received a MacArthur Foundation "genius" grant in 2004 for her work using fabric, needlepoint, paint, ink, charcoal, clay, and found objects to craft vast paintings, sculptures, and freestanding objects that dramatize and celebrate her childhood neighborhood, travels, family, and the concept of home.

Many artists are at the height of their powers past traditional retirement age. More notable, though, is that our culture not only recognizes but reveres their work, based on demand and the accolades they receive. That's something new: a growing recognition that though the young may have a callow beauty, what they don't (and can't) have is a time-honed under-standing of the very things that Aminah Robinson's work is about—family and heart, life and death, tragedy and joy. Our society is finally beginning to acknowledge what artists have always known: time is the final ingre-dient that allows creative people to enrich the world.

> *While we have the gift of life, it seems to me the only tragedy is to allow part of us to die, whether it is our spirit, our creativity, or our glorious uniqueness.*[8]
>
> —GILDA RADNER

Senior Achievers

The Cast of the Fabulous Palm Springs Follies

The cast often changes from year to year, but some things don't change. You still have to be at least fifty-five to perform in the Follies; you'd better be a top stage professional with decades of experience on the boards, and you're going to be playing before packed, delighted houses of all ages.

The Follies were the brainchild of Riff Markowitz, the producer/impresario who still emcees each performance with his brand of humor (sample joke: "The *most* often used pick-up line in a senior citizens bar is, 'So . . . do I come here often?'"). Fifteen years after the first curtain, they are world-famous.

Although we interviewed four of the cast members from the 2005 Follies, every performer from every year deserves to be recognized as extraordinary. In their 60s, 70s, and even 80s, they dance with the grace and agility of people half their age, sing like birds, and connect with their audience in an intimate way rarely seen in the Broadway mega-shows of today.

What makes the men and women of the Follies such an inspiration to so many older people is that they're not just up on stage trying gamely, but that they're up there putting on one heck of a show. The ladies are shapely and gorgeous; the gentlemen are debonair and funny. Together they swing, jitterbug, tap, and kick their way into the hearts of thousands each year, defying every stereotype of age as they go.

If you haven't seen the Fabulous Palm Springs Follies, see it. If you have, take an older friend who hasn't. It will show you what's possible. Find out more at www.psfollies.com.

Finding Your Inner Grandma Moses

Anna Mary Robertson Moses didn't begin serious painting until age seventy-eight, but she kept it up until one hundred, becoming, along with ceramicist Beatrice Wood, the symbol of the idea that "it's never too late" to express your creativity. Moses' extraordinary, colorful expressions of folk life in rural Vermont—country markets, harvest time, and much more—are priceless today, proof not only of her talent but her marketing savvy. A model of stubborn Yankee pride, Moses switched to painting with her left hand when arthritis cramped her right and was mourned as an American treasure at her death in 1961. She remains a marvelous role model for any senior who dreams of turning his or her later years into a fount of poetic verse, handmade furniture, or watercolor landscapes.

Do you have an inner Grandma Moses? Or perhaps an inner Mozart? There are many ways to discover your creative side or to enrich it if you're already engaged in something creative. And there's no better time than in your Second Prime when you have not only the time but also the motivation to do everything you can to stay connected and challenged and keep mind and body sharp and vibrant. If you're already spending part of your time on a creative pursuit, you simply need to ask yourself how you can not only continue but expand it after you leave full-time work for someone else. Can you take your work to the next level with more time? Can you take courses at a local university to take your work from hobby quality to near-professional? Can you find other "refirees" who also practice your avocation and form a group or circle?

If you don't think you have a creative side, think again. Everyone does. Remember, creativity is expressed in more ways than painting, singing, dancing, and writing. Gardening is one example we've used, but crafts, collecting, storytelling, home decorating, photography, and simply applying your mind creatively to otherwise noncreative tasks all qualify. Here are a few ways you could explore your dormant creative side:

- Join a writing workshop.
- Audition for a community theater company.
- Get some books on painting and try in the privacy of your home.
- Write a poem in one long session of work, not stopping to edit yourself.
- Take your camera and record the things you see in a typical day.

- Join a local chorale or barbershop group.
- Take up an instrument you played as a child.
- Write down the story of how your parents met or about your first home as a child.
- Redesign the décor in a room of your home.
- Find an interesting recipe and cook something you've never made before.
- Take piano lessons.
- Make up stories and tell them to your grandchildren.
- Volunteer to build and paint sets for a theater group or to build floats for a parade.
- Create a rock garden in your front yard.
- Take a class in making clay pots.
- Make a collage.
- Start collecting stamps, coins, models, or anything that strikes your fancy.
- Get your video camera and make a short film.
- Restore an old car.

There's really no limit to creative expression. It can be any endeavor that challenges you to envision something out of thin air, fires your passions, is something you love doing, and that other people can enjoy. Remember, creativity exists to be shared. If you stick to these criteria, you can't go wrong.

How Many of These Are You Old Enough to Remember?

- Blackjack chewing gum
- Wax Coke-shaped bottles with colored sugar-water
- Candy cigarettes
- Soda-pop machines that dispensed bottles
- Coffee shops with tableside jukeboxes
- Home milk delivery in glass bottles with cardboard stoppers

- Party lines
- Newsreels before the movie
- P. F. Flyers
- Butch wax
- Telephone numbers with a word prefix (e.g., Olive-6933)
- Peashooters
- Howdy Doody
- 45-RPM records . . . and 78-RPM records
- S&H Green Stamps
- Hi-fi systems
- Metal ice trays with lever
- Mimeograph paper
- Blue flashbulbs
- Packards
- Rollerskate keys
- Cork popguns
- Drive-in theaters
- Studebakers
- Washtub wringers

You Don't Have to Make a Living, Just Live

The big question we hear when we talk about creativity is, "Do I have to make a living at it?" The answer is a resounding *no*. If you can make a living at the creative work you love, it's a wonderful, invigorating thing to be able to do. It marks you as one of the truly blessed. But if you can't—or you choose not to—so what?

It's important to know what you want from your creative life. As we said in an earlier chapter, continuing to work in some way is vital to longevity. And continuing to earn an income can make old age far more secure and pleasurable. Do you want to earn an income from your creativity? Do you have what it takes to sell your paintings to galleries, send articles to magazines, or market your craftwork in local stores? Creative work can become a business for you if you choose to make it so. But know if that's what you want.

If it's not, that's fine. Creativity is its own reward, after all. It opens your eyes to new ways of seeing the world, fine-tunes your mind and keeps it young and sharp, reaches out to other people, and most important, gives you joy and purpose. Creativity is life force. It's not an accident that some people call God *the Creator*.

Second Prime Strategy—Creativity

1. Things to Do
- Look for opportunities to be creative in your community.
- Take stock of the hobbies you loved when you were younger.
- Look for people around you who are engaged in the type of creativity you'd like to do.
- Look for classes in things like writing, painting, and voice.
- Find ways to practice being creative in total privacy until you're comfortable.
- Make a list of people you trust to whom you can show your work first.

2. Changes You Need to Make for a More Creative Life
-
-
-
-
-

3. Your Creative Goals for Your Second Prime
Example: "Discover the filmmaker inside of me."
-
-
-
-
-

4. Creativity Resources

- Fabulous Palm Springs Follies (www.psfollies.com)
- How Much Joy (www.howmuchjoy.com)
- Senior Theatre (www.seniortheatre.com)
- The House of Elder Artists, Inc. (www.theainc.org)
- Eldergivers (www.eldergivers.org)
- Creative Class (www.creativeclass.org)
- New Lifestyles (www.newlifestyles.com)

chapter eleven —————————————————————————

Purpose *or* They Don't Need
Preachers in Heaven

How does one keep from "growing old inside"? Surely only
in community. The only way to make friends with time is to
stay friends with people . . . Taking community seriously not
only gives us the companionship we need, it also relieves us
of the notion that we are indispensable.[1]

—ROBERT MCAFEE BROWN

To hold the same views at forty as we held at twenty is to have
been stupefied for a score of years, and take rank, not as a
prophet, but as an unteachable brat, well birched and none
the wiser.[2]

—ROBERT LOUIS STEVENSON

The Reverend Billy Graham was talking to Art Linkletter when Art
mentioned that after he went to heaven, the reverend would need to
find a new line of work, a new purpose. A bit taken aback, Graham asked
why. Art replied, "Well, they don't really need preachers in heaven, do they?"

The moral? Everyone, even the most accomplished people in the
world, needs a purpose in life. After you've lived for decades, it takes
something very powerful to make you confront every day with energy
and enthusiasm. Money doesn't do it because money on its own is
meaningless. Family doesn't do it because the whole idea of raising a
family is so they can make it on their own. What keeps us moving forward, what gives our lives meaning, is *purpose*. People need purpose.

Something noble, difficult, and bigger than ourselves that pushes our limits, tests us, and makes our town, county, or country a better place.

What goes on inside your mind has as much to do with your life span, soulspan, and healthspan as what goes on in your arteries, gastrointestinal tract, and kidneys. At the core of what lab researchers might call the "soft" factors in living long and living well is something that may be the ultimate determiner of length and quality of life: *will.* The will to live seems to influence life's outcome more than practically any other factor.

The evidence for this is anecdotal and intuitive. No university has done a clinical trial, testing how being willful helps you live to a hundred. But think about the people we all know of who have lived and worked into their 80s and 90s while smoking, drinking, and defying all modern health wisdom. We call them "health reprobates." What do they have in common? A will to keep living their own way and a sense of purpose, something that gets them out of bed in the morning.

Bob Proctor, seventy-one, speaker and author of *You Were Born Rich*, once said to Mark, "I look into what I am doing, not what I am getting everyday. Doing is an expression of what is going on inside my mind. I keep upgrading within and keep evolving without." Bob has been speaking to millions of people for forty years and says he is more turned on, enthusiastic, and effective than ever. He plans to die working, but he won't tell anyone until five years after he is gone. Proctor says, "As one ages and sages, he should not slow down, rather he should speed up and calm down. Like it says in the last chapter of James Allen's *As a Man Thinketh*, 'Self control is strength. Right thought is mastery; calmness is power. Say unto your heart, 'Peace, be still.'"[3]

> *Nothing contributes so much to tranquilizing the mind as a steady purpose—a point on which the soul may fix its intellectual eye.*[4]
>
> —Mary Wollstonecraft Shelley

Purpose Is the Reason for Long Life

Why do you want to live long? It isn't simply not to die, is it? If you believe in an afterlife, why not check out at fifty-five and enjoy your eternal reward? What keeps you here beyond the simple biological drive to live? That's a question not often asked but one worth answering. For most of us, the answer is *purpose*. We have things we simply must accomplish on this earth, and we're not ready to go until we've done our best to accomplish them.

Writes life coach Richard J. Leider in *The Purpose Project: An Incomplete Manifesto for Retirement*:

> The common theme at the core of every single interview I have conducted over the past thirty years with conscious elders is this: purpose is essential to staying alive! If there is no contact with purpose, there is an almost spiritual sadness inside us—a deep disappointment—a retreat into self-absorption. Without a renewed sense of purpose, we feel stuck in our past, and the future looks like more of the same. We desperately need a new reason to get up in the morning. The unwavering truth about retirement is: change or wither into aging; grow or die within.[5]

Some of the effect of purpose is knowable. When you're excited about doing something, adrenaline and endorphins flood your body, creating exhilarating sensations of strength and vitality. But that's not enough to explain purposeful seniors living to ninety-five when equally healthy folks with no sense of purpose barely reach eighty. There must be something else going on here. As reported in detail in *National Geographic's* long-term Quest for Longevity study, the natives of Okinawa are renowned for living long, healthy lives with an average life expectancy of eighty-two years. Okinawans suffer from only 20 percent of the heart disease and 25 percent of the breast and prostate cancer of Americans, and senile dementia is also less common.[6]

The secrets? There are many: Okinawans eat a low-calorie, plant-based diet, and their land-based culture leads to lifelong physical exertion. But they also possess a strong sense of purpose, known as *ikigai*, which roughly translates in English to "that which makes one's life worth living." Okinawans have one of the longest life spans and healthspans of any group, and purpose is unquestionably part of it.[7] Purpose gives their lives meaning, a center, a reason beyond simply weathering the passage of time. Any rock in the ocean can do that; it takes a ship to actually get somewhere.

Purpose defines the vast empty space of our lives like furniture defines a room. It lends shape and color to our days and gives a propulsive force to our lives, so instead of drifting, we move proudly and confidently in a direction of our own devising.

When You Deny Purpose . . .

In his seminal book, *Man's Search for Meaning,* psychologist Viktor Frankl makes the case that every individual is hard-wired to search for the meaning of his own existence. He uses the example of his own experience in the World War II Nazi concentration camps to show how a sense of purpose—a sense that one's life has a reason for existing and continuing—can grant the ability to survive even under the most horrific circumstances. Frankl created a therapeutic process called "logotherapy." (*Logos* is Greek for "meaning.") Such therapy sessions center on helping the patient discover the meaning in his or her life. In this way, individuals discover their own unique significance.[8]

Many people believe that the purposes of their lives have been ordained by God. It's the search for meaning that counts. As Frankl states (and we concur), when a person is obstructed from connecting to his meaning, the result is frustration, depression, and hopelessness. It is the struggle to find meaning that frustrates us and creates discontent and anger in our lives. Deny your own sense of purpose and you guarantee decay of body, mind, and spirit. Frankl stated that people who live without purpose tend to live in an existential vacuum filled with drug abuse, alcoholism, and other self-destructive habits.[9]

Nature abhors a vacuum. If you deny the need for purpose in your own life, something else will fill that space: rage, denial, or, maybe worst of all, the sad conviction that this is all there is, you have outlived your usefulness, and the rest of your days are merely an exercise in not dying.

THE THREE TYPES OF PURPOSE

So how do you go about bringing purpose into your life? First of all, you probably already have it. Whether or not you're living that purpose is another matter. If you are, you're doing what we call "living on purpose," that is, living with a direction in mind, not just existing. That's the kind of healthy approach that will keep you in your Second Prime for decades.

But if you don't know your purpose or what to do about it, the first step is to understand what purpose is. We've heard plenty of definitions, but we like ours best:

Purpose is that activity that you will overcome all obstacles to do.

There are plenty of things we'd do for free, but there aren't many activities that get you so charged with energy that you will go without sleep, working until the wee hours of the morning, completely unaware of the passage of time. You might forgo other pursuits for the sake of a vacation or dinner out with friends, but with purpose there's nothing you'd rather do. When you're living with purpose, even aches, pains, and illness can't stop you. You find yourself aware and performing at your best on little sleep, being awakened in the middle of the night by thoughts and ideas. You're running on all cylinders, and it feels wonderful.

There are three types of purpose:

1. Things you've always wanted to do. These could be sailing around Cape Horn, learning to play the saxophone, or just about any other pursuit that fires your passion.

2. Things you feel called to do. These are activities that compel you in a way you don't necessarily understand. You feel pulled toward them.

3. Things that make a positive difference. You might not feel a passion for these activities, but you are passionate about their effects, from saving endangered wetlands to reading to children after school.

Notice that one purpose can fit all three categories. If you have that kind of purpose, that's your "meta-purpose"—the overpowering act that's the meaning of your life, the thing you simply can't *not* do. If you have an idea of what your purpose might be, see into which category it falls. That's the start of your adventure.

And get this: it does not matter whether your purpose aligns with the goals of society. It's wonderful if both align; it multiplies your joy and satisfaction to do something meaningful for yourself that also improves your community or sheds light into the life of one person. But that should not be the guiding force behind your search for meaning. In the end, your purpose is your purpose, and you can't change it. You've got to listen to and serve that voice inside you. You cannot worry about what others think or what society will make of you. You've probably spent too many years doing that already.

When you're seeking your purpose, your goal should be to have a sense of *healthy inspirational discontent*. That is, you're not unhappy, but you're restless. You know there's more you can be, more you can do, and more you can have, and you hold yourself to a high enough standard that you *simply cannot rest* until you've tried with all you've got to achieve that standard.

Agelessness Secret #11

Give Blood Regularly

You know that giving blood is a wonderful charitable act that saves lives. You may have even donated your share of pints. But did you know that giving blood actually benefits your health?

An increasing amount of evidence suggests that giving blood actually reduces damage to your arteries, reduces the risk of cardiovascular disease, and creates new cells that are more life giving. Here's how it works: when you give blood, you also lose some iron. Iron has been shown to increase the oxidation of cholesterol, which is thought to damage blood vessels. So when you reduce the iron level in your blood, you reduce that risk.

University of Florida researcher Dr. Jerome Sullivan argues that this is one of the reasons why the risk of heart disease is lower for women than for men. For decades, women menstruate, losing iron and keeping it at controlled levels. But after menopause, women's risk rises to match that of men. And giving blood may be the solution.

There's still some skepticism about the lifesaving effects of giving blood in the scientific community, but the small studies that have been done so far show that donating may offer real benefits. A 1998 Finnish study that appeared in the *American Journal of Epidemiology* showed that of 2,682 men tested, those who donated blood at least once a year had an 88 percent lower risk of heart attack than non-donors. Another study from 1997 showed that men who donated blood were less likely to show signs of cardiovascular disease than nondonors.[10]

In addition to what appear to be real health benefits from giving blood regularly, there's also another benefit. Giving blood is an act of pure charity, something that can and does save lives every day. When you give blood, you're giving something positive to the world. You're creating a new opportunity for abundance, compassion, and positive energy to come back to you.

Besides, giving blood may be one of the only things you can do for your heart that has almost no risk. As spokesperson for the American Red Cross, Mark asks that you call 1-800-GIVELIFE and give blood now. If you want blood to be there for you and your loved ones, you must give it in advance. While we have brilliant doctors and scientists, none have invented pseudoblood. If you cannot give, please encourage three of your friends or your entire organization to schedule a blood drive and help out. We thank you in advance.

Become a "Quester"

"Questers" are people who have made sudden career or life changes because they reassessed their lives and decided they needed a different direction. So says Carole Kanchier, PhD, a psychologist and internationally syndicated columnist who coaches individuals on finding purpose in their lives. For Kanchier, author of *Dare to Change Your Job . . . And Your Life*, the later stage of life should be defined not by retirement, but *reassessment*, a natural part of our life cycle.

"Retirement is a life cycle transition," she told us in an interview. "Periodically, we reassess where we are and where we want to go. Whether we make the transition at fifty, sixty, or seventy, these are questioning times. We should reassess who we are and where we want to go. Take time out, go back to school, go to another job. Why wait for the traditional concept of retirement to do what you want to do?"

Kanchier insists that people don't lose their purpose; it just becomes hidden, buried beneath a lifetime of excuses, other priorities, and societal expectations. In fact, you're born with your purpose; it's innate to you, and you can't change it. You can only give it voice or deny it. That means that even if you're seventy-five and have never listened to that voice inside telling you to find your purpose, it's not too late. It's never too late, says Kanchier.

"Some people know what their purpose is, but they're afraid to follow it because of spouse, parents, friends," she says. "Some people don't know what their purpose is because they've covered it up. But you can find it if you want to. You've got to please yourself. You're no good to anybody if you don't do what makes you happy. It's like when you're on an airplane and they ask you to put the oxygen mask on yourself before you help someone else."

How do you become a quester? Start by refusing to listen to the "shoulds" in your life, Kanchier advises. "People listen to 'should' rather than to who they are. It's funny, but the people who have the least education are often the ones who best grasp the concept while the ones who are most educated tend to be more distant from it because they're trying to please the 'shoulds' in their lives."

Seventy-year-old George went for his annual physical. All of his tests came back with normal results.

Dr. Smith said, "George, everything looks great physically. How are you doing mentally and emotionally? Are you at peace with yourself, and do you have a good relationship with God?"

George replied, "God and I are very close. He knows I have poor eyesight, so he's fixed it so that when I get up in the middle of the night to go to the bathroom (poof!) the light goes on when I go, and then (poof!) the light goes off when I'm done."

"Wow," commented Dr. Smith, "that's incredible!"

Later in the day, Dr. Smith called George's wife. "Thelma," he said, "George is just fine. Physically he's great, but I had to call because I'm in awe of his relationship with God. Is it true that he gets up during the night and (poof!) the light goes on in the bathroom, and then (poof!) the light goes off?"

Thelma exclaimed, "That old fool! He's going to the bathroom in the refrigerator again!"

Learning to Love Risk

If we close our ears to the voice inside trying to tell us the meaning of our lives, the reason we refuse to listen is often fear of risk. Defying the conventional wisdom of society, going against the expectations of our family, sinking our money into a new business or a year of world travel— they all represent risk, and risk is scary. Risk represents the uncertain, the possibility of failure. Old age comes with a predetermined set of expectations from children, friends, and our culture: old folks fear change, stick to their habits, play it safe, and adhere to their usual roles of wise counselor, doting grandparent, and rocking chair jockey. And if you step outside those roles, society inflicts punishment: the scorn of friends, the disapproval of relatives. The longer you've stuck to your role, the harder it is to break free of it and risk punishment.

So many seniors resign themselves to the status society has designated for them and ignore the compulsion that calls them to pursue their purpose. They do it because it's the path of least resistance. It's much easier to play golf and learn shuffleboard—to meet the low expectations of others—than to shatter the mold, step out of your comfort zone, and announce that you are going to become an actor, start a farmers' market, or get your bachelor's degree. When you risk, you open yourself to failure, and that's terrifying.

But when you step out of your comfort zone, that's when you're most alive. Taking risks brings out your creativity and brings change into your life. Risk is a force for change and a creator of opportunity. If you want a rewarding Second Prime, it's vital that you remember that without risk, there is no reward. That's not to say you have to take foolish risks. What good is the wisdom of age if you're going to ignore your experience and throw your money away on a bad business venture, for instance? With decades of life lessons, you're in a better position than anyone to gauge a situation and decide if it's a worthwhile risk. Pursuing your purpose may mean taking a smart, calculated risk, such as quitting a job or alienating friends of a particular political or religious persuasion.

You should always be asking, "Is this worth the risk?" Balance the nature of the risk with the opportunity that springs from it because:

All risk is opportunity in disguise.

When you first consider pursuing a purpose that's lain dormant inside you for years, you will also face some risk. There is always risk in momentous change. But instead of worrying about failure, think about the challenge. How much will facing the risk and triumphing build your confidence and skills? How much stronger will you become? How much joy and electricity will success add to your life? With each risk you face, you'll relish the next one even more. The potential energy of risk becomes the kinetic energy of purpose realized.

Senior Achiever

Tom Begert-Clark, 53, professional speaker and founder, Even As We Speak

Tom Begert-Clark tired of being in a corporate environment, so he did something most folks wouldn't even consider: he launched his own speaking business at age fifty-three. Today, he travels around the country, speaking to groups on issues ranging from elder care to developing your business.

"I was speaking while I was working for a corporation, and I was getting a lot of calls, 'Gee Tom, can you come to our conference, consult with us,' and so on. But my corporate job didn't allow that," he says. "So I decided if I was going to make the change, I'd better do it now. So I left the security of corporate America, and it's been just unbelievable."

Begert-Clark has begun writing a book he's had in mind for years, and he maintains a relentlessly positive attitude while building his corporation and brand and speaking across the country. But that doesn't mean he received universal support when he announced his decision. His employer was shocked.

"Professionals said to me, 'Are you sure you want to do this?' 'Do you know how many businesses fail?' Always negative," he says. "But friends and family said, 'Well, it took you fifty-three years to decide that it was right for you to do this; what took so long?' They knew it was the right decision for me before I did."

Begert-Clark says that friends tell him now that he looks happier than they have ever seen him. And while he took an income hit in the beginning, savings got him through the early period, and he has a plan to get back to the level of income he was at in his corporate position. "I want money. Everybody wants money," he says. "But I was making good money, and I wasn't happy. And that was affecting everything I was doing. Am I ever going to retire? No way. You never know what's going to develop tomorrow."

Find Tom Begert-Clark at www.evenaswespeakonline.com.

BE A TRIBAL ELDER

For the tens of thousands of years that there have been human collectives, there have been tribal elders. In most societies, elders have been venerated, treated as sources of wisdom and knowledge. From the Sioux of the Great Plains to the feudal culture of Japan, the elders of many cultures have held places of honor. Even though our age tends to be obsessed with youth, many cultures in this modern world still treat the old with reverence.

In your search for your personal meaning and sense of purpose, don't discount the beauty of becoming a tribal elder. Your experience, wisdom, and perception are assets no one can take from you, and they have value to others. Talk to younger people. Offer them your knowledge. Become a mentor or advisor. Be a storyteller and refuse to let the lessons, people, and events of the past turn to dust. Keep a journal. Preserve your photos and writings. Become a living library. Work with organizations like Elder Wisdom Circle (www.elderwisdomcircle.org) to share your wisdom with others.

Most important of all, blend your wisdom with the energy and courage to change as your life enters a new phase. "Change is a part of the natural cycle of living, just like the seasons change," says Carole Kanchier. Following your purpose can mean disruptive change, but change means you're alive and growing, and isn't that the point?

Second Prime Strategy—Purpose

1. Things to Do
- Figure out what's important to you.
- Think about how you would be willing to change your life.

- Look for the factors that have been stopping you and figure out why they have power over you.
- Decide what you would do if money was not an issue.
- Identify your strengths, your passions, and the things that fascinate you.
- Use this information to determine your purpose.
- Make a plan to live by that purpose.
- Set goals.

2. Changes You Need to Rediscover or Pursue Your Purpose

-
-
-
-
-

3. Your Purpose Goals for Your Second Prime

Example: "Teach myself to take greater risks without fear of failure."

-
-
-
-
-

4. Purpose Resources

- Real World University (www.rwuniversity.com
- ServiceLeader (www.serviceleader.org)
- Helpguide (www.helpguide.org)
- How Much Joy (www.howmuchjoy.com)

Age Is Wasted on the Old

Young people don't know what age is, and old people forget what youth was.[1]

—IRISH PROVERB

I find that a man is as old as his work. If his work keeps him from moving forward, he will look forward with the work.[2]

—WILLIAM ERNEST HOCKING

Supposedly, playwright George Bernard Shaw quipped, "Youth is wasted on the young." There's some dispute over whether he actually said that, but what's important is the counterpoint, which is that "Age is wasted on the old," which is to say, the gift of long life is often wasted on people who accept the idea that getting to sixty and beyond means becoming corpulent, indigent, and incontinent. Living long is perhaps the greatest gift of all, if you make the most of it. Mr. Spock, of the original *Star Trek* television series, had it right when he said, "Live long and prosper."[3] There's never been a better salutation, and there's never been a simpler, clearer idea of what being in your Second Prime is all about. Your old age can be about living long and prospering in your body, mind, finances, sex life, relationships—every aspect of your life. As we've said from the beginning, it's all up to you—to use your mind and spirit for the future you choose.

What Can You Do? Everything!

We couldn't include even the smallest percentage of the incredible, groundbreaking seniors around the country who are doing amazing, age-defying things. Consider, for example:

- Norman Vaughan, 99, the last surviving member of Admiral Byrd's 1925 Antarctic expedition, who is planning a one hundreth birthday party atop Mt. Vaughn, the forbidding 10,000-foot Antarctic peak named for him.
- Gene Glasscock, 71, who in 2005 completed a horseback ride to all forty-eight state capitals in the continental United States, traveling more than 20,000 miles in three years to raise money for the children of Paraguay.
- Bill Anderson, 80, who in 2004 completed a bicycle ride from San Diego, California, to Jacksonville Beach, Florida, to raise $3,000 and national awareness for the homeless.
- Lucille Borgen, who at 91 in 2004 won the Women 10 slalom and tricks event at the Annual Water Ski National Championships.
- John Meeden, the 64-year-old former homeless man who's now one of the best softball players in the country. (Read the entire story at http://www.seniorsoftball.com/news.php?story=133&phpSID=c10b2542552fe85bf533662ba10905d8).
- Ray Strong, 105, a landmark California landscape painter, cofounder of the San Francisco Art Students League and the Oak Group in Santa Barbara, and still active as an artist.
- Gertrude Friedman, 84, who wrote and self-published her first novel, *Tushika*, about her Romanian aunt.
- Julius Shulman, 95, the world's leading architectural photographer, still works and sells his work around the globe.

- Ray Sutton, 73, who bills himself as "the world's oldest living blogger."
- "Papa Joe" Paterno, at 79 the oldest active college football coach, still leading the Penn State Nittany Lions to the Big Ten title.
- Dale Glenney of Pennsylvania, 55, who, after discovering power lifting at 43, set a world record in his age group by lifting 418 pounds.
- Leonard McCracken, 102, who flew back to his boyhood home of Warren, Ohio, in 2005 to finally receive his high school diploma, 85 years after dropping out to help his family cope with the Spanish flu epidemic of 1918–1920.

This is merely scratching the surface. If you want to read about even more of what we call Senior Achievers, you can find their stories at www.SecondPrime.com. But here, each one of these amazing men and women is a living testament to the possibilities that await every one of us, no matter how old we are. Is there something physical, mental, or genetic that gave these people an edge in staying active and creative into their Second Prime? Not really. Mostly, they're people who have simply refused to play by society's rules of getting old. They've decided to *grow old* instead—to learn and expand their minds, push themselves to the peak of their professions, and never quit keeping body and brain active and alive. With US life expectancy at an all-time high of 77.6 years, today's Baby Boomers, if they can avoid the traps of obesity, inactivity, and diabetes that already afflict half of Americans age fifty-five to sixty-four, can look forward to lives of almost limitless potential.

The fabric of our culture is shifting, and ever more power and influence are flowing to older Americans. That means you have more ability than any midlife generation in history to take control of your future and ensure that you remain independent as you age. That's vital; there is evidence that those having a concept of control over the outcome of their aging are more likely to make lifestyle choices that increase their longevity. Margie E. Lachman, professor and chair of Psychology and director of the Life Span Developmental Psychology Lab at Brandeis

University, writes in an article for *Psychological Science Agenda*: "Many studies show that those who believe aging-related outcomes are at least somewhat under their control are more likely to engage in adaptive behaviors."[4] More than one controlled study has indicated that control beliefs are associated with successful aging.

By embracing the idea of a Second Prime and following the principles of this book and the experts featured in it, you will gain that sense of control. You will refuse to allow society's expectations to determine how you age, or to let the choices of your past affect the healthy, vital choices of your future. You'll become stubborn about living in a way that makes others gasp and delivers you the greatest joy, excitement, challenge, and love. You'll become ferociously independent, determined to take care of your physical and financial affairs until the day you drop. You'll become an activist for the rights of seniors, if not in Washington, in your own community. Because you'll realize that everyone has a right to live with the purpose and passion that you do.

An elderly lady was stopped, waiting to pull into a parking space when a young man in his new red Mercedes went around her and parked in the space she was waiting for.

The sweet little old lady was so upset that she went up to the man and said, "I was going to park there you rude man!"

The man sneered, "That's what you can do when you're young and bright."

This upset the lady even more, so she got in her car, backed it up, stomped on the gas, and smashed into the front of the Mercedes.

The young man ran back to his smashed car and asked, "What did you do that for, you crazy old woman?!"

The little old lady smiled. "That's what you can do when you're old and rich!"

THERE'S SO MUCH OUT THERE FOR YOU

If you have even the slightest doubt about all this, just look around. Thousands of news stories run each year trying to figure out the impact the Baby Boomers will have on society, the economy, values, the family. You're already running things whether you realize it or not! Ignore the advertisers who obsess about the eighteen- to twenty-four-year-olds; we all know they're not the ones with the money. You are. That's why the world is slowly coming around to the truth that Boomers and seniors are the future. Just surf the Internet. According to the Pew Internet and American Life Project, as of 2004, 22 percent of Americans sixty-five and older were using the Internet, up from 15 percent in 2000. That's about eight million seniors online, sharing their experiences and ideas at wonderful destinations like Lost in Time (www.jlkuntz.com) and Time Goes By (www.timegoesby.net).[5]

Far, far beyond blogs is an entire universe of senior-oriented Web sites, books, periodicals, and organizations, some of which we've already talked about and more of which you'll find in the Resources section. There's an American Association of Baby Boomers (www.babyboomers.com) and a Web site that covers trends and news in the Boomer world at www.aginghipsters.com. There's *GRAND* Magazine, dedicated to grandparents everywhere, and a book by Joe West, Paul Jofe, and Ken Leebow called *300 Incredible Things for Seniors on the Internet*. There are even the Senior Pages (www.seniorpages.com), a business and professional directory for people fifty-five and over. Organizations are launching that tap the wisdom of older people to help individuals and businesses through tough times while around the country, day care centers are being started where elders care for toddlers, giving incredible benefits to both. People who claim that the older generation is being marginalized just aren't looking closely enough.

A FUTURE OF INCREDIBLE TECHNOLOGY

Of course one of the most exciting aspects of entering your Second Prime is that you'll be around to see advances in medicine and science that promise to improve the ability to be independent and possibly extend human life by decades.

Genetic discoveries are being made all the time: in late 2005, a study by the National Institutes of Health through the University of Pittsburgh revealed the discovery of a gene, APOE E2, that appears to be directly related to reaching age ninety without a significant decline in mental function.[6] Genetics offers unbelievable promise. But two of the most promising advances that are just beginning to develop are *assistive technology* and *nanotechnology.*

Defined by US law, assistive technology is any item or product that can assist a person with disabilities in maintaining independence. But in its highest form, assistive technology uses sophisticated systems like sensors and micromotors to help seniors remain more mobile, live more easily on their own, and give seniors with disabilities the opportunity to function as close to normal as possible. Assistive technology includes devices for personal mobility, driving, wellness, independent living and care giving, and worker productivity. Here are a few examples:

- Electronic pets that use play and emotion to remind seniors to take needed medications
- "Smart" phones that can provide directions, signal others for assistance, and even turn lights and alarms off and on
- "Gait mats" laid on the floor that can sense changes in an older person's walking pattern that indicate an increased risk of falling
- Artificially intelligent robots that help cognitively impaired seniors navigate their daily living spaces

Assistive technology is about "helping people as they get older maintain their independence, even in the face of impairment and disabilities," says Dr. William Mann, OTR, PhD, professor and chair of the Department of Occupational Therapy at the Rehabilitation Engineering Research Center at the University of Florida. In an interview conducted for this book, he says, "The goal is to have people able to remain living at home and enjoy a quality of life even if they have a disability." Mann's work covers everything from wheelchairs and walkers to special computer interfaces and what's known as a "pervasive computing environment," in which computers, actuators, and sensors are invisible beneath the surface of an everyday environment, performing their functions and essentially unseen until needed.

According to Mann, this advanced "smart" technology can often be controlled by voice, body movement, or simple commands. "We have a 'smart house' that we've built here that does all kinds of things that would help somebody with mild impairment to severe disability," says Mann. "Some of it is related to the entertainment system, some of it is prompting of tasks for somebody with cognitive impairment. We have a smart microwave that can read the RFID (radio frequency identification) label on a food package. The microwave knows what the food package is and automatically sets up the cooking for it and also talks to the person and shows a short video on a screen right above the microwave."

> *When life has been well spent, age is a loss of what it can well spare,— muscular strength, organic instincts, gross bulk, and works that belong to these. But the central wisdom, which was old in infancy, is young in fourscore years, and dropping off obstructions, leaves in happy subjects the mind purified and wise.[7]*
>
> —Ralph Waldo Emerson

Smart House

Mann told us he compares the experience to being in one of today's high-tech cars. "When you're in a car, you're in a pervasive computing environment," he says. "There are chips all around you. The same with an airplane. Sensors, chips, applications that are going on, and you're not even aware of it. What we've focused on is developing applications for people who have difficulties in movement, in mobility, might fatigue easily, applications that can help people with visual impairment and people with cognitive impairment." The university has already built a prototype "smart house" within an innovative retirement community called Oak Hammock (www.oakhammock.org). In the Gator Tech Smart

House, says Mann, "you walk up to the door and ring the doorbell, and the resident inside will not just hear a doorbell, but the screen in the room where the resident is will come on and a picture of who is outside will be pictured on the monitor. If the resident chooses to let the person in, they can talk to them by intercom and say, 'I'm going to unlock the door,' then instruct the house by voice command to let the person in. For somebody with mobility impairment, that eliminates the need to get up."

Pressure-sensitive floors that monitor location and sense falls, systems that automatically call for help, voice-controlled media and entertainment centers, solar-sensitive blinds and lighting systems, and more are all part of this "science-fictionesque" technology. Mann expects to see such technologies reach the mass market in three to five years, both via developers and consumers who can buy "assistive technology in box" at the local Costco. Affordability will be a question, but since the technology will be modular, people will be able to buy what they can afford, and there's the possibility of insurance covering some of the cost; the government and private insurers pay more than 50 percent of the cost for today's basic assistive devices. There's a powerful incentive for insurers and entitlement programs to evolve to pay for advanced assistive technology. "We did a study that we published in the *Archives of Family Medicine* in 1999 that showed that . . . if you give people the tools to live independently, overall, in terms of health-related costs, you'll save a ton of money," Mann says. "An approach that gives people the means to be independent is not simply good for them, it's less expensive."

NANOTECHNOLOGY

Even more "science fictiony," but quite real, is the world of nanotech—molecule-sized machines and devices such as nanotubes and "Bucky balls" (named for Buckminster Fuller) that can actually manipulate individual cells and, if perfected, show enormous promise for repairing and preventing the damage of aging. Nanotech is immensely popular with aggressive antiaging advocacy groups such as Fight Aging! (www.fightaging.org), but it's gaining more and more notice in the mainstream.

In an article for Salon.com, Alan H. Goldstein speculates on where nanotech will be in 2016—specifically, with the human genome fully mapped, your doctor will be able to pull your genetic profile from a national database then use nanomedicine to read the gene sequence from a single cell in an area he suspects might be cancerous, all the work taking place in a laboratory no wider than a human hair. Next, nanobots could be turned loose to seek and destroy only the cancerous cells—at their size, they would be able to take on the rogue cells hand-to-hand—while leaving healthy tissue untouched. This technology is under development right now and could usher in an era of extraordinary "personal medicine."[8]

SELF SECURITY AND INSTEADICARE: MAKING YOUR OWN PLANS

Technology is tomorrow. Today, you have a decision to make. Do you depend on the government to take care of you, or do you assume the programs of today will not remain the same, hope for the best while preparing for the worst, and take control of your own financial and health future? You know which choice we recommend. In his interview, futurist Dan Burrus concurs. "If I'm a Baby Boomer, I need a strategy," he says. "My strategy is that I need to start thinking about my future and taking control of it. That means I have to get in action mode rather than a passive mode—I would call it more of an opportunity mode than a crisis mode—solving problems before they happen. I suggest spending an hour thinking about your future. What are the problems that I can see in that hour of the week? What are the problems that I can see that will be opportunities? Because every problem I can see is an opportunity in disguise."

Your opportunity is to create your own Self Security and Insteadicare plans—life strategies that use what you've learned about work, opportunity, and money to plan wisely today and find enjoyable ways to earn an income tomorrow, so if Social Security lets you down, you're still financially secure. It's also to exercise, eat right, reduce stress, take supplements, and do everything else you can to keep your biological machine fit, trim, agile, and operational—and to find alternative health coverage that focuses on wellness—so you don't need to take prescription drugs for cholesterol, high blood pressure, or arthritis, and if Medicare collapses under its own weight, you won't miss it.

If Social Security and Medicare are around in twenty-five years, fine. We have no doubt they will be, but rest assured they won't be the same programs they are today. Something's got to give, and it's very likely that the safety net you thought you had won't be there, not in the same way. The technology, opportunity, health care, science, entrepreneurial resources, and social changes are in place for you to seize control and determine how the next twenty-five, thirty-five, or forty-five years will shape up. All that remains is for you to have the mind-set to do it.

To get you started, we've created a Self Security and Insteadicare Worksheet:

My Self Security and Insteadicare Worksheet

Self Security Plan

1. Expected monthly income from retirement investments if you keep saving at your current rate.	$
2. Current expected income from Social Security.	$
3. How much you would need monthly to live the lifestyle you want.	$
4. Assuming a 50 percent drop in your Social Security payout, how short will you be?	$
5. How much more do you need to earn and save per month to get by in your Second Prime?	$

6. Now, how much more do you want to earn and save monthly to live the life you really crave? $

7. Check the measures you're willing to include in your Self Security plan to help you reach your goal:

Job ○   Start a business ○   Buy rental property ○
                Cut costs ○   Invest ○

8. Write down details of how you will accomplish each of the measures you selected:	9. Your Self Security benefits. Example: Consistent income and equity from rental property.
• Job	•
• Start a business	•
• Buy rental property	•
• Cut costs	•
• Invest	•

10. Track your progress weekly.

Insteadicare Prescription Plan
(we could have made it complicated, but that's the government's job)

Exercise/Moderate to heavy dose, 4–5 times weekly Description: Example: Three four-mile morning walks	Effective for: Example: Weight control

•	•
•	•
•	•
•	•
Diet/Fruits, vegetables, grains, nuts, lean meats; dose/3 times daily Description: Example: Fruit for breakfast every morning	Effective for: Example: Lower cholesterol
•	•
•	•
•	•
•	•
Sleep/7–8 hours; dose/daily Description: Example: Regular 10 p.m. bedtime	Effective for: Example: Increased energy
•	•
•	•
•	•
•	•
Supplements/as determined by physician or dietician; dose/daily Description: Example: 1000 mg selenium	Effective for: Example: Lower heart attack risk
•	•
•	•
•	•
•	•

Stress reducers/at least one method; dose/2-3 times per week minimum Description: Example: Quiet time alone	Effective for: Example: Reduced blood pressure
•	•
•	•
•	•
•	•
Appearance improvement/ multiple methods; dose/ask practitioner Description: Example: Monthly manicure	Effective for: Example: Improved confidence
•	•
•	•
•	•
•	•
Attitude/multiple methods; dose/unlimited Description: Example: Social gatherings	Effective for: Example: Avoiding depression
•	•
•	•
•	•
•	•

Cost? This is the best part:
$

The Second Prime Club

Use these worksheets or create your own; the goal is to plan and take steps to remain independent as you age. As you take control of your future well-being, you'll find yourself developing the attributes of a person truly in his or her Second Prime: a fierce self-reliance, confidence, a sense of achievement, and a feeling that the only limits you have are those you set for yourself.

When that happens, you're ready. Ready to join the Second Prime Club, an organization we've created for Boomers and seniors who refuse retirement to embrace refirement, who know that sixty is the new forty and seventy the new fifty, and who are using their time to explore, create, laugh, love, give back, and connect in ways previous generations never even imagined. If you're part of the group that's redefining age, you belong in the Second Prime Club.

The slogan says it all: "Old age. Schmold age." Members don't care about the calendar, but about the travel schedule, the number of weight plates on a bench press machine, the amount of olive oil in a gourmet recipe. When you join at www.SecondPrime.com, you're joining with a community of seniors and Boomers who approach their later years with fire, enthusiasm, adventure, and a thumb to the nose toward the traditional concepts of old age. Second Primers are cheerfully defiant of stereotypes and love every minute of it.

Join the Club and you'll get your very own Self Security Card, Insteadicare Benefit Plan, and a lot more. On SecondPrime.com, you'll also find articles, interviews, products, event calendars, ways to connect with other members, and a lot more. It's a great thing to be in your Second Prime, and it's even better when you're in the club. Try it out.

Things That Bring Joy at Any Age

• Falling in love
• Laughing so hard your face hurts

- A hot shower
- No lines at the supermarket
- A special glance
- Getting mail
- Taking a drive on a pretty road
- Hearing your favorite song on the radio
- Lying in bed listening to the rain
- Hot towels fresh out of the dryer
- Chocolate milkshakes (or vanilla or strawberry)
- A bubble bath
- Giggling
- A good conversation
- The beach
- Finding a twenty-dollar bill in your coat from last winter
- Laughing at yourself
- Midnight phone calls that last for hours
- Running through sprinklers
- Laughing for absolutely no reason at all
- Having someone tell you that you're beautiful
- Laughing at an inside joke
- Friends
- Accidentally overhearing someone say something nice about you
- Waking up and realizing you still have a few hours left to sleep
- Your first kiss (either the very first or with someone new)
- Making new friends or spending time with old ones
- Playing with a new puppy
- Having someone play with your hair
- Sweet dreams
- Hot chocolate
- Road trips with friends
- Swinging on swings
- Making eye contact with a cute stranger

- Making chocolate chip cookies
- Having your friends send you homemade cookies
- Holding hands
- Running into an old friend and realizing some things never change
- Watching the expression on someone's face as they open a much-desired present from you
- Watching the sunrise
- Getting out of bed every morning and being grateful for another beautiful day
- Knowing that somebody misses you
- Getting a hug from someone you care about
- Knowing you've done the right thing, no matter what other people think

A Final Word

"I think that a lot of people in their later years, rather than just remaining in their own home or moving to a specific community where they stay anchored for the rest of their lives, [will be trying] new models of timeshares and floating condominiums and house swapping," aging expert Dr. Ken Dychtwald told us. "It's the idea of a generation of people who are more willing to try new things and more comfortable relocating, and are going to take big bites out of world culture and have fun doing so."

That's the vision we have for you: of a life that's rich and crazy and audacious and passionate and brilliant and giving. More than any other generation in the modern world, you have the ability to shape the future. Your generation has the numbers, the money, the experience, and the wisdom. Now all you need is the desire. Your Second Prime is waiting. Go get it.

—Mark Victor Hansen
Art Linkletter
June 2006

Second Prime Resources

General
- Preferred Consumer Senior Living
  (www.preferredconsumer.com/senior_living)
- Mature Resources (www.matureresources.org)
- *GRAND* Magazine (www.grandmagonline.com)
- Gerontological Society of America (www.geron.org)
- Academy of Achievement (www.achievement.org)
- Cool Grandma (www.coolgrandma.com)
- The Senior News Source (www.theseniornewssource.com)
- FirstGov for Seniors (www.firstgov.gov/Topics/Seniors.shtml)
- Today's Seniors (www.todaysseniors.com)
- Real World University (www.rwuniversity.com)

Work and Money
- American Institute of Financial Gerontology (www.aifg.org)
- *Entrepreneur* Magazine (www.entrepreneur.com)
- United States Small Business Administration (www.sba.gov)
- Paladin Registry (www.paladinregistry.com)
- Wiser Advisor (www.wiseradvisor.com)
- Startup Bank (www.startupbank.com)
- SCORE (www.score.org)
- Preferred Consumer Small Business Channel
  (www.preferredconsumer.com/small_business)

Body

GENERAL HEALTH
- Eternal Health (www.eternalhealth.org)
- National Institute on Aging (www.nia.nih.gov)
- Alliance for Aging Research (www.agingresearch.org)
- Infoaging (www.infoaging.org)
- The Okinawa Centenarian Study (www.okinawaprogram.com)
- American Academy of Anti-Aging Medicine (www.worldhealth.net)
- Mayo Clinic (www.mayoclinic.com)
- Medline Plus (www.nlm.nih.gov/medlineplus)

MOVEMENT
- National Senior Games Assn. (www.nsga.com)
- *Geezerjock* magazine (www.geezerjock.com)
- International Council on Active Aging Fitness Facility Locator (www.icaa.cc/facilitylocator.htm)
- Fifty Plus (www.50plus.org)
- Senior Fitness (www.senior-fitness.com)
- About Exercise (exercise.about.com/od/exerciseforseniors)

DIET
- The World's Healthiest Foods (www.whfoods.com)
- Diabetes Danger (www.diabetesdanger.com)
- Nutrition Action Healthcenter (www.cspinet.org/nah)
- WholeHealth MD (www.wholehealthmd.com)

SUPPLEMENTS
- Office of Dietary Supplements (http://ods.od.nih.gov)
- US Food and Drug Administration (www.cfsan.fda.gov/~dms/supplmnt.html)
- NatureMade (www.naturemade.com)

SLEEP
- National Sleep Foundation (www.sleepfoundation.org)

- Sleepnet (www.sleepnet.com)
- The Better Sleep Council (www.bettersleep.org)

Health Insurance

- The New Health Insurance Solution (www.tnhis.com)
- Extend Benefits (www.extendbenefits.com)
- eHealthInsurance (www.ehealthinsurance.com)
- Alternative Health Insurance Services
  (www.alternativeinsurance.com)
- Society for Innovative Medical Practice Design
  (www.conciergephysicians.org)
- Fitness and Wellness Insurance Agency
  (www.fitnessandwellness.com)

Books

- *121 Ways to Live 121 Years and More!* by Dr. Ronald Klatz, President, American Academy of Anti-Aging Medicine, and Dr. Robert Goldman, Chairman, American Academy of Anti-Aging Medicine
- *The New Health Insurance Solution* by Paul Zane Pilzer
- *Dare to Be 100* by Walter M. Bortz II, MD
- *Diabetes Danger* by Walter M. Bortz II, MD
- *Younger Next Year* by Chris Crowley and Henry S. Lodge, MD
- *Merchants of Immortality* by Stephen S. Hall
- *Aging Well* by Andrew Weil, MD
- *Healthy Aging* by Andrew Weil, MD
- *Eternal Health* by Dr. Michael Elstein
- *Simple Health Value* by Dr. Andrew Myers
- *The Memory Bible* by Dr. Gary Small
- *The Memory Prescription* by Dr. Gary Small
- *The Adult Years: Mastering the Art of Self-Renewal* by Frederic M. Hudson
- *The Miracle of Tithing* by Mark Victor Hansen
- *Put Old on Hold* by Barbara Morris, RPh

- *The Power Years* (and others) by Dr. Ken Dychtwald
- *AgeLess* by Edward Schneider
- *The Boomers' Guide to Good Work—An Introduction to Jobs That Make a Difference* by Ellen Freudenheim and published by MetLife Foundation and Civic Ventures
- *The Passion Centered Professional* by Gary Zelesky
- *The Automatic Millionaire* by David Bach
- *Finish Rich* by David Bach

Mind

- Bernard Osher Foundation (www.osherfoundation.org)
- Elderhostel (www.elderhostel.org)
- Learning Annex (www.learningannex.com)
- American Association of Community Colleges (www.aacc.nche.edu)
- SeniorNet (www.seniornet.org)
- UCLA Center on Aging (www.aging.ucla.edu)
- John Douglas French Alzheimer's Foundation (www.jdfaf.org)
- Alzheimer's Association (www.alz.org)
- Alzheimer's Disease Education and Referral Center (www.alzheimers.org)
- Family Doctor (www.familydoctor.org)
- Dementia (www.dementia.com)
- Neurology Channel (www.neurologychannel.com)
- Internet Mental Health (www.mentalhealth.com)
- The Human Brain (www.fi.edu/brain)
- Elder Wisdom Circle (www.elderwisdomcircle.org)
- Mentoring (www.mentoring.org)

Sex

- Sallie Foley (www.salliefoley.com)
- His and Her Health (www.hisandherhealth.com)
- The all-in-one Christian Web Site Community (www.praize.com)
- eHarmony (www.eharmony.com)

Spirituality

- Sojourners (http://sojo.net)
- Christian Community Health Fellowship (www.cchf.org)
- Women of Faith (http://womenoffaith.com)
- The Intersection of Faith & Life (www.crosswalk.com)
- Christianity Today (www.christianitytoday.com)
- Elder Hope (www.elderhope.com)
- Christian Answers (www.christiananswers.net)

Attitude

- AARP (www.aarp.org)
- Time Goes By (www.timegoesby.net)
- Fearless Aging (www.fearless-aging.com)
- Positive Attitude Institute (www.positiveinstitute.com)
- Dr. Wayne Dyer (www.drwaynedyer.com)

Creativity

- Fabulous Palm Springs Follies (www.psfollies.com)
- How Much Joy (www.howmuchjoy.com)
- Senior Theatre (www.seniortheatre.com)
- The House of Elder Artists, Inc. (www.theainc.org)
- Eldergivers (www.eldergivers.org)
- Creative Class (www.creativeclass.org)
- New Lifestyles (www.newlifestyles.com)

Purpose

- VolunteerMatch (www.volunteermatch.org)
- Help Your Community (www.helpyourcommunity.org)
- ProLiteracy (www.proliteracy.org)
- Idealist (www.idealist.org)
- World Volunteer Web (www.worldvolunteerweb.org
- ServiceLeader (www.serviceleader.org)
- Helpguide (www.helpguide.org)

Glossary of Second Prime Terms

Catastrophizer—A person who is always predicting disaster and expecting the worst; someone to avoid.

Disease deflective—Maintaining optimal health so disease passes you by instead of getting a disease and then trying to cure it.

Empowerments—The ten joyful, positive aspects of old age to which you're entitled . . . if you make the right choices.

Futurepathic—Focusing on future wellness by maintaining lifelong health of mind, body, and spirit.

Healthspan—The span of your life during which you enjoy vigor, strength, endurance, and agility enough to do whatever you want to do.

Insteadicare—Our alternative to Medicare, in which you keep your body in top shape so you need Medicare as little as possible.

Light Partner—A friend who sticks with you for years, bringing light to your life.

Lovespan—The span of your life during which you have meaningful relationships and pursue your passions.

Mindspan—The span of your life during which your mind and brain are healthy and thought and reason are sharp.

Prayscription—Maintaining a spiritual center to life to keep yourself healthy, connected, and filled with a sense of meaning and hope.

Quizzically Fit—In good mental shape for puzzles, games, curiosity, and discovery.

Re-Great—The opposite of regret; the state of learning from the past but looking to the future with wisdom and perspective.

Sageing—Aging with greater wisdom, judgment, and experience, taking advantage of them all and passing them down to the younger generations.

Self Security—Our alternative to Social Security, in which you save wisely, make smart lifestyle choices, and continue earning after you leave full-time work, so you are always financially secure.

Seniorpreneur—One of the millions of Americans over fifty who are starting businesses.

Soulspan—The span of your life during which you have a strong spiritual life, connection with a congregation, or do your most giving back to others.

Workspan—The span of your life during which you're actively working, earning, and creating; it doesn't have to be about money but about productivity.

Notes

Foreword *by Art Linkletter*

1. U.S. Department of Health and Human Services, "Effects of Health Care Spending on the U.S. Economy," February 25, 2005; Congressional Budget Office, "The Economic and Budget Outlook: Fiscal Years 1999–2008," January 1998; Economic Policy Institute, "Collision course: The Bush budget and Social Security," March 16, 2005.
2. www.brainyquote.com/quotes/authors/j/john_wooden.html, accessed March 13, 2006.

Foreword *by Mark Victor Hansen*

1. www.satchelpaige.com/quote2.html, accessed March 13, 2006.

Introduction: Forget Entitlements—Introducing the Ten Empowerments

1. Social Security Administration, "Status of the Social Security and Medicare Programs," March 23, 2005.
2. Ibid.

Part I: It's Not "How Old Are You?" But "How Are You Old?"

chapter one: The Eight Great Myths About Growing Old

1. Franklin P. Adams, *Nods and Becks* (New York: Whittlesey House, 1944), 53.
2. Philip James Bailey, *Festus* (B. B. Mussey & Co.; 8th American edition, 1849), Scene V.
3. *USA Today/ABC News* poll quoted in "Centenarian Envy," Fight Aging, October 23, 2005, http://www.fightaging.org/archives/000644.php.
4. Donna L. Hoyert, Hsiang-Ching Kung, and Betty L. Smith (ed.), *National Vital Statistics Reports*, Vol. 53, No. 15, "Deaths: Preliminary Data for 2003," February 28, 2005, http://www.cdc.gov/nchs/data/nvsr/nvsr53/nvsr53_15.pdf.
5. Kathleen Fackelmann, "Centenarians Increase in Age and Numbers," USAToday.com, October 23, 2005, www.usatoday.com/tech/science/2005-10-23-aging-centenarians_x.htm.
6. Samuel Ullman, "Youth," *The Silver Treasury, Prose and Verse for Every Mood*, ed. Jane Manner (New York: Samuel French, 1934), 323–24.

7. "World's Oldest Person," AVirtualDominica.com, October 14, 2003, www. avirtualdominica.com/mapampo.htm.

8. Dan Buettner, "The Secrets of Long Life," *National Geographic*, November 2005, 2–27.

9. The Stowe Foundation, http://www.thestowefoundation.org/index.htm.

10. Steve Chawkins, "At 105, He Still Throws Self Into Sports," *Los Angeles Times*, November 26, 2004.

11. Margie M. Donlon, Ori Ashman, and Becca R. Levy, "Re-Vision of Older Television Characters: A Stereotype-Awareness Intervention," *Journal of Social Issues* 61 (2), 2005, 307–319.

12. Linda Langley, Rebecca Thurston, Wythe Whiting, and James Blumenthal, "Interaction of Blood Pressure and Adult Age in Memory Search and Visual Search Performance," *Aging, Neuropsychology, and Cognition*, 10 (4), 241–254.

13. Gary Small, *The Memory Prescription* (New York: Hyperion, 2004), 8.

14. M. F. K. Fisher, *Sister Age*, "Afterword" (New York: Vintage, 1983).

15. J. G. Bretschneider and N. L. McCoy, "Sexual interest and behavior in healthy 80- to 102-year-olds," *Archives of Sexual Behavior*, April 1988; 17(2):109–29.

16. Xenia Montenegro and Linda Fisher, "Sexuality at Midlife and Beyond," *AARP the Magazine*, July/August 2005.

17. Gary R. Andrews and George C. Myers, Australian Longitudinal Study of Aging, Waves 1–5 (1992-1997), Adelaide, South Australia: Flinders University of South Australia, Centre for Ageing Studies, 1999, distributed by Inter-university Consortium for Political and Social Research, Ann Arbor, Michigan, 2000; Gary R. Andrews and George C. Myers, Australian Longitudinal Study of Aging, Wave 6 (1999–2000), Adelaide, South Australia: Flinders University of South Australia, Centre for Ageing Studies, 1999, distributed by Inter-university Consortium for Political and Social Research, Ann Arbor, Michigan, 2003.

18. Buettner, "The Secrets of Long Life," 19–20.

19. Robert H. Coombs, "Marital Status and Personal Well-Being: A Literature Review," *Family Relations*, 1991, 40: 97–102.

20. Frederic M. Hudson, *The Adult Years: Mastering the Art of Self-Renewal* (San Francisco: Jossey-Bass, 1999), 219.

21. Martin E. P. Seligman, C. Peterson, and S. Maier, *Learned Helplessness: A Theory for the Age of Personal Control* (New York: Oxford University Press 1993), 4–7.

22. Kathleen Pender, "Everyone, Start Saving," *San Francisco Chronicle*, February 2, 2006, C-1; U.S. Department of Commerce, Bureau of Economic Analysis, "National Economic Accounts," http://www.bea.gov/bea/dn1.htm.

23. "Rule of Conduct," *Letters of John Wesley*, ed. George Eayrs, (London: Hodder and Stoughton, 1915), 423.

chapter two: Final Score: Lifestyle 70, Genes 30

1. Ida Husted Harper, *The Life and Work of Susan B. Anthony* (Indianapolis: Bowen-Merrill, 1899), ch. 46.

2. Antoine de Saint-Exupéry, *Wartime Writings* (New York: Harvest/HBJ Book, 2002), 114.

3. John W. Rowe and Robert L. Kahn, *Successful Aging* (New York; Random House, 1998), 30.

4. "Seventieth Birthday Speech," *Mark Twain: Collected Tales, Sketches, Speeches, & Essays, 1891–1910* (New York: Library of America, 1992), 716.

5. Quoted in "Books," *Sunday London Times*, May 10, 1992.

6. World Health Organization, *The World Health Report 2003*, "Global cancer rates could increase by 50% to 15 million by 2020" (press release) April 3, 2003.

7. "Supplements: Turmeric," WholeHealthMD.com, www.wholehealthmd.com/refshelf/substances_view/1,1525,10062,00.html.

8. Chisato Nagata, Naoyoshi Takatsuka, and Hiroyuki Shimizu, "Soy and Fish Oil Intake and Mortality in a Japanese Community," *American Journal of Epidemiology*, November 2002, 156: 824–831.

9. Gary E. Fraser, "Associations between diet and cancer, ischemic heart disease, and all-cause mortality in non-Hispanic white California Seventh-day Adventists," *The American Journal of Clinical Nutrition*, Vol. 70, No. 3, 532S–538S, September 1999.

10. J. M. Marijke and Chin A. Paw, Wageningen University, The Netherlands, "Immune Response in Elderly Depends on Physical Activity Rather Than Enriched Diet," *Medicine & Science in Sports & Exercise*, Vol. 32, No. 12, page 2005.

11. R. Jorde & K. H. Bønaa, "Calcium from dairy products, vitamin D intake, and blood pressure: the Tromsø study," *American Journal of Clinical Nutrition*, 71:1530–1535; A. Flood, U. Peters, N. Chatterjee, J. V. Lacey, C. Schairer, and A. Schatzkin, "Calcium from diet and supplements is associated with reduced risk of colorectal cancer in a prospective cohort of women," *Cancer Epidemiology, Biomarkers and Prevention*, Vol. 14, January 2005, 126–132.

12. William Strawbridge, "Frequent attendance at religious services and mortality over 28 years," *American Journal of Public Health*, Vol. 87, Issue 6 (1997), 957–961.

13. Sandra L. Reynolds, Yasuhiko Saito, and Eileen M. Crimmins, "The Impact of Obesity on Active Life Expectancy in Older American Men and Women," *The Gerontologist* (2005) 45:438–444.

14. Kathleen Fackelmann, "Omega-3 Gets Another Boost," *USA Today*, July 21, 2003, http://www.usatoday.com/news/health/2003-07-21-fish-usat_x.htm.

15. Becca Levy, Martin D. Slade, Stanislav V. Kasl, Suzanne Kunkel, "Ohio Longitudinal Study of Aging and Retirement," *Journal of Personality and Social Psychology*, 83: 261–270, 2002.

16. Michael D. Lemonick, "The Ravages of Stress," *Time*, December 13, 2004, 45.

17. Richard Corliss and Michael D. Lemonick, "How to Live to Be 100," *Time*, August 30, 2004, 43.

18. Victor Hugo, "Thoughts," *Victor Hugo's Intellectual Autobiography*, trans. Lorenzo O'Rourke, (Funk and Wagnalls, 1907).

19. "Vitamin Pills Do Not Stop Cancer," BBC News, October 1, 2004, http://news.bbc.co.uk/2/hi/health/3703498.stm.

20. Leonard W. Poon (ed.), *The Georgia Centenarian Study* (Amityville, NY: Baywood Publishing Co., 1992).

21. Lisa Chippendale, "Toward a Fountain of Health, Not Youth," American Federation for Aging Research, http://websites.afar.org/site/PageServer?pagename=IA_feat4.

22. Stephen S. Hall, *Merchants of Immortality* (Boston: Houghton Mifflin, 2003), 204.

23. National Cancer Institute, *Antioxidants and Cancer Prevention: Fact Sheet,* January 8, 2003, www.cancer.gov/newscenter/pressreleases/antioxidants; The George Mateljan Foundation for The World's Healthiest Foods, "The World's Healthiest Foods List, A-Z," http://www.whfoods.com/foodstoc.php.

24. Hugo L. Black, *Think,* February 1963.

25. Leonard Hayflick, comments from "Briefing on Anti-Aging Medicine," New York Academy of Sciences, June 23, 2004.

chapter three: It's Who You Know

1. André Maurois, *The Art of Living,* trans. James Whitall (New York: Penguin, 1960), 282–83.

2. Ambrose Bierce, *The Devil's Dictionary* (New York: Bloomsbury USA, 2004), 20.

3. Eric W. Kaplan, "Seniors and Depression," *Medical Moment,* July 1, 2003, www.medicalmoment.org/_content/signs/jul03/151175.asp.

4. Thomas A. Glass, Carlos Mendes de Leon, Richard A. Marottoli, and Lisa F., Berkman, "Population based study of social and productive activities as predictors of survival among elderly Americans," *British Medical Journal,* August 1999; 319: 478–483.

5. A. Faber and S. Wasserman, "Social Support and Social Networks: Synthesis and Review," *Social Networks and Health, Advances in Medical Sociology* (J. Levy and B. Pescosolido, eds.), 8, 29–72.

6. "Communications as Therapy: The Science behind CaringFamily," CaringFamily.com, 2005, www.caringfamily.com/public/service/science.cfm.

7. "People," Jule Styne, lyrics, and Bob Merrill, music (New York: Chappell-Styne, Inc.), 1963.

8. Walter M. Bortz II, *Dare to Be 100: 99 Steps to a Long, Healthy Life* (New York: Fireside, 1996), 37.

9. Charles Dickens, *Barnaby Rudge,* Ch. 2 (London: Chapman and Hall, 1841).

10. Thomas Rutledge, Karen Matthews, Li-Yung Lui, Katie L. Stone, and Jane A. Cauley, "Social Networks and Marital Status Predict Mortality in Older Women: Prospective Evidence from the Study of Osteoporotic Fractures," *Psychosomatic Medicine,* 2003, 65:688–694.

11. Jeannette Haviland-Jones, "The Flowers & Seniors Study," 2001, quoted in "Mother Nature's Social Security," Society of American Florists, AboutFlowers.com, www.aboutflowers.com/seniorstudy.htm.

12. Edward Schneider, *AgeLess* (New York: Rodale, 2003), 68–70.

13. American College of Clinical Thermology, "Overview of Digital Infrared Thermal Imaging," www.thermologyonline.org/patients_overview.htm.

14. Abby Adams, *An Uncommon Scold* (New York: Fireside, 1989).

Part II: You Can't Turn Back the Clock, But You Can Rewind It

chapter four: Work & Money *or* The Only Thing You Should Re-Tire Is Your Car

1. Pearl S. Buck, *My Several Worlds* (New York: Pocket Books, 1960), 337.

2. Anaïs Nin, *The Diary of Anaïs Nin, Volume 3,* (New York: Harvest/HBJ Book, 1971).

3. André Maurois, *The Art of Living,* trans. James Whitall (New York: Penguin, 1960), 282–83.

4. Julia Boorstin, "Get Real About Your Future," *Fortune,* July 11, 2005, p. 42.

5. Labor Research Association, "The Pension Crisis Hits the Fan (July 29, 2004)," LRA Online, www.laborresearch.org/story2.php/360.

6. Peter Coy and Diane Brady, "Old. Smart. Productive. Voices of Experience," *Business Week,* June 27, 2005.

7. "Baby Boomers Envision Retirement II: Survey of Baby Boomers' Expectations for Retirement," AARP (study conducted by RoperASW), www.aarp.org/money/careers/employerresourcecenter/researchanddata/a2004-08-10-envisionret.html.

8. Kathy M. Kristof, "More Senior Citizens Are Opting to Stay Employed," *Los Angeles Times,* August 1, 1999.

9. Hesther Lynch Piozzi, *Anecdotes of the Late Samuel Johnson LLD* (London: 1786).

10. Minnie Holmes-McNary and Albert S. Baldwin, Jr., "Chemopreventive Properties of trans-Resveratrol Are Associated with Inhibition of Activation of the I{kappa}B Kinase," *Cancer Research,* 60:13, 3477–3483.

11. Ellen Freudenheim, *The Boomers' Guide to Good Work—An Introduction to Jobs That Make a Difference* (Washington, D.C.: MetLife Foundation and Civic Ventures, 2005), 3.

12. Jim Hopkins, "The New Entrepreneurs: Americans Over 50," *USA Today,* January 17, 2005.

13. Lynn A. Karoly and Julie Zissimopoulos, "Self-Employment and the 50+ Population," AARP Public Policy Institute Issue Paper, March 2004, 93.

14. William D. Novelli, "How Aging Boomers Will Impact American Business," (speech presented at meeting of the Wisemen), The Harvard Club, New York, NY, February 21, 2002.

15. "As Entrepreneurs, Seniors Lead U.S. Start-Ups;" "The Image Of Senior Start-Ups Is Making Businesses Re-Think Their Options," *Franchising World,* August 2005.

16. "Seniors in the Workforce," NationalCity.com, http://www.nationalcity.sbresources.com/SBR_template.cfm?DocNumber=PL18_0200.htm.

17. Karen E. Spaeder, "9 Senior Businesses to Start," *Entrepreneur,* November 18, 2004.

18. Freudenheim, *The Boomers Guide,* 3.

19. Oscar Wilde, *The Picture of Dorian Gray* (New York: Modern Library, 1998), 245.

20. Ruth Helman, Mathew Greenwald & Associates, Dallas Salisbury, Variny Paladino, and Craig Copeland, "Encouraging Workers to Save: The 2005 Retirement Confidence Survey," Employee Benefit Research Institute, April 2005, 5.

21. Robert B. Avery and Michael S. Rendall, "Estimating Size and Distribution of Baby Boomers' Prospective Inheritances," *American Statistical Association's 1993 Proceedings of the Social Statistics Section,* 1993, 11–19; "Fast Facts About the Largest

... Most Lucrative ... Most Active Market ... BOOMERS," JWT Mature Marketing Group, http://www.beyondthenumbers.com/btn5.html.

22. U.S. Congressional Budget Office, "The Retirement Prospects of the Baby Boomers" (special report), March 18, 2004.

23. Cait Murphy and Julia Boorstin, "Five Threats to Your Financial Security," *Fortune*, July 11, 2005: 90–96.

24. "Top Ten Ways to Prepare for Retirement," National Retirement Planning Coalition, www.retireonyourterms.org.

25. David Bach, *The Automatic Millionaire: A Powerful One-Step Plan to Live and Finish Rich* (New York: Broadway, 2003).

chapter five: Body or Never Let Anyone Help You Out of a Chair

1. Dave Barry, "Your Disintegrating Body," *Dave Barry Turns 40* (New York: Ballantine Books, 1990), 17.

2. Harry S. Broudy, "Education for Leisure," *Paradox and Promise: Essays on American Life and Education* (Danville, IL: Vero Media, 1961).

3. Tom Stoppard, *Rosencrantz and Guildenstern Are Dead* (New York: Grove Press, Reprint edition, 1991).

4. Chris Crowley and Henry S. Lodge, *Younger Next Year* (Ontario: Thomas Allen & Son Limited, 2005), 13–15; Jon W. Williamson, Peter G. Snell, C. Gunnar Blomqvist, Bengt Saltin, "A 30-Year Follow-Up of the Dallas Bed Rest and Training Study: II. Effect of Age on Cardiovascular Adaptation to Exercise Training," *Circulation: Journal of the American Heart Association*, Sep 2001; 104: 1358–1366.

5. "Eat 'Super Foods,'" *Nutrition Action Healthletter*, Center for Science in the Public Interest, www.cspinet.org/nah/10foods_good.html.

6. Agatha Christie, *An Autobiography* (New York: Berkley Publishing Group, 1996).

7. Carolyn C. Armistead, "5 Smarter Ways to Lose Weight: Follow These Guidelines and You Will Drop Pounds, Just As Our Writer Did," *Shape*, June 2003.

8. To purchase Joyce Shaffer's e-book, *Bone Health Guide: Osteoporosis & Thinning Bones*," please go to http://www.kickstartcart.com/app/netcart.asp?setCookie= TRUE&MerchantID=56187&ProductID=2124101.

9. "Diabetes Epidemic Could Claim 622,000 Lives Annually by 2025," SeniorJournal.com, November 9, 2005, www.seniorjournal.com/NEWS/Health/5-11-09DiabetesEpidemic.htm.

10. Walter M. Bortz II, *Diabetes Danger* (New York: Select Books, 2005), 1.

11. Claudia C. Collins, "Water: Fountain of Life," Fact Sheet 99-30, University of Nevada, Reno Senior Wellness Series.

12. Gabrielle "Coco" Chanel, *Ladies' Home Journal*, September 1956.

13. Andrew Weil, "Aging Naturally" (book excerpt), *Time*, October 17, 2005, 64–65.

14. Oliver Wendell Holmes, radio address, March 8, 1931, *His Book Notices and Uncollected Letters and Papers* (ed. Harry C. Shriver), (Cambridge, MA: Da Capo Press, 1936), 142.

15. Rob Stein, "Study Is First to Confirm That Stress Speeds Aging," *Washington Post*, November 30, 2004, page A01.

16. *2003 Sleep in America Poll*, National Sleep Foundation, http://www.sleepfoundation. org/hottopics/index.php?secid=16&id=207.

17. "Survey Reveals Older Americans' Attitudes Toward Sleep" (news release), International Longevity Center-USA, Sleep and Healthy Aging Scientific Consensus Conference, November 3, 2005.

18. Ibid.

19. Walter M. Bortz II, *Dare to Be 100: 99 Steps to a Long, Healthy Life* (New York: Fireside, 1996), 197–198.

20. Oscar Wilde, *Lady Windermere's Fan*, Act III, 1893.

21. Crowley and Lodge, *Younger Next Year*, 29–30.

chapter six: Mind *or* Are You "Sageing" or Aging?

1. Abigail Van Buren, *Editor & Publisher*, quoted in *Reader's Digest*, May, 1980.

2. Marilyn Ferguson, *The Aquarian Conspiracy* (New York: Tarcher, 1980).

3. Take a Brain Sip! s.v. "Jeanne Calment," jeanne-calment.brainsip.com.

4. Adlai Stevenson, "The Educated Citizen," an address to the class of 1954, Princeton University, March 22, 1954.

5. Andrew Weil, "Aging Naturally" (book excerpt), *Time*, October 17, 2005, 64–65.

6. Gary Small, *The Memory Prescription* (New York: Hyperion, 2004), 8.

7. Michael Elstein, *Boosting Memory, Preventing Brain Aging* (special report), p. 4; for more information, visit Dr. Elstein's Web site at www.eternalhealth.org.

8. Ibid.

9. R. Katzman, T. Brown, P. Fuld, et al, "What Is the Significance of the Neurotransmitter Abnormalities in Alzheimer's Disease?" *Neuropeptides in Neurologic and Psychiatric Disease*, J. B. Martin and J. Barchas, eds. (New York: Raven Press, 1986), 279–286; "Risk Factors for Alzheimer's Disease," AlzheimersDisease.com, www.alzheimersdisease.com /hcp/about/pathophysiology/risk-factors.jsp.

10. R. Brookmeyer, S. Gray, and C. Kawas, "Projections of Alzheimer's Disease in the United States and the Public Health Impact of Delaying Disease Onset," *American Journal of Public Health* 88 (1998): 1337–1342.

11. Parvoneh Poorkaj, Vikram Sharma, Leojean Anderson, Ellen Nemens, Ma Elias Alonso, Harry Orr, June White, Leonard Heston, Thomas D. Bird, Gerard D. Schellenberg, "Missense mutations in the chromosome 14 familial Alzheimer's disease presenilin 1 gene," *Human Mutation*, 11: 3, 1998, pp. 216–221.

12. Lester Packer, *The Antioxidant Miracle* (New York: Wiley & Sons, 1999) 156, 73.

13. Hugh W. Pinnock, "We Will Go with Our Young and with Our Old," *Ensign*, November 1979, 74.

14. Audie G. Leventhal, Yongchang Wang, Mingliang Pu, Yifeng Zhou, Yuanye Ma, "GABA and Its Agonists Improved Visual Cortical Function in Senescent Monkeys," *Science*, May 2, 2003, 812–815.

15. Kelly Griffin, "Stay Sharp Longer," *AARP The Magazine*, September/October 2005; *Staying Sharp* (e-books), NRTA: AARP's Educator Community along with the Dana Alliance for Brain Initiatives, www.aarp.org/about_aarp/nrta/staying_sharp.

16. Louisa May Alcott, *Little Women*, 1869.

17. J. L. Kuntz, *Lost in Time* (blog), www.jlkuntz.com/archives/2005/11/old_jokes.html.
18. "Looking Ahead: A Baby-Boomer Perspective," U.S. Society & Values, *Electronic Journal of the U.S. Information Agency*, Vol. 4, No. 2, June 1999.
19. John Dewey, *Democracy and Education* (The Macmillian Company, 1916).
20. Rush University Medical Center, "The Religious Orders Study, 1993–2006," www.rush.edu/rumc/page-1099611542043.html.
21. Kelly Griffin, "You're Wiser Now," *AARP The Magazine*, September/October 2005.

chapter seven: Sex *or* Still Enjoying It While Everybody Else Is Just Talking About It
1. D. H. Lawrence, letter, Dec. 27, 1928, to Lady Ottoline Morrell, Heinemann, *The Letters of D. H. Lawrence* (1932), 773.
2. Amusing Quotes s.v. "Bob Hope," http://www.amusingquotes.com/h/h/Bob_Hope_1.htm.
3. Xenia P. Montenegro and Linda Fisher, "Sexuality At Midlife and Beyond: 2004 Update of Attitudes and Behaviors," commissioned by *AARP the Magazine*, 2004.
4. "Elexa™ by Trojan® Survey of Women and Desire," conducted by StrategyOne (news release), September 13, 2005, www.elexabytrojan.com/news.aspx?type=news.
5. Emily Carlson, "Study shows brain activity influences immune function," University of Wisconsin, Madison, September 2, 2003, www.news.wisc.edu/8849.html; Erik J. Giltay, Johanna M. Geleijnse, Frans G. Zitman, Tiny Hoekstra, and Evert G. Schouten, "Dispositional Optimism and All-Cause and Cardiovascular Mortality in a Prospective Cohort of Elderly Dutch Men and Women," *Archives of General Psychiatry*, November 2004, 61: 1126–1135.
6. Alan Farnham, "Is Sex Necessary?" Forbes.com, www.forbes.com/2003/10/08/cz_af_1008health.html.
7. Ibid.
8. "Sex, the Cold Cure," *BBC News*, April 14, 1999, http://news.bbc.co.uk/1/hi/health/319070.stm.
9. Farnham, "Is Sex Necessary?"
10. "Intimacy and aging: Tips for sexual health and happiness," MayoClinic.com, September 27, 2005, www.mayoclinic.com/health/sexual-health/HA00035.
11. Rita Rudner, from her comedy routine.
12. "Aging Does Not End Sex, Relationships, Says Expert," SeniorJournal.com, http://www.seniorjournal.com/NEWS/Sex/5-09-21AgingDoesNotEndSex.htm.
13. Sallie Foley, *Sex and Love for Grownups: A No-Nonsense Guide to a Life of Passion* (Washington, D.C.: AARP, 2005), 153.

chapter eight: Spirituality *or* Plugging Into a Higher Power
1. Mark Twain, "What Is Man?" (1906), *Complete Essays*, ed. Charles Neider (Cambridge, MA: Da Capo Press, 2000).
2. Mark Water (ed.), *The New Encyclopedia of Christian Quotations* (Grand Rapids, MI: Baker House, 2001).
3. Po Bronson, "A Prayer Before Dying: The Astonishing Story of a Doctor Who

Subjected Faith to the Rigors of Science—And Then Became a Test Subject Herself," *Wired*, December 2002.

4. Water, *Encyclopedia of Christian Quotations*.

5. H. G. Koenig, H. J. Cohen, L. K. George, J. C. Hays, D. B. Larson, and D. G. Blazer, "Attendance at religious services, interleukin-6, and other biological parameters of immune function in older adults," *International Journal of Psychiatric Medicine*, 1997; 27(3): 233–50.

6. John H. Christy, "Prayer as Medicine," *Forbes*, March 23, 1998.

7. D. B. Larson, H. G. Koenig, B. H. Kaplan, R. S. Greenberg, E. Logue, and H. A. Tyroler, "The impact of religion on men's blood pressure," *Journal of Religion & Health*, 1989; 28: 265–78.

8. W. J. Strawbridge, R. D. Cohen, S. J. Shema, and G. A. Kaplan, "Frequent attendance at religious services and mortality over 28 years," *American Journal of Public Health*,1997 87: 957–961.

9. Nic Fleming, "Spiritual Meditation 'May Reduce Pain,'" (London) *Telegraph*, September 1, 2005, http://www.telegraph.co.uk/news/main.jhtml?xml=/news/2005/09/01/wmed01.xml&sSheet=/news/2005/09/01/ixworld.html.

10. Kenneth I. Pargament, Harold G. Koenig, Nalini Tarakeshwar, June Hahn,"Religious Struggle as a Predictor of Mortality Among Medically Ill Elderly Patients: A 2-Year Longitudinal Study," *Archives of Internal Medicine*, 2001;161:1881–1885.

11. Terrence D. Hill, Jacqueline L. Angel, Christopher G. Ellison, and Ronald J. Angel, "Religious Attendance and Mortality: An 8-Year Follow-Up of Older Mexican Americans," *The Journals of Gerontology Series B: Psychological Sciences and Social Sciences*, 2005 60: S102–S109.

12. Christie Aschwanden, "Mass as Medicine?" http://www.sagecrossroads.org/Default.aspx?tabid=28&newsType=ArticleView&articleId=115.

13. Hill, et al, "Religious Attendance and Mortality."

14. Harold Koenig, *The Healing Connection* (West Conshohocken, PA: Templeton Foundation Press, 2004).

15. Frederick Buechner, *Wishful Thinking* (San Francisco: HarperSanFrancisco, 1993).

16. Water, *Encyclopedia of Christian Quotations*.

17. Sharon O'Brien, "Lower Body Exercise for Seniors: Improve Strength and Balance," (Senior Living), About.com, http://seniorliving.about.com/od/basicexerciseseries/ss/balanceexercise.htm; George F. Fuller, "Falls in the Elderly," *American Family Physician*, April 1, 2000, www.aafp.org/afp/20000401/2159.html.

18. Michael Shermer, "Faith-Medicine Connection Challenged," *Skeptic Magazine*, November 10, 2005.

19. Paul T. P. Wong, "A Course on the Meaning of Life," International Network on Personal Meaning, www.meaning.ca/articles05/mol/course-mol-12sept05.htm.

chapter nine: Attitude *or* Be Regretless

1. E. B. White, "Life Phases," *New Yorker* (February 20, 1937), reprinted in *Writings from the New Yorker 1927–1976*, ed. Rebecca M. Dale (New York: HarperCollins, 1991).

2. Francis Bacon, "No. 97," *Apothegms*, 1925.

3. Sok-Ja Janket, Markku Qvarnström, Jukka H. Meurman, Alison E. Baird, Pekka Nuutinen, and Judith A. Jones, "Asymptotic Dental Score and Prevalent Coronary Heart Disease," *Circulation*, March 2004; 109: 1095–1100.

4. Marya Mannes, *More in Anger* (New York: Lippincott, 1958).

5. Becca Levy, Martin D. Slade, Stanislav V. Kasl, Suzanne Kunkel, "Ohio Longitudinal Study of Aging and Retirement," *Journal of Personality and Social Psychology*, 83: 261–270, 2002.

6. Amy Scholten, "Attitude About Aging May Affect Longevity," St. Francis Hospital & Health Centers, 2005, http://www.stfrancishospitals.org/DesktopDefault.aspx? ID=28743&tabindex=3&tabid=37.

7. Candace Pert, *The Molecules of Emotion* (New York: Touchstone, 1997), 167, 276–77.

8. Samuel Ullman, "Youth," *The Silver Treasury, Prose and Verse for Every Mood*, ed. Jane Manner (New York: Samuel French, 1934), 323–24.

chapter ten: Creativity *or* What's Grandma Moses Got That You Ain't Got?

1. Leonard S. Marcus, "Why Is Maurice Sendak So Incredibly Angry?" *Parenting*, October 1993.

2. Harold Rosenberg, *The Tradition of the New* (Cambridge, MA: Da Capo Press, 1994), preface.

3. Nohl Martin Fouroohi and Ellen Liu Kellor, "Creativity, Activity, and Longevity." Click "Press" link at http://www.mynewfriend.com.

4. Gene D. Cohen, *The Creative Age: Awakening Human Potential in the Second Half of Life* (New York: Avon Books, Inc., 2000), 3.

5. Ray Bradbury, "Run Fast . . . ," *Zen in the Art of Writing* (New York: Capra Press, 1989), 13.

6. Lawrence Katz and Manning Rubin, *Keep Your Brain Alive* (New York: Workman Publishing Company, Inc., 1999), 31–35.

7. "Hot Topic: Calorie Restriction," The Longevity Meme, http://www.longevity meme.org/topics/calorie_restriction.cfm.

8. Gilda Radner, *It's Always Something* (New York: Simon & Schuster, 1989), 130.

chapter eleven: Purpose *or* They Don't Need Preachers in Heaven

1. Wisdom Quotes s.v. "Robert McAfee Brown," http://wisdomquotes.com/cat_ age.html.

2. Robert Louis Stevenson, "Crabbed Age and Youth," *Virginibus Puerisque and Later Essays* (Sheridan, OR: Heron Books, 1969), 67.

3. James Allen, *As a Man Thinketh* (Camarillo, CA: DeVorss & Company, 1979).

4. Mary Wollstonecraft Shelley, *Frankenstein*, 1831.

5. Richard J. Leider, *The Purpose Project, An Incomplete Manifesto for Retirement*, published on the Web site of the Center for Spirituality and Healing, http:// www.csh.umn.edu/img/assets/8100/manifesto1.pdf.

6. Dan Buettner, "The Secrets of Long Life," *National Geographic*, November 2005, 2–27.

7. Ibid.

8. Viktor Frankl, *Man's Search for Meaning* (Boston: Beacon Press, 1959), 121–122.

9. Ibid. 128–130.

10. Michael Alvear, "Evidence suggests that giving blood has health benefits," CNN.com Health, April 26, 2000, http://archives.cnn.com/2000/HEALTH/04/26/give.blood. wmd.

chapter twelve: Age Is Wasted on the Old

1. *Columbia World of Quotations,* www.bartleby.com/66/96/2496.html.

2. Helen Exley, *Wisdom for Our Times* (Spencer, MA: Helen Exley Gift Books, 2003).

3. An ad lib by Leonard Nimoy, on the set of the *Star Trek* television show in 1966, adapted from a traditional Jewish benediction.

4. Margie E. Lachman, "Aging Under Control?" *Psychological Science Agenda,* Volume 19: No. 1, January 2005.

5. Susannah Fox, "Older Americans and the Internet," Pew Internet and American Life Project, March 25, 2004, http://www.pewinternet.org/PPF/r/117/report_display.asp.

6. Jessica Rowlands, "Genes Related to Longevity Identified," MedicalNewsToday.com, December 13, 2005, www.medicalnewstoday.com/medicalnews.php?newsid=34869.

7. Ralph Waldo Emerson, "Old Age," *Society and Solitude,* 1870.

8. Alan H. Goldstein, "Nanomedicine's Brave New World," Salon.com, November 28, 2005, www.salon.com/tech/feature/2005/11/28/nanomedicine/index.html.

About the Authors

Mark Victor Hansen is best known as "that *Chicken Soup for the Soul*® guy." The Chicken Soup idea is just one of many that have propelled him into a worldwide spotlight as one of the most dynamic and compelling personalities of our time. A premier motivational and inspirational speaker. Mark's other best-selling books include *The Power of Focus* and *The One Minute Millionaire*.

For more information, visit www.markvictorhansen.com.

Art Linkletter, cultural and TV icon, has lifted our spirits for more than sixty years, performing in such shows as *House Party* and *Kids Say the Darndest Things*. As Chairman of the Board of Linkletter Enterprises, Art oversees several building and management enterprises around the world. A best-selling author, he has written more than twenty books, including his recent bestseller, *Old Age Is Not for Sissies*, which is also the title of his lecture tour.